Praise fo
Tell Me How You Lou

"Ed is a great bear of a man, full of en€ making and filmmakers. We have been in the trenches together and shared the heat of the battle. He has watched my back. I love him."
  —**Harrison Ford**

"Ed Feldman is a Hollywood institution. From the unique perspective of his remarkable career, he paints a vivid, passionate, shrewd, funny, and ultimately affectionate picture of movies and the people who make them."
  —**Glenn Close**

"Feldman's stories about the film industry's moguls past and present will keep you in stitches. If you want to have a good time, read this book."
  —**Laura Linney**

"Brilliant and too true!"
  —**Bob Woodward,** *New York Times* **bestselling author of** *Plan of Attack* **and** *All the President's Men*

"Ed Feldman has no mercy—he keeps you laughing from start to finish. His work with and for stars spans fifty years and he spares no one their particular folly."
  —**Steve Shagan, Oscar-nominated screenwriter of** *Primal Fear*

"Risk management is an imperative for the leadership of any organization today. Filmmaking, where the United States is the world leader by far, is exceedingly risky. Ed Feldman is the consummate risk manager, skillfully managing the many uncertainties in producing a movie and, concurrently, the studio's enormous financial risk."
  —**William G. Shenkir, Ph.D., world-renowned enterprise risk management expert and professor and former dean of the McIntire School of Commerce, University of Virginia**

Publishers Weekly: "From the buttoned-down world of the old studio system to the freewheeling global media business of today, film producer Feldman has seen it all. With Barton's help, he spins an entertaining, often hilarious yarn of bottom-line obsessed executives, impossibly vain movie stars and hardworking, even courageous filmmakers... Told in a breezy style, this tale of the pleasures and pains of life in the Hollywood food chain will delight casual readers and give more serious film-business buffs yet another reason to love the movies and the people who make them."

Hollywood Reporter: "Feldman's memoir... reads like a friendly chat, skipping from anecdote to anecdote, while also discussing the challenges posed by specific movies."

Produced By (Producer's Guild): "Ultimately... is a great read for anyone interested in producing, or Hollywood history in general. It is a revealing, no-holds-barred account from an industry icon on what it takes to make it as a producer. It's conversational, humorous and anecdotal style makes it a brisk and enjoyable read."

Kirkus: "An enthusiastic... memoir about navigating Hollywood egos... Feldman's memoir is engaging, especially his rules of producing."

Tell Me How You Love the Picture

A Hollywood Life

Edward S. Feldman

with Tom Barton

Creative Book Publishers International

Beverly Hills

TELL ME HOW YOU LOVE THE PICTURE. Copyright © 2007 by Edward S. Feldman. All rights reserved, reprinted by arrangement with St. Martin's Press Inc. Printed in the United States of America. No part of this book may be used or reproduced in any manner whatsoever without written permission except in the case of brief quotations embodied in critical articles or reviews. For information, address Creative Book Publishers International, 280 S. Beverly Dr. Ste 306, Beverly Hills, CA 90212

www.bookpubintl.com

Library of Congress Control Number 2007928514

Feldman, Edward S.
    Tell Me How You Love The Picture: A Hollywood Life / Edward S. Feldman with Tom Barton
    ISBN-13: 978-0-9779131-3-8

For Lorraine,
who has shared this journey with me

CONTENTS

ACKNOWLEDGMENTS

WE WOULD LIKE TO THANK MARC RESNICK, OUR EDITOR AT St. Martin's Press, for his generosity and support; and our literary agent, Joe Veltre, for his steadfast belief in the project. Also thanks to Becki Heller, Marc's very able assistant. We appreciate the excellent transcription work of Leanna Payne.

From Ed Feldman:
My thanks to Winship Cook, my longtime associate and friend, who was invaluable in putting this book together.

To Kenneth Hyman for his friendship and the opportunity to come to Hollywood.

My appreciation to the great many actors, directors, writers, production designers, directors of photography, and staff persons who have made my career possible.

To Tom Barton, my friend and collaborator, for his creativity and insight, who made this book possible.

To my children, Shari, Mark, and Richard, who have listened to these stories too many times without raising their eyebrows.

From Tom Barton:

It has been one of the greatest privileges and honors of my life to work with Ed Feldman on this book. Ed is a tough-minded, successful movie producer. Yet he is a compassionate, caring gentleman. How he is able to reconcile the two is one of the themes of this book.

Harrison Ford once called Ed "a walking repository of Hollywood history." This is certainly true—Ed has shared much of his amazing knowledge and insights here. But Ed is also an active producer. This rang true to me when, during a writing session around Ed's dining room table, he had to take a call from John Travolta's agent about a big movie project.

I would like to thank the administrators at the University of North Florida for their support of my research and writing over the years, especially related to the business of entertainment and to risk management—most notably Ed Johnson, Earle Traynham, Charlie Calhoun, John MacArthur, and Gary Fane. Also, thanks to Larry Thoele of KPMG for the funding of my research fellowship for twelve straight years. My sincere appreciation to the former UNF students who assisted me with entertainment and risk management research projects, especially Terah Deveraux, Elizabeth Johnson, Guy Jackson, Elvie DeGuzman, Keely Mitts, Mike Price, Mandy Brady, and Janet Dahlseid.

I was fortunate that, over the years, generous and talented professionals helped me understand concepts and ideas integral to this book: Bill Shenkir and Paul Walker of the University of Virginia; Bill Scharninghausen, former controller of Lucasfilm; Ken Scherer, former chief operating officer of Lynch-Frost Productions; and Jim Merrill, a noted authority on the entertainment industry. I owe a debt of gratitude to Enid Graham for helping me understand the art and craft of professional acting.

Most especially, my warm thanks to my wonderful children, Robbie, Hayley, Grant, and Ted, for their love and support during this project— and always.

Success in Hollywood isn't about making money.
It's about survival.

Tell Me How You Love the Picture

WHAT I DO IS PRODUCE

I GAVE THE DOOR A CONFIDENT KNOCK. I HAVE *ARRIVED,* BOTH literally and figuratively.

My employer, 20th Century Fox, had sent me over to the St. Regis Hotel to discuss a marketing campaign on a film with truly one of the giants of the business, the legendary, almost mythical producer David O. Selznick.

Selznick had produced one of the great films of all time, *Gone with the Wind,* as well as classics such as *Rebecca* and *A Star Is Born.* And now at age twenty-seven, I was meeting with him one-on-one. Pretty good for a kid from the Bronx in his first real job, making all of $112.50 a week. Yes, I had *arrived.*

"Ed Feldman to see Mr. Selznick," I said to the assistant when the door opened. I was ushered into the sitting room to have breakfast and talk business with the great Selznick.

A few moments later, Selznick strides in and offers me his hand. "Ed, I'm David Selznick. A pleasure to meet you."

The breakfast meeting went well. I explained what we had in mind for the campaign. Selznick listened attentively, gave me feedback, ideas. We talked about the picture—a remake of *A Farewell to Arms*—and then about the film business in general. I was feeling *really* confident now. Why, we were almost equals.

From out of the blue, Selznick says, "You know, Ed, this is probably the most important moment of your life."

And I reply, "Why do you say that, *David*?" No *Mr. Selznick* for me.

"Because you are having breakfast with the most important man in the history of this business."

God, I thought, no one told me Selznick was a kidder. Well, if it's witty banter he wants, I can deliver. So I said quickly and jauntily, "David, it's such an ironic thing for you to say that here because three weeks ago in this very same suite, Darryl Zanuck told me the exact same thing."

Now, here's where the scene switches to slow motion as I absorb every agonizing detail—a real your-life-passes-before-your-eyes moment.

Selznick says nothing. He glares at me. Without missing a beat, he leans over, picks up the phone, and dials a number. I don't get the impression he's planning to tell the folks back at the office what a damn funny guy Feldman is.

"Mr. Spyros Skouras, please. This is David Selznick. I'll hold."

I'm frozen, paralyzed. Some half-chewed toast just sits there in my mouth.

"Spyros, I want Ed Feldman *fired!*" he screamed.

Now, Spyros Skouras ran Fox. I saw him all the time. In the hall, in his office, in the screening room. I'm doomed.

I could hear Skouras clearly through the phone because he was talking very loudly. "David, I can't fire Ed Feldman. You're asking me to do the impossible."

Thank God, I thought. Fox is sticking up for me. One of the heavy hitters of the film business is asking for my head and they're backing me up. What a great company.

Selznick is getting angrier and angrier. "Why *can't* you fire him, Spyros? Tell me. Why not?"

"I would fire him, David, if I knew who the hell you were talking about. How can I fire him and I don't even know who he is?"

Exit Feldman. I quietly got up, set my napkin down, and walked through the front door. Selznick never noticed—too busy yelling at Skouras.

I worked for Fox—for Skouras—for nine years. He spoke with me often, greeted me in the hall, saw me at meetings, saw me in the steam room. But usually he saw me with other people, a producer or director or someone. He would say to me, "You're a smart young man. Someday you'll work for me."

So for the entire nine years, before and after Selznick, he never knew who I was or that I was employed by Fox.

And you know what? After my disastrous encounter with "the most important man in the history of the business," that was just fine with me.

I'm a producer.

That young kid, nearly fired for mouthing off to a self-important big shot producer, now produces feature films for a living. For the record, these films are called feature films because they're shown in movie theaters before they reach home video and cable TV.

And they tend to be very, very expensive. The average production budget of the last four pictures I produced was in the neighborhood of $85 million each.

And lately they tend to feature big stars. Over my career, I've produced movies with Harrison Ford, Mel Gibson, Jack Lemmon, Glenn Close, Jim Carrey, and Eddie Murphy. This partly explains why the movies have been so pricey.

But working with stars goes far beyond that. Take Harrison Ford. He is much more than a big movie star. He's a generous, talented actor whose tremendous contributions to the making of a film are well over and above his considerable acting skills. Harrison is very smart—he's someone you always want to be in business with.

It's amazing that the general public often knows so little about what a producer actually does on a picture. Part of this is because a producer's role on a film depends on the particulars of the project itself. Some individuals are given a producer credit if they helped acquire the script or arranged financing but had little to do with the development and production of the film. A person is sometimes granted a producer's credit because he or she was involved with an early version of the project and has contractual rights that carry over.

Some people confuse the movie's producer with the director, and that's not unreasonable when directors also produce their own films. On most projects, the producer is the general manager and the director actually makes the picture. If you drew an organizational chart of a typical movie, the director would report to the producer. (With superstar directors like a Steven Spielberg, it's probably the other way around.) But in the workaday making of the movie, the producer and the director are more like partners.

So what *do* I do as a producer?

Well, one thing I *don't* do is put up my own money. And it's not that I don't believe in the projects. It's that producing a movie and financing a movie are two different things. Financing a movie is for investors who analyze the risks and potential returns of a number of projects, then invest their capital accordingly.

There was one scary time when my house was on the line to help pay for one of my movies. It was a little low-budget flick called *Hot Dog . . . The Movie.* But I don't do that anymore.

What I do as a producer is pretty simple, when you get right down to it. I'm the guy the studio hires to bring them a completed movie.

Many times, I acquire a script myself. It might be complete and ready to go, or in need of a rewrite or the like—*Witness, The Golden Child, Save the Tiger,* for example. Other times, I'm brought in to literally supervise the making of the film after someone else has developed it—*The Truman Show, Forever Young,* and *Green Card* were like that.

In both cases, the studio basically says, "Ed, here's $70 million. Go off and make this movie. Probably the script needs work, so we'll need you to consult with the director, the writers, and us. We might even need a second or third rewrite. Use good people on the picture but watch your spending—you have $70 million to spend and it's basically up to you to spend it wisely. If you run into problems, let us know. In fact, we'll be looking over your footage and production reports a lot to see how things are going. But you're in charge. We're there to help and we may show up once in a while but we won't hover around. Now good luck, Ed. Godspeed and all that. We're counting on you. Win one for the Gipper."

It's not really *that* simple, but that's the gist of it.

Moviemaking is one of the riskiest commercial activities on the planet. No one really knows how a movie is going to do. After screening *The Truman Show* for the first time, Sherry Lansing, then head of Paramount, turned to me and said, "Ed, you've made the most expensive art film in history."

Now Lansing is a top-flight movie executive. To call a movie an "art film" is to say that it's a good, high-quality work but that it seems to appeal to a very limited, specialized audience. Art films will typically play in small, possibly stand-alone theaters appealing to a more sophisticated audience. You know the type of theater I mean. When they're not showing the latest art film, they're running a Fellini retrospective, drawing a few film buffs who debate why the director used such-and-such a camera filter.

Studios categorically do *not* spend $50 million to $70 million on "art films."

MGM has a famous motto, *"ars gratia artis"*—art for the sake of art—that dates back to 1928. A retooled version could apply to all the major studios (and I don't mean this cynically): "art for the sake of money." (Mel Brooks even joked about this in one of his movies.)

Well, *The Truman Show* ended up a huge hit, financially and critically. We hit a home run, out of the park, and the ball finally landed three miles away.

I was a producer on another film, *K-19: The Widowmaker*, which starred Harrison Ford and Liam Neeson. It told the compelling true story of the Soviet Union's first nuclear submarine, a vessel so ramshackle that it nearly caused a nuclear explosion in the North Atlantic. The film was well made and directed. It was tense and gripping. Harrison and Liam were wonderful in very tough roles (they played Russian submarine commanders). The critics loved it. Paramount released it in prime time, midsummer 2002, with a huge, expensive marketing push. Our ace in the hole—Harrison Ford, one of a select few superstars who can bring people to a film with his persona.

But the audience stayed away in droves. The film cost its backers $90 million (Paramount was only distributing it) and took in $35 million in North America box office and even less abroad.

With *K-19,* we tapped the ball up in the air and it fell right into the catcher's mitt. *Yer out!*

Meanwhile, in this tortoise and hare pennant race, *My Big Fat Greek Wedding,* staffed with talented unknowns and costing a mere $5 million, grossed over $240 million at the North American ticket booths, becoming one of the top romantic comedies of all time. We—*K-19*—outgrossed it for three weeks starting in July 2002, right after we opened. Then we were almost gone completely two weeks later and *Greek Wedding* was still trotting along.

And all the major studios—I mean *all*—had turned *Greek Wedding* down. Try explaining *that* to your stockholders, Mr. Movie Mogul.

Now that's a risky business to be in.

Everyone looks back on *Titanic* as if it was always destined to be a hit—the highest-grossing film in history—from the get-go. But people have selective memories.

A friend of mine once tried to arrange a conference call with James Cameron, *Titanic's* writer and director. Cameron was hard at work on the script and his time was very, very scarce. Cameron's assistant was apologetic and explained that Cameron was writing a script based on the sinking of the *Titanic,* something not that many people were aware of early in the effort. My friend was incredulous—what an odd choice for the great action director James Cameron. Besides, the Titanic story had been filmed several times before and everyone already knows the ending!

During the filming of *Titanic,* the cost went wildly over budget, making 20th Century Fox, the lead studio on the film, look like it had an out-of-control train wreck on its hands. Another *Waterworld.* Hollywood tongues were wagging at a furious pace and the words were not kind. Fox's very survival, or at least the tenure of its senior executives, was questioned.

Then an odd thing happened. It opened and people went to see this three-hour-plus mega-epic and loved it, especially teenage girls and young women. They went back again and again, sobbing each and every time over Leonardo DiCaprio's tragic, selfless love for Kate

Winslet. You just know there was many a young man who "got lucky" after taking his date to see *Titanic*.

The money rolled in, and Fox and Cameron were now *geniuses.* (The real geniuses were at Paramount, who put up a fixed amount to partner on *Titanic,* then split the take with Fox. Fox had to shoulder the cost overruns alone.)

At the end of the day, a good producer is valuable to movie studios because he or she helps them tame the risk of moviemaking. The studios pay me very well to manage these mega-dollar productions competently, keep problems to a minimum, come in at the budgeted cost figure plus a standard contingency allowance, and deliver a high-quality movie to them, so they can market it to the masses.

With all the other risks they face, they don't need a big-dollar headache happening three thousand miles away. It costs over $200,000 a day to shoot a big movie on location. If the picture runs five days behind, that's more than $1 million down the drain. The studio chiefs like to get a sound sleep at night and that's why they need good producers.

And *that's* what I do for a living.

And the work—well, sometimes it goes like this . . .

In late 1996 through mid-1998, I produced *The Truman Show* for Paramount and Scott Rudin with my friend the extraordinary Australian Peter Weir directing. As most people know by now, the film centers around a young man and his life. He seems very ordinary—except that his life is really a television show and he is the show's unwitting star. All of his friends and family are paid actors. He is an international phenomenon but he doesn't know it. Hidden cameras are everywhere, following him constantly. Jim Carrey played the man, Truman Burbank, in his first dramatic role.

There are two central characters to the piece, Truman and the director of the television show, the enigmatic Christof.

The movie was fully cast by the time we began shooting in Seaside,

Florida, on the Florida Panhandle near Panama City. Seaside is the ultimate planned community, looking something like an idealized version of a 1950s American town. Idyllic, worry free, controlled. Most of the film's principal photography occurred in and around Seaside.

Now, because of the nature of the story, Christof is never actually seen in Seahaven Island, Truman's fabricated hometown. Throughout the film, Christof sits in an elaborate TV control room, behind the fake sky that looms over the island.

So there was no need to film any of Christof's scenes in Florida. Later we would move the production to the Paramount studio lot in Hollywood and shoot all of Christof's scenes together on a soundstage. Then the scenes would be combined with the Florida footage to tell the story.

Dennis Hopper was playing Christof as we began the control room shooting at Paramount. Hopper had had mixed success over his career but he was capable of delivering strong, magnetic performances in unconventional roles. David Lynch's *Blue Velvet* was one of his best.

But it was well known that during phases of his life, he had been a heavy drug user. He had talked about it publicly. The word we had on him in 1996 was that he was drug-free and reliable. The last thing a big $70 million picture needs is a secondary lead who shows up late or delivers an erratic performance. And God forbid we would ever find him stoned in his dressing room. With those fears behind us, Peter Weir and Paramount were satisfied that Hopper would work out fine.

But he didn't, and it wasn't because he was using drugs. On Day 1 of the Christof scenes, we knew we were in trouble. Hopper was not off to a good start in the role. For one thing, he was having difficulty remembering his lines.

Keep in mind that much of the movie was shot and rough-edited by the time Hopper arrived. We knew we had a winner. Almost all of Carrey's performance was finished and he was terrific, exceeding a lot of people's expectations.

All it took was that one day of shooting to question Hopper as the right actor for the role. Peter Weir was exasperated but passive. But I didn't wait for Peter. I called Paramount and Scott Rudin, and told them we might need to replace Hopper and that we should start looking around. They said fine—we'll pay him off and go with someone else if necessary.

Hopper wasn't needed again on the set for a while. Then one day we call on him to read lines off-camera as Christof while we filmed Jim Carrey in the water tank on the Universal studio lot. Christof and Truman have a dramatic exchange as Truman escapes from his imprisonment by boat at the end of the picture. In the scene, Truman hears Christof's voice through a loudspeaker—Christof is still in the TV control room behind the fake sky.

Hopper's delivery wasn't what we anticipated. We had to replace him.

Peter was reluctant to release Hopper. I told him, "Look. He's going to bring down the whole picture. If you continue with Hopper, believe me, you will be back here reshooting the last three weeks of the movie."

Peter finally said, "All right. But *you* handle it."

Dennis Hopper is a great actor. No person relishes this sort of thing but it had to be done. This is what they pay me for.

I called Hopper and here's what I said: "Dennis, no one in the world is more impressed by your talent and films than Peter Weir and I. But sometimes the magic doesn't work."

Immediately he said, "OK." That was that. A classy guy and a classy exit.

So now we have no Christof and no really good prospects either. Luckily, there was still plenty to do—beach scenes, water scenes. But finally we reached the point where there was nothing else to film. We would have to shut down production pending a new Christof, and believe me, that sort of thing is very, very expensive.

There are plenty of good actors out there but the problem was, we couldn't find a Christof we were all happy with and who was available right then. Many names were bandied about. No luck.

Paramount had its list. Peter Weir doesn't pay much attention to lists.

Finally, I'm at wit's end. It's Thursday and the following Tuesday is the shutdown point.

I'm in my office ruminating about what to do now, when I get a call from an agent with CAA—Creative Artists Agency—and he says, "Ed, what do you think of Ed Harris for the part?"

And at that moment, God smiled down on me.

I say, "I think Ed Harris is *fabulous.* We're going to shoot at Zuma Beach tonight. Have him come over to meet Peter Weir. He lives near there."

So Harris drives over in his truck, gets out of the truck, meets Peter for the first time. And it's love at first sight. He's the one.

So that night I immediately put him into wardrobe, makeup, hair, and everything . . . without a deal. That's a mistake. All you budding film producers out there, *that's a mistake.* The next day, after he was cast and ready to go, CAA "killed me" with the deal. We paid him $800,000 for six days' work on the film. Plus there was a penalty of $50,000 a day for every day over that.

But it was money well spent. Ed Harris is one of the most talented actors in the business. And because of his professionalism and speed, we didn't go over the six days.

Harris has moments in the movie that are amazing, such as when he goes up to the movie screen and touches sleeping Jim Carrey's face. One of the highlights of the film, in my mind. That was pure Ed Harris.

Harris went on to be nominated for an Academy Award for *The Truman Show,* one of the three Oscar nominations we received. (The others were writing and directing.) He won the Golden Globe award, as did Jim Carrey.

The picture itself became a huge hit for Paramount, taking in $240 million in worldwide box office.

Who knows how it would have done without Ed Harris. Scott Rudin and I would prefer not to contemplate that.

You know, any tough guy can come along and say, I'm going to bring this movie in on time and on budget, no matter what. And then he browbeats the director, bullies the actors, and terrorizes the crew. What kind of movie do you think he'll get? I'll tell you. A bad one, a rotten one, an unwatchable one. And that's assuming everyone doesn't walk off before shooting finishes. And no one will want to work with him again. Take it from me—the word gets around and quickly.

That sort of abusive behavior doesn't work well in assembly-line manufacturing, and it sure as hell isn't going to work in something as delicate as the process of assembling creative elements in manufacturing movie magic.

I firmly believe the following:

You have to respect the creative process.

Call it the Second Rule of Producing.

(I know, I know, I can count. I'll get to the first one later. Trust me.)

There's a famous story of Donald Sutherland considering the lead male role in Nicolas Roeg's now classic thriller *Don't Look Now.* On the telephone, Sutherland told Roeg that he wanted to discuss changes in the script before he accepted the part. Roeg replied, "Do you want to do the film as it is written or not?"

Now, this sounds very authoritarian and didactic: *My way or the high-way.* But Roeg later explained to a friend of mine what he really meant in that conversation with Sutherland: "Obviously I want to hear what you have to say, but the film isn't on the page, the film is in my head. If it were on the page, it would be a novel."

The film is in my head.

That's a big part of the risk of moviemaking. Anyone who reads a script before the movie is made is drawing mental images of how the finished product will look and sound. But it's the director's vision that counts. He's the one in charge of blending all the creative elements and turning those words on a page into a magical cinematic experience.

We all know that excellent movies are magical. There's nothing quite like sitting in a darkened theater with four hundred or so other people watching a film that intrigues us, saddens us, surprises us, makes us laugh, makes us cry with tears of joy. The communal experience, the wide screen, the breathtaking photography and rich sound, the enchanted performances. It's simply magic. No other way to describe it.

And to get that magic, you have to let the creative process evolve without a lot of interference and micromanagement. It needs nourishment, not oppression.

Hire good people and let them do their jobs.

But a delicate high-wire act is always going on. A huge amount of money is at stake and the producer cannot let the filmmaking process get out of control, no matter how creative the results.

A big issue in moviemaking is when to spend money and how much. These are some of the most difficult, thorny decisions in producing. There has been horror story after horror story about directors spending money foolishly during the shooting of a picture. Entire books have been devoted to out-of-control productions like *Heaven's Gate,* the 1981 film that sank United Artists.

The studio pays people like me to keep this from happening.

A hand goes up.

"Ed, I'm a director. How do *you* know if it's foolish or not? Some of the best moments in a picture have been created spontaneously on the set. That's part of the process. Would anyone want Cameron to have changed anything in making *Titanic,* the biggest grossing film in history?"

Good question. You could write a whole book on that general subject. So I did. Covering that and many other things. Here it is.

For now though, I'll give you an example of the wise use of money. We tested an almost complete *K-19,* the Harrison Ford submarine picture, with test audiences in movie theaters. Two things rang out from these sessions, loud and clear. Harrison's character needed to be (a) more heroic and (b) more sympathetic. Everyone agreed. The studio, the director, Harrison—everybody.

Harrison is playing the commander of a doomed Russian submarine and much of the film focuses on his character flaws. He is overly stubborn and reckless in protecting Mother Russia at the expense of his men's safety and the possibility of a nuclear catastrophe.

But the test results were clear: he needed to be more balanced. At the eleventh-and-three-quarter hour, there's not really that much you can do about fixing the movie's main character.

But you can do something. In this case, it was reshoots. Here's what we did . . .

The scenes in the interior of the submarine were originally shot on an elaborate, realistic set built in an old factory in Toronto during spring 2001. The set was demolished about two months after we finished. We had to reconstruct from scratch the parts of the interior we needed on a soundstage in Hollywood in January 2002. The preparation for the new shoot took about two weeks.

Then we brought Harrison and some of the other actors back to film some very short sequences that supplemented or altered scenes shot in Toronto. In one sequence, we amplified Harrison's rescue of a crewman from the contaminated submarine reactor room. The original scene was shorter. The new footage played up the heroic angle.

The other major sequence—we gave Harrison an emotional speech in the sick bay to radiation-poisoned, very sick crewmen, but we focused on the crewman who had behaved cowardly but then rose to the occasion. The redone scene softened Harrison's character tremendously and made him more sympathetic.

The actual shooting took about three days and the total cost was close to $1 million.

Did it save the movie? No.

But it was important to make the picture as good as we could. Plus it positioned us better for the home video and cable releases.

I started my career in the world of big-time movie publicity in 1950. Now let me forewarn you about the publicity business back then—it was very freewheeling. In the pages that follow, I will describe things we did to promote movies that can only charitably be called "bending the truth." But that was the way things were done then, no matter how it looks today. If a big company did now what publicity guys did in the 1950s, there would be no shortage of scandal and lawsuits.

Look what happened to Sony and Microsoft in 2001 and 2002, respectively. Sony was plenty red-faced when *Newsweek* discovered that Sony marketing people had invented a phony critic, then quoted from the critic's "reviews" in ads. The state of Connecticut fined Sony $326,000 for deceptive advertising. Why Connecticut? Because the fake critic "worked" for a small newspaper based in Ridgefield, Connecticut.

(That's really kind of funny. If Sony had employed its fake critic at an Idaho paper, then Idaho would be $326,000 richer, not Connecticut.)

Microsoft got a shiner when it was revealed that its marketers had posted a fake story on the company website. They were trying to counter Apple's successful ad campaign featuring stories of why Windows users switched to Apple products. Problem was, Microsoft's story was bogus and the accompanying photo was from a stock-picture house. Ouch.

We would have done stuff like that routinely in 1952 and not thought twice about it. And nobody would have cared. But not now.

It is one of the ironies of my career that I started out making a success by *bending* the truth, and in much later years, I built a much bigger success by *telling* the truth, the whole truth, and nothing but.

I'll use the Third Rule of Producing to explain:

When producing a big-budget picture, you are always better off telling the studio the truth, no matter what.

I am convinced that a huge chunk of my producing success is that I am a straight shooter with the studio. I tell them the good and the bad, unvarnished. I'm not an alarmist, but if there's a problem, I want them to know about it.

Mainly because studio executives hate surprises. They don't much like bad news in general but they *really* hate surprises. I had no hesitation about calling Paramount immediately with the Hopper problem. If I had delayed or been wishy-washy, it could have been very costly.

I have had bigger and bigger movies assigned to me over the last few years. And I firmly believe much of this owes to my directness with the studios.

They say the truth shall set you free.

If you had been in Nottingham, England, on a certain day in 1995, at the National Dalmatian Festival, there is a good chance you would have seen movie producer Ed Feldman kissing every dog he could get his hands on. And cuddling them and caressing them and whispering sweet nothings in their floppy ears. You might have thought, "My gracious, what a dog fancier that Feldman is."

Or maybe, "My God, Feldman has lost his bloomin' mind!"

And you would be wrong on both counts.

The truth is, I had just been told off at lunch by two prominent leaders of U.K. Dalmatian clubs. The chief of the Scottish club stood up after five minutes at the lunch table and declared, "You know something, I don't even want to break bread with you people." And storms out. Not even time for a "Hoot, mon."

At the other end of the table, the head of an English Dalmatian club tells me, "Why don't you take your little picture and go back to America with it?"

They had me pegged for Cruella DeFeldman.

And all I was trying to do was make a picture called *101 Dalmatians* for Disney, and I really wanted the help and goodwill of the Dalmatian clubs and every other Dalmatian lover in Great Britain. Because we needed three hundred Dalmatian puppies—triple the number Cruella wanted to make into a fur coat in the movie.

Not many people know that kissing dogs is part of the job description of a movie producer. But on this picture, it certainly was. The ill-starred lunch was at a meeting and show of the Dalmatian clubs of the United Kingdom. After my dressing down, I thought it was a good idea to tour the show area and demonstrate to the British Dalmatian world that I wanted only the best for my little spotted friends . . . a little smooching couldn't hurt.

For Disney *101 Dalmatians* was a huge picture. The original animated feature from 1961 is one of the crown jewels of the Disney library, and they spared no expense on this live-action remake. In its scope, it was as if we were making a canine *Raiders of the Lost Ark*.

Disney had hired me to supervise the movie. One of my specialties in the 1990s forward was producing big-budget, complicated movies in locales far away from headquarters.

Budgeted at $67 million, *101 Dalmatians* starred Glenn Close, one of the world's great actresses, as the evil Cruella DeVil. Filming would be in England, with massive interior sets at Shepperton Studios near

London.

By far the biggest challenge in the film was the Dalmatian puppies. We had decided early on not to use special effects to create the illusion of ninety-nine puppies because we wanted to draw a clear distinction between the animated version and our dogs—which would be real. (Add the two adult dogs for 101.) When we did the sequel, though, we used some computer-generated puppies to speed things up.

The Dalmatian clubs were concerned that some or most of the three hundred puppies would end up being put to sleep after the filming. I had told them firmly and strenuously that it would never happen, but they were skeptical. Think about the public relations nightmare for Disney if any of those cute little Dalmatian puppies from the movie were killed when no longer needed.

We came up with a good solution. I guaranteed to the Dalmatian clubs that the adoption of every single puppy used on the film would be prearranged, so when a puppy was finished on the set, it would go off immediately to a loving home. With this, the problem went away, and we were off and running.

The Royal Humane Society in England wasn't equipped to provide an observer on the set every day of filming. So we brought over an American Humane Society observer and she was very meticulous about her job.

We built a Dalmatian hotel at Shepperton and the dogs were treated like royalty. Thirteen trainers were assigned to the puppies, and a veterinarian was on site twenty-four hours a day. The kennels were thoroughly cleaned twice a day. On the set, no one except a trainer could touch a dog. We cordoned off the stage so that you had to dip your shoes in disinfectant before you entered the filming area.

We needed three hundred puppies because we could use them for the production only when they were five or six weeks old and at their cutest. They grew so quickly that we required two groups of puppies to complete the picture.

Here's the way it worked. About four weeks into production, we stopped everything and filmed the first group of puppies for a week. Then they went off to their new homes. About five weeks later, regular filming again stopped and we brought in the second group of puppies for another week of filming. And then resumed regular production.

You can imagine the logistical nightmare of providing the right number of puppies at exactly the right time. This feat of prowess was expertly handled by Birds and Animals Unlimited, an American company.

101 Dalmatians was a big hit and three hundred adorable little Dalmatian puppies found three hundred loving homes. All's well when a movie producer can supply a Disneyesque happy ending in real life.

I'll talk in detail later about the riskiness of filmmaking and how I help manage it, but I'd like to discuss one risk right now that has its own unique twist in the entertainment industry: the "people risk." (As you saw, the "dog risk" wasn't that bad.)

Few business ventures are as dependent on individual high-priced people as moviemaking. I mentioned earlier that we viewed Harrison Ford as our ace in the hole on *K-19* because he is one of a select few movie stars who can actually "open" a picture. This means that folks see his name and want to buy tickets to the movie because he's in it. The opening-weekend boost the film gets is enormously valuable and can lift the picture like it's on wings.

It's no secret that these A-List movie stars make upwards of $15, $20, or even $25 million per picture.

This gives the A-List actors enormous power in the industry generally, in picking projects, and on the set of the movie. I am happy to report that most of the A-List are responsible professionals who rarely, if ever, abuse this power. I've found the A-Listers I've worked with as a producer to be surprisingly pleasant and cooperative.

But I'll give you the Fifth Rule of Producing anyway:

You can manage the people risk about 99 percent of the time. It's the other 1 percent that will get you.

Now, in my business, you can have a people risk from directors, crew, and actors who are not at the very top, not just the A-Listers. But there is a much heavier concentration of risk in the A-List.

I'll tell you about a man who once thought he had the people risk under control. Think of him as a 99-percenter.

I was sent to Rome in 1966 to check on John Huston's *Reflections in a Golden Eye,* which was shooting there. I was then the vice president for advertising and publicity for the film's producer, Seven Arts.

The film starred Elizabeth Taylor and Marlon Brando. Based on the novel by Carson McCullers, it was a melodrama set on an army base in the Deep South, circa late 1940s. Brando played an officer on the base, a repressed homosexual, and Taylor was his wife, a not-so-repressed nymphomaniac. John Huston was directing.

Why film in Rome, about three thousand miles and three million cultures away from the 1940s Deep South? Because that's where Elizabeth Taylor wanted it to be filmed.

You must understand that in 1966, Elizabeth Taylor was a goddess. Starting with the filming of *Cleopatra* in the early 1960s, Taylor was *the* female movie star and sex symbol of the era. Many believed her to be the most beautiful woman in the world. Her face was everywhere—magazine covers, movie posters, glitzy movie premieres. The media couldn't get enough of her.

Her romance with costar Richard Burton during the making of *Cleopatra*—both were married to other people—was a story for the ages. (*Cleopatra* was so expensive that it nearly brought down my old employer, 20th Century Fox.) After that, Taylor and Burton's stormy, very public marriage was another story for the ages.

So if Elizabeth Taylor wanted a film set in the Deep South to be filmed in central Italy, then that was that. No more questions.

I arrive on the *Reflections* set at the studio Dino De Laurentiis built to compete with the venerable Cinecittà. I was tickled to be seeing my old friend John Huston again.

The phrases "a man's man" and "hale fellow well met" must have been invented for John Huston. He was gregarious, funny, charming. Tall and distinguished, yet friendly and open. A wonderful man and a wonderful human being.

But I came to Rome in the middle of a crisis. I was the Seven Arts studio man on site right then, so naturally I became involved.

It seems that *Reflections* was running behind. Elizabeth Taylor may have been a goddess but she was a very difficult goddess. She seemed to be always late or ill or some other damn thing.

Anyway, there's a production meeting this one morning at the studio. The line producer, C. O. "Doc" Erickson, explains to Huston and me that they can get back on track if they can alter the shooting schedule. We had been filming six days a week all along, but Taylor's contract specified that she had to work only five days a week. Now if she would agree to work for three Saturdays, everything would be fine. In fact, not only would the movie be back on schedule but the production could wrap up by Christmas. Everyone could leave for the holidays and be done with the picture. Otherwise, they would be stuck in Rome for Christmas and away from their families.

After this is explained at the meeting, we all turn to Huston.

"Just leave everything to me. I'll take care of it," he says.

My account here doesn't do justice to Huston's voice and delivery. When Huston spoke, you heard these deep, mellifluous words in those wonderfully expressive tones of his. It wasn't for nothing that he was the voice of God in *The Bible*. Plus he was dramatic and convincing, a natural actor. He also played the part of Noah in *The Bible*.

As Huston and I walk over to the set, he explains that he and "Elizabeth" have a wonderful relationship and he is absolutely certain she will agree to the Saturday work.

I knew about Elizabeth Taylor, so I was skeptical. But how can God *and* Noah be wrong, I ask you?

Taylor is seated with her assistant as Huston and I approach. He turns his head and looks at me with a confident "Watch and Learn" expression.

"Elizabeth, my darling, may I have a brief word with you." And he takes her hand and kisses it.

"Why certainly, John, my sweet." And she flashes him a thousand-megawatt smile.

"Elizabeth, my love, I have been having a little talk with the Production Department. If we could impose upon you to work just three Saturdays in the next eight weeks, we could finish the picture in time for Christmas. So that everyone can go back to home and hearth. To spend the holidays with their loving families. It would make their Christmases oh, so much merrier."

Huston was really laying it on thick but it was a masterful performance. God, he was good. (A lot of those guys on the crew didn't have families at all, much less loving ones.)

But Taylor just sits staring at him. Nothing.

Surely she is turning over in her own mind how she might phrase her response to Huston's entreaty. Certainly she would wish to match his legendary eloquence.

But still she is silent, her expression blank.

Huston pipes up, "Just three Saturdays. What do you think about that, Elizabeth?"

Finally the Goddess Elizabeth answers:

"John, why don't you go fuck yourself."

And lo, the cast and crew of *Reflections in a Golden Eye* were greeted by a bright Rome sunrise—come Christmas morning.

WELCOME TO SHOWBIZ

I PUSHED ON THE STEAM ROOM DOOR TENTATIVELY, THEN opened it a few inches. Thick clouds of hot steam billowed out, enveloping me and making me turn my head and blink. Now I'm standing there, with the door cracked open, dressed in a wool suit, buttoned-down shirt, tie, nice leather shoes, the works. I look really sharp.

But my assignment right then was to meet with Fox muckety-mucks in the executive steam room about some big movie launch.

Why couldn't I meet with them in a conference room?

Because they were in the steam room!

I pulled myself together, straightened my tie, and went in.

The steam was almost impenetrable. I inched along for a few feet, swiping my hand in front of my face, trying to make a visual path for myself.

Finally, I could make out some figures sitting on ledges at various levels, a few standing or pacing.

Almost to a man, they were overweight and bald. A few had towels around their midsections but . . . omigod, most of them were totally naked, their privates fully exposed.

As I crept along, the only sounds were water dripping and the occasional sharp report of flatulence. It *was* right after lunch.

I walked slowly, surveying each face, careful to keep my gaze at eye level until I found my man. He looks up.

"Oh, Feldman. You're here. Pull up a chair." Har, har.

I'm holding a legal-sized pad of paper but I need to retrieve my fountain pen from my pocket. So I try tucking the pad under my arm while I fumble for the pen. Whoops. The legal pad hits the floor, paper side down. I grab the pen, bend down, pick up the pad quickly and . . . I can't avert my eyes fast enough. A big, hairy—hairy everywhere but the head—Fox exec gets up just then and, of course, he had to be one of the ones with the towel around his shoulders instead of his waist.

Sights like that have been known to scar lesser men for life.

I get myself together, tear off the soaked top sheet of the pad, gingerly uncap the pen, and now I'm poised to take notes.

Wool suit and tie, standing next to some hairy, three hundred-pound guy with his privates exposed.

A few anxious minutes later, the meeting is done and I'm creeping toward the door. I glance down and am horrified to see that my meticulous notes are running down the wet legal pad in an inky, ruined mess.

Then I have that creepy sensation that someone is staring at me. You know that strange, almost psychic feeling—you want to turn around and see who it is.

I whirl around—no one is looking up. But I do think I perceive one set of exposed private parts turn its head away, guiltily.

I need to get more sleep.

No matter what I say, here or anyplace else, my first job out of Michigan State with 20th Century Fox was terrific. Not only did it help me develop skills and contacts that I could draw on for the rest of my working life, but the job set me on a permanent career trajectory that allowed me to fulfill my wildest dreams and ambitions.

I owe those fat, naked guys a lot. I really do.

I had more meetings in the executive steam room but I learned to manage them better. Use a pencil, not a fountain pen. Schedule them before lunch, not after. And just ignore those pesky, curious private parts. They mean no harm.

I was initially hired as a writer in the Fox press book department. A press book for a movie was a collection of advertisements, news stories, pictures, even reviews of the movie, all in camera-ready, printable form. The studio would send these out to the theater owners, who would use them as they wished in local newspapers or other media outlets. Press books often included suggestions for promoting a picture—if we were pushing a Betty Grable movie, we might include a plan for having a local department store sponsor a Betty Grable look-alike contest. Some small newspapers would even reprint our review of the movie word-for-word. A good press book could be an invaluable aid to selling the movie and, we hoped, result in a higher box office take. Modern-day press kits incorporate elements of the old press books and usually contain electronic or video media.

I rose quickly in the ranks of Fox's publicity department in New York. From press book writer, I became fan magazine contact, then trade paper contact, then New York newspaper contact. I was one of Fox's "men of tomorrow." What that actually meant was I'd better work really hard today for a pittance so I could make some decent money tomorrow.

People and situations would come and go, but there were two main constants in my rise up the Fox ladder, both industry legends: Spyros Skouras and Charles Einfeld.

Skouras ran Fox. I told you a little about him earlier—he was the man who would fire Ed Feldman if he knew who Ed Feldman was. Einfeld was the head of advertising and publicity at Fox, a very important position.

His department could make or break a film in a heartbeat. It was Einfeld's job to get fannies into theater seats and he was good at it. Einfeld was making $2,500 a week back in the early 1950s, which would be close to $1 million a year now.

Skouras was the son of a Greek shepherd. He was penniless when he came to this country in 1910 with two brothers, George and Charles. As uneducated immigrants, they worked menial jobs initially, but over a few years they managed to scrape together $4,000 to build a St. Louis nickelodeon theater. Before long, they owned every movie theater in town and eventually sold out to Warner Bros. in the 1920s. Skouras helped engineer the 1935 merger of Fox Metropolitan Theaters with 20th Century Films that resulted in 20th Century Fox. Skouras became the company's president in 1942.

Skouras spoke in a thick Greek accent that never became easier to understand in all the years I knew him. Now he had an executive assistant named Lemuel Jones. Once, he told a new secretary, "Get me Lem Jones." But in his accent, it came out as something like, "Get me Lam Jobs." The secretary puzzled over this and finally decided she knew what he wanted. So Skouras is sitting at his desk—it's 9 A.M.—and a waiter arrives with a plate of, you guessed it, *lamb chops.*

"No, no, no," he screams. "I don't want this. I want Lem Jones, Lem Jones!"

I probably couldn't have done much better than that poor beleaguered woman. If it had been me, a pair of long johns might have shown up on his desk.

Around the office, we had a theory that Skouras could speak perfect English if he wanted to but he kept the Greek accent because it made him much more of a character.

Skouras was a smart if rough-hewn businessman, but his skills as a visionary sometimes were lacking in a big way. Here are some things Skouras passed up while I was at Fox:

★ The classic film *On the Waterfront*—Skouras was committed to the new wide-screen process, CinemaScope. "We only make CinemaScope films in color!" he said. *On the Waterfront* was in black and white. It went on to win eight Academy Awards including Best Picture. It generated a box office gross of ten times its cost . . . for Columbia Pictures.

★ Buying the ABC television network for a song—"We're in the movie business, not the television business!"

★ The first rights to In-Flight motion pictures—"Tell me who's going to sit through a picture in an *airplane*!"

Skouras could be very out of touch at times. Once we wanted to show him how successful our advertising department was. He would get his hair cut once a week at exactly the same time. We bribed the barber to put on a certain radio station during the hour he was in the chair. And then we would just pile on the commercials and the publicity into one hour. He thought we were *geniuses*!

All the major studios had the same unwieldy geographic arrangement then. The movies were made on the West Coast in Los Angeles while everything else, including company headquarters, was on the East Coast in New York. Why was this? Well, it made some sense because the big media—radio, television, major newspapers, magazines—were based largely in New York. Much of what Fox did was selling and the close media contacts were essential. Plus I guess the moguls just preferred living in New York. It's interesting—I've made my living in the film business all my adult life, and I didn't move to California until the late 1960s, almost twenty years after I started.

My immediate boss at Fox was Charles Einfeld. He was more polished than Skouras, but just as much of a character. Einfeld is the man who assembled his advertising and publicity staff at Warner Bros., some fifty or sixty people, and told them on December 5, 1941, "I keep hearing that some of you are nervous there will be a war. I will tell you categorically, there will be *no war*! And you can quote me." OK, Charlie, I just did.

Peace in Our Time by Charles Einfeld. For all of two days.

Einfeld had been the high-profile chief of advertising and publicity at Warner Bros. for many years, then left and formed Enterprise Pictures with David Loew, the son of MGM founder, Marcus Loew. Enterprise's films showed mixed results during the mid-1940s but it was eventually brought down by one film, *Arch of Triumph,* starring Ingrid Bergman and Charles Boyer from the Erich Maria Remarque blockbuster novel. The picture lost $2 million on its $4 million cost, causing one studio executive at the time to call it "the greatest commercial failure in the history of motion pictures." After this debacle, Einfeld went back to a career in advertising and publicity, this time with Fox.

Einfeld was one tough SOB. He always kept you on your toes by demeaning you. You'd place a front-page story in *Daily Variety* and he would berate you because it was below the fold.

And sentimentality, unless it could sell a movie ticket, was for sissies.

We were releasing the picture *With a Song in My Heart,* the story of singer Jane Froman, starring Susan Hayward. We were just getting ready to hold the world premiere at the Roxy Theater in New York, when word came through that Froman's real-life husband, commercial airline pilot John Burn, had just survived the harrowing crash of his plane, Pan Am Flight 526-A, in San Juan Harbor, Puerto Rico. Fifty-three people out of sixty-nine on board perished.

The tragic event was doubly significant because Burn had rescued a badly injured Froman from a USO plane crash during World War II, and they had fallen in love and married. That sequence of events was portrayed very dramatically in the film, with Rory Calhoun as Burn.

Stunned, I bring the *New York Journal-American* into Einfeld's office, the plane crash headline blaring off the front page.

"Charlie, you have to see this!"

Einfeld takes one look, slams his fist down on the desk, and exclaims in an excited voice, "My God! Ed, you can't buy publicity like this for a *million dollars!*"

Then there was the time Einfeld was worried about the tone of an ad campaign pushing one of Fox's new releases. "Boys," he said, "we gotta get some fun into this campaign. We gotta make sure people know they're gonna have a good time at this movie." So we paid a famous husband-and-wife radio team, Dorothy Kilgallen and Dick Kollmar, of the *Breakfast with Dorothy and Dick* show, $2,000 a week for two weeks to chat up all the funny moments in the picture.

The film was *The Diary of Anne Frank.* A laugh a minute it wasn't.

But Einfeld really was a top-notch advertising and publicity executive, the best. He's the one who coined the famous Fox slogan of the day, "Movies Are Better Than Ever!"

Einfeld had an edict then that male stars could appear at premieres only in tuxedos. If a guy should happen to show up without a tuxedo, before we could run a picture of him in the press an artist had to airbrush a tuxedo on. Well, I get a call one morning from a star who had a bit of a drinking problem. We'll call him Sy. "Ed," Sy asks sheepishly, "did I wear a tuxedo last night? I don't remember that."

I smile to myself.

"You must have, Sy. I saw you in it in the *Daily News.*"

Einfeld taught me a great deal about the business but he was also the most anti-Semitic *Jew* I ever met. His son was marrying one of the daughters of the Spiegel Catalogue people in Chicago. And all Einfeld was worried about was that it shouldn't be a Jewish wedding. Now the Fox publicity department—I included—was making the wedding arrangements. We finally found a "Christian" (read non-Jewish) place to hold it—the Town Tennis Club in New York, which didn't have air conditioning.

I bring Einfeld the wedding announcement we're sending to the *New York Times.* He looks it over and frowns. I know what the problem is. In the second paragraph, it says rabbi so-and-so will perform the service. And he looks at it and he looks at it, the frown deepening. Finally I said, "You know, Charlie, it *is* appropriate to refer to a Rabbi as the Very Reverend Doctor." The frown disappears. He puts the paper down, stands up, grabs me by the shoulders, and with a big grin, he says, "Ed, you're a *genius*! Why aren't *you* my son?"

Now at the Town Tennis Club, everybody knew it was not to be a Jewish wedding . . . except the bandleader. With all our careful 20th Century Fox planning, no one had thought to talk to the bandleader. And in the middle of this Christian wedding, all of a sudden the band strikes up the "Hava Nagila." And there is that old Greek Orthodox Spyros Skouras, sweating like a stallion, dancing the Horah in the middle of this WASPy tennis club.

These early years working publicity at Fox were never dull. And I was learning the movie business from the best teachers in the world. But my greatest, happiest, most satisfying successes happened nine miles north of Fox headquarters, in the Bronx.

Dad and I got into the gray DeSoto parked along the 1800 block of Harrison Avenue. Even though we lived in a pretty nice apartment building, in the Bronx in 1952 you had to park on the street. But it was OK. Safe street, good neighbors. No vandalism. The car would still be sitting there in the morning.

"Thanks for driving me in, Edward."

"Glad to, Dad."

Actually, this worked out well for me. Dad was a traveling salesman for ladies handbags, and he normally took the DeSoto on a Willy Loman trek through upstate New York and New England, gone from Monday through Friday. But this week, he was working at the company showroom in Manhattan. So I would drop him off on Thirty-third Street and then drive to the 20th Century Fox building on Fifty-sixth Street. This would give me some quality father-son time with him, a rarity then, what with his schedule.

Plus I didn't have a car of my own, so I could use the DeSoto to run some errands during the day.

And truthfully, driving through Manhattan was a nice change from taking the subway. Traffic then was heavy but bearable, much easier than today.

I was taller than Dad and had to adjust the mirrors and the seat. Finally we took off down Harrison Avenue. We had driven only fifty yards before Dad had me pull over.

"Let's give her a ride," he said. And he nodded toward a young woman walking along the street toward the trolley stop.

Did I say *woman*? Make that *girl*. Woman? Girl? No, teenager. On second thought, woman.

Anyway, she's now riding in the backseat of the DeSoto as we make our way to Manhattan. We drove down the Grand Concourse, rode past Yankee Stadium, crossed over on the Macombs Dam Bridge, rode through Harlem, entered Central Park at 110th Street, and then exited the park on Seventh Avenue headed downtown.

I'm a good driver but I was a pretty dangerous driver that morning because I couldn't keep my eyes off the rearview mirror. ("Car turning, Edward. . . . *Edward.*")

This *person* in the rearview mirror had lived on our block in the next apartment building for several years but I remembered her only as a little fourteen-year-old neighbor kid before I went off to college.

A kid no longer.

A young Elizabeth Taylor.

That was it. The face in the rearview mirror was a young Elizabeth Taylor. The *National Velvet* Elizabeth Taylor.

No. Too young.

The *Father of the Bride* Elizabeth Taylor.

Driving through Central Park in the early morning with Elizabeth Taylor in my view, leafy shadows bouncing off her radiant face. Died-and-gone-to-heaven time.

Some small talk and long, long glances later, we pulled up at the headquarters of Kute Kiddie Koats Incorporated on Thirty-fourth Street. Miss Taylor got out.

"Thank you for the ride, Mr. Feldman," she said to Dad. "And thank you, too, *Edward*." And she gave me a smile and a little wave.

"You're welcome, Lorraine," Dad said.

My eyes were glued to her back until she disappeared into the building. I looked over at Dad and he flashed me a big grin. He knew exactly what I was thinking so I didn't have to say anything. But I said it anyway.

"Wow, she is beautiful!"

Dear Mom,
I have just met the girl I'm going to marry.
Love,
Edward

OK, so I've got things a bit out of order. The note came later.

Two months after dropping the young Elizabeth Taylor off at Kute Kiddie Koats Incorporated, I needed a date for a classy party at Peacock Alley at the Waldorf-Astoria. Fellows my age just didn't date girls from the neighborhood. We didn't want everybody knowing our business. And believe me, the romantic details would get around Harrison Avenue at light speed.

My usual girlfriends—all from beyond the neighborhood—were busy that night so I took a chance and called Lorraine. She was surprised, to say the least, but agreed to go.

I picked her up in the gray DeSoto and we headed to the shindig, arrayed in our finest. She looked stunning. Elizabeth Taylor should wish to ever look as good as Lorraine did that night.

We danced, partied, and got to know each other. The evening was perfect—except for one thing. I took her to Rueben's, a high-class eatery on the East Side, and she ordered a $5 sandwich. At the time, I was making $62.50 a week. That one sandwich was almost 10 percent of my pay for the entire week. *And* she left half the sandwich (worth 5 percent of my pay) on her plate. Suddenly, I wasn't very hungry.

But pricey sandwich or no, I was smitten.

I came home with stars in my eyes and a lump in my throat. And *now* I wrote my mom the note.

Lorraine was going out with another guy then, so our first real, official date was later. It was on Lincoln's Birthday. I took her to the Russian Tea Room for lunch, then *This Is Cinerama* at the Broadway Theater.

Lorraine and I started dating exclusively but I quickly learned something about her that sent chills through me. Even today, five decades later, I *still* cringe. Well, here goes . . .

Lorraine was still in high school.

I thought her job at Kute Kiddie Koats Incorporated was a permanent one she had gotten after graduation. Instead it turned out to be a summer job between her junior and senior years.

Now this was going to be tricky. I may have been a young guy, just starting out, making $62.50 a week, a low man on the Fox totem pole. But remember that Fox was a *very* big-time totem pole. In my publicity job, I traveled sometimes in pretty rarified circles.

Lorraine and I were at a 20th Century Fox party one night with some awfully sophisticated people. Lorraine probably had her Algebra II midterm the next day or something. I introduce her to Herman Raucher, soon to be a big novelist and screenwriter. Raucher says, "Lorraine, what do you do?"

Before she can answer, I say, "Lorraine's a nurse, Herman."

Lorraine looks at me with the strangest look, like I've lost my marbles.

"Oh, how very interesting. And where is it that you work, Lorraine?"

I say quickly, "Mt. Sinai."

Before Raucher could finish saying, "And what do you do at Mt. Sinai?" it was, "Excuse us, Herman, I must talk with . . ." And we were off.

Now, it's the night of Lorraine's senior prom, for God's sake, at the

Roosevelt Hotel, no less. And I'm doing the Grand March, head down, muttering frantic prayers that no one from Fox sees me.

Here's a nightmare to rouse a guy from a deep sleep, in a cold sweat: In a dream, I'm walking down a deserted hallway at Fox. A ghostly Skouras steps in front of me and, still not even knowing my name, loudly asks, in that fractured accent of his, "So, your girlfriend graduate high school yet?"

As for keeping things quiet on Harrison Avenue, forget it. My mother used to be the Guardian of the Street. She would hang out the window of my bedroom on the ground floor, and she would converse with everybody who passed by. So did everyone know about Lorraine and me in the neighborhood? Had it existed then, CNN couldn't have been any more effective than the GFNS—the Gertrude Feldman News Service.

I'll have to say that Mom was leery of Lorraine at the very first. You see, Mom had a thing that anyone who wasn't born in this country was a foreigner. Lorraine's parents were from Hungary and Mom was suspicious of them for that reason. But it was a funny generational thing—my mother's parents came from Minsk, Russia, and my father's parents came from Alsace-Lorraine, then part of Germany. But *my* parents were born here and, to Mom, that made a difference. Eventually, Lorraine and Mom became good friends, and Mom was thrilled at the prospect of welcoming Lorraine into the family.

Lorraine and I were married on November 28, 1953, in a beautiful catering hall at 163rd Street and Jerome Avenue in the Bronx, right down from Yankee Stadium. I used to tell people we were married at third base, Yankee Stadium.

Lorraine looked like Elizabeth Taylor, natch, and I looked like . . . oh, what the hell, Montgomery Clift.

We took a one-week honeymoon to Miami Beach—Delano Hotel. Back then, someone had had the bright idea that flying was safer if you flew backward, with the seats facing to the rear. So we flew south, while headed north.

The Delano gave all the honeymoon couples their own little cabana by the ocean, and they were all clustered together under the sign Delano Honeymooners Colony. When a couple would retire to their room in midafternoon, the entire place would yell "Matinee, matinee!" behind them.

After then flying north, facing south, we moved to our own apartment below Harrison Avenue, on the swankier Grand Concourse. You could describe it as a one-and-a-half-room apartment. It had a doorman but no separate bedroom.

But we were in love and I was a happy man.

Part of learning the movie business was learning to deal with the personalities of the business. Some of the biggest, most celebrated names in the world passed through the publicity department of Fox, in one way or another.

One evening I'm working late by myself, almost dozing at my desk, when I sense someone at the door. I look up and there is this beautiful young blond woman, dressed to the nines, high heels, ample bosom pushing on low-cut bodice, extremely form-fitting, very short dress.

I do a double take. Shake my head a little. This must be a dream because . . .

It's Marilyn Monroe.

In her trademark, breathy, little-girl voice, she asks, "Can you help me? Where will I find Mr. Bush?" And she smiles that patented billion-dollar smile of hers.

I hesitate for a second.

"I'm here to discuss my publicity tour with him."

I recover quickly. With a big grin, I say, "Oh, I'm so sorry but Mr. Bush has left for the day, Miss Monroe. I'll be happy to tell him you were here. And how are you this evening?"

I escort her down the hall toward the elevator. We're all alone. Any second, I might expect an unseen fan in the floor to blow her skirt up around her waist while I look on with a Tom Ewell expression of admiration and amusement.

But alas, only in the movies.

Now, in the Fox New York office, we used to handle Howard Hughes's work just as a personal favor to Perry Lieber, who was a big Fox publicity executive on the West Coast. And one day I pick up the phone and my secretary says, "Ed, Howard Hughes is on the line." At first, I thought someone was joking around with me, but then I got really nervous. Howard Hughes was the richest and most powerful man in the world—the biggest of the big shots.

Hughes says, "Ed, this is Howard. You know, I've been having an affair with Gina Lollobrigida. I'm sure you know about that."

I said, "No, no, Mr. Hughes, I don't know anything about that." But of course, I did. Everyone did.

"Well, Ed, she's just finished a picture that I helped finance called *Beautiful But Dangerous,* the story of Lina Cavalieri, the Italian opera star. And I want you to just throw a gigantic world premiere of the movie in New York for charity and give Gina a big night."

And I said, "Whatever you say, Mr. Hughes." But he doesn't tell me that the picture is in Italian and it's awful. In fact, it's so awful that I cannot get a charity to sponsor the premiere.

So I made up a charity called the Daughters of Italy. And my wife, Lorraine; Dorothy Brodsky, wife of my Fox buddy Jack Brodsky; and the girlfriend of Dick Winters, another Fox buddy, were the committee pictured in the *New York Times* as they planned the premiere for the Daughters of Italy. The film died but Mr. Hughes got his premiere.

A couple of years later Hughes calls me up again with another request . . . but with a new twist. He says, "Ed, I've been having a thing with this singer and I just cut an album with her and I want to send her to New York for a week of publicity activity."

I said, "Certainly. That'll be no problem, Mr. Hughes."

He says, "But there's one *caveat*—I don't want anything to appear in print."

I had to think about that one. We're to throw big press conferences, photo shoots, everything. But nothing is to appear in the press. Impress the hell out of the singer, then he'll whisk her out of town with no trace. Brilliant. That's why he's Howard Hughes and I'm Ed Feldman.

So we meet her plane with ten photographers who have no film in their cameras and are just running flashbulbs. Then we hire our friends—one will represent the *New York Times*; another, *Billboard*; another, *Variety*; and so on. And they interview her and we pay each guy $100. She did day after day of interviews with all our friends and she never caught on. We pull it off without a hitch. Almost.

I had an eighteen-year-old intern from Princeton working in my office that summer, and he sees a photograph of the girl and thinks he's going to impress me. And he takes the photograph off my desk, and goes down and plants it in the *New York Journal-American*. To my terror, the picture appears and I'm fully expecting to be "whacked" by Howard Hughes. Fortunately Hughes never saw the picture. And it was the only thing that ever appeared about the girl.

I'll never forget. I had started work at Fox on a Monday. Then on that Thursday, they said be up in the projection room at ten o'clock for a screening.

Ten o'clock arrives and I go up and they're showing a new Fox movie called *All About Eve*. Directed by Joseph L. Mankiewicz, starring Bette Davis and Anne Baxter.

It turned out to be the best movie I saw in nine years at the company. But I was so impressed that they were *paying me* to sit through a movie—it was thrilling.

Skouras's wife had designed the projection room with imported Egyptian artifacts and tapestries. And I'm sitting underneath all the gilt, thinking this has got to be the greatest job in the whole world.

The picture ends and, of course, it's a wonderful movie. I go into the elevator and Skouras comes in before the door closes. Now it's just Skouras and me, riding down.

And he doesn't know who I am. But that's no surprise because remember, he *never* knew who I was during my entire Fox career.

He looks at me, smiles, and says in his broken English, "Tell me. Tell me how you *loved* the picture."

CHASING THE ELECTRIC
RABBIT

THE MAN SITTING ACROSS FROM ME AT BREAKFAST IS ONE OF THE richest, most powerful men in Hollywood. At one point, we hated each other but over time, we became friendly. It's 1978 and this man, my old boss Ray Stark, has invited me over to his house for breakfast and pleasant conversation. But Stark's house wasn't just a *house*—it was the former Humphrey Bogart estate in the exclusive Holmby Hills section of Los Angeles. Having breakfast there is like dining at the White House: servants bowing and scraping, crystal, exquisite china, crisp linen. One of the finest private art collections in the country. Why, I had just been admiring a Monet that's larger than any of the ones I saw in France. An original Utrillo covers the projection booth window in his living room.

Stark definitely lived it up.

While Stark and I are sitting there, an assistant comes over and whispers something to him. Stark nods and turns to me. "Ed, I'm so sorry, but Bob Redford is on the phone. You know, I'm doing *The Electric Horseman* with him. And with Jane Fonda. I'll need to take this."

I begin to get up out of my chair—I'll just disappear for a while and give Stark some privacy. Robert Redford is the biggest male star of this era, and whatever he wants to talk with Stark about must be pretty important and doesn't concern Ed Feldman.

But Stark motions to me to keep my seat and picks up the receiver of the phone. "Good morning, Bob. How are you?"

Now I couldn't hear what Redford was saying but I could tell Stark wasn't very happy about it.

"Bob, please understand that Margaret Booth is one of my closest friends in the business. She's already assigned to the picture."

Stark told me later that Redford was unhappy that Stark was using Booth, a longtime supervising film editor, to work on *The Electric Horseman*. Booth really was a very good friend of Stark's and now Redford wanted her released. "I don't want her around," Redford said. Stark suspected that Redford was worried that Booth would be a conduit—an information channel—back to Stark during production of the film.

The conversation now turns tense. Redford tells Stark that if Booth is on the picture, then he's off. He would walk.

Now it's Stark's turn. "Bob, you're an actor. You go from picture to picture. You sell yourself to the highest bidder. You're loyal to whoever is paying you right then.

"Margaret Booth is an old, cherished friend of forty-two years. I will simply not forgo her friendship *for an actor.*"

After Stark puts the phone down, he smiles at me and shakes his head. "Just another actor . . . trying to push me around."

I can assure you that very few movie producers would ever call a super-star like Robert Redford "just another actor." But Ray Stark would and didn't blink an eyelash over it either. He was that *tough*. Stark was even one of the producers who "discovered" Redford back in the 1960s, casting him opposite Natalie Wood in *This Property Is Condemned*. One of Redford's most successful dramatic films was Stark's *The Way We Were* with Barbra Streisand, years before *The Electric Horseman*.

My relationship with Ray Stark dates back to 1960. In 1960, Ray Stark was something I aspired to be—a movie producer. I was a publicist for him then, and I had been a publicist with 20th Century Fox in New York for most of the 1950s. I can tell you that publicity is about hundred million light-years from producing. A career in publicity sounds exciting—rubbing shoulders with stars, planning glitzy premieres and parties. Working for a major, well-known movie studio.

That is certainly true; much of it *was* exciting and glamorous. But then there are assignments like this one—

Fox was releasing *The Egyptian* in 1954, a big-budget historical epic starring Edmund Purdom and Bella Darvi, who also happened to be studio chief Darryl Zanuck's girlfriend. Naturally, we were going to give it a big push. So they decide to send out two tractor trailer museum trucks of Egyptian memorabilia, artifacts, and costumes around the country to promote the picture. One truck will cover a northern route and the other, a southern route. Sixty-six cities each. Well, I get assigned to be the advance man on the southern tour. So Fox puts me in an un-air-conditioned sedan, gives me a map, and sends me out to visit the sixty-six cities two weeks ahead of the truck to complete the arrangements.

This isn't a plum assignment. I'm a newlywed and it's summer—the heat would be sweltering—and I'll be gone eleven long weeks. But I'm a company man and game, so I turn the sedan south and off I go.

By this stage in my life, I hadn't done much traveling. But I would now. My route took me as far west as San Antonio, Texas. And as expected, the heat was almost unbearable. Fortunately, my bride, Lorraine, was able to fly to Houston to meet me and stay with me until New Orleans.

This trip was a real cultural eye-opener for New Yorker Ed Feldman. In rural Louisiana, I saw snakes crossing the road. Never saw that in the Bronx.

More ominously, I saw signs all over that I had never seen before. Unpleasant signs:

COLORED RESTROOM

NO COLOREDS ALLOWED ON THE MAIN FLOOR OF THE THEATER

I encountered one lady newspaper publisher in Pensacola who had a problem with the likes of me. Here's what she said: "You're a press agent, aren't you? A *northern* press agent. And I think you're also a *Jewish* northern press agent. And we don't cotton to those kind of people down here."

But I won her over, and she did a lot for us. Call me a goodwill ambassador to the South for northern Jewish press agents.

We had a model traveling with the tractor trailer. She and a cheetah (*yes, a model and a cheetah*) were sent along to provide atmosphere for the Egypt-themed display. She was from Chapel Hill, North Carolina. That was our last stop, so I thought it might be fun to arrange a big celebration for her during the stay there—big homecoming, keys to the city. Well, here's what the mayor told me: "Why, Mr. Feldman, that girl was asked to leave town. Do you think this is a good idea?"

That cinched it. Now I thought it was a *great* idea. But I didn't want to embarrass the model, so I canned that plan.

The cheetah and I both had one thing in common—we didn't like the stifling heat at all. The display is in Nashville at a department store and the cheetah decides the air conditioning is just fine. They can't get it to leave. The trainer pulls and pulls, the cheetah digs in and holds on. Finally, a big section of mangled department store carpeting is dragged to the front door along with the cheetah.

On this trip, I did find out for sure that I had picked the right industry to work in. The manager of the Fox Theater in Atlanta taught me a lesson I never forgot. He held up an empty paper cup from his concession stand. "Ed," he said, "this is a great business we're in. Look at this paper cup. When I fill it with soda, I'll sell it for fifty cents. The soda costs me a penny and the cup costs me a penny. So I've made a profit of forty-eight cents."

With those kinds of profit margins, Ed Feldman has found a home.

Now if I can just get my share of the forty-eight cents.

"Lieutenant Feldman, I hear you're a hot shot press agent. I've been a full colonel in the air force for ten years, since I was twenty-seven years old. You have got two years to make me a general. Now get to work!"

"Yes, sir, Colonel Gideon."

And I saluted sharply, turned, and exited Gideon's office.

It seems my movie-business career has taken a little detour. I would have to wait to get my share of the forty-eight cents. After finishing my sixty-six-city tour of the South for Fox and *The Egyptian,* I was called up to active duty in the air force for two years. I had been in ROTC at Michigan State, so my "Greetings from the President" telegram shouldn't have been too much of a surprise.

My family gave me a big send-off party on a Friday and then the next Friday, I was back home on leave from fighting the Battle of Delaware. I was stationed at Dover Air Force Base in Delaware and my C.O. was Col. Francis Gideon.

Gideon was serious about the assignment he had given me. He fully expected me to get him promoted to general in two years through force of publicity. Well, if I could successfully promote *The Egyptian* in Selma, Alabama, then why not? I like a challenge.

The first thing I did was put Gideon Bibles aboard every plane in the command. But wait, there's more. I get a picture of Col. Gideon putting the first Bible in a plane on the front page of the *Air Force Times.* Now, this would be like the *New York Times* back home. It was a big deal.

This kind of success gave me power at Dover you just wouldn't believe. I could give myself temporary duty anywhere I wanted—no orders from anyone. Just the fact that Col. Gideon wanted me to do some work for him.

On Armed Forces Day, I got pretty young female reservists called up. So visitors to Dover that day would be greeted by a sea of beautiful women in uniform.

I was doing such a good job for Gideon, I thought I deserved a raise. He set me straight. "Lieutenant, in the service, they don't give you *raises.*"

"Well, Colonel, I *am* doing the work a major should be doing." A promotion would certainly give me a raise.

So Gideon promotes me to first lieutenant after only six months in the service.

Now I get word that the National Sweet Pea Festival of Great Britain is being held, for the first time in forty years, in Dover, England, instead of London. And they're inviting all the Dover sister cities from around the world to send or bring flowers to the festival. I go to the air force and suggest that we fly the mayor of the city over to the festival, representing Dover, Delaware.

"Lt. Feldman, the United States Air Force is not going to fly the mayor of Dover to some sweet pea festival in England."

So with Gideon's blessing, I made the trip instead, a large box of sweet peas balanced on my lap as I crossed the Atlantic on my first trip abroad.

Just so you know, sweet peas—*Lathyrus odoratus*—are highly scented annuals of the Leguminosae family. They are a climbing plant with fragrant pastel-colored flowers.

The captain of the plane, Austin Totterdel, had orders that in the event of trouble during the flight, the last thing he is to ditch are those fragrant sweet peas.

My prized box of sweet peas starts leaking: it was over the Azores, I think.

Because of a NATO exercise, they couldn't take me directly to Dover, so we land in Burtonwood, England, near Liverpool, in the dead of night. Dover is a three-hundred-mile train trip ahead. The next morning, the aide to the commanding general of Burtonwood Air Force Base picks me up and takes me to the general himself. In front of a whole group of senior officers, this two-star general addresses me: "Lieutenant, I cannot emphasize enough the importance of your mission today. Today, you don't just represent the United States Air Force. You represent every man, woman, and child in the United States of America."

I'm not sure they got a more dramatic send-off on D day.

I arrive at the National Sweet Pea Festival by train with my box of dripping, drooping sweet peas. I was greeted at the station by three hundred people and a marching band. I was the only sister-city representative to make the trip, although some had sweet peas delivered by local florists in their names. Sir Edwin Weston, a town official, insists that I stay with his wife and him in their house, literally on the White Cliffs of Dover.

My puny sweet peas were pathetic next to the big, healthy, vibrant local sweet peas. But that didn't matter. The society was just happy I showed up. In fact, they made me an honorary member of the National Sweet Pea Society, the first American "ever thus honored."

I was the guest of honor at a luncheon attended by two thousand people under a massive tent. They seated me between the lord mayor of Dover—who looked like the square-jawed English character actor Victor McLaglen—and his wife—who also looked like Victor McLaglen.

They start toasting up a storm—To the Queen! *Drink.* To country! *Drink.* To the President of the United States! *Drink.* To the Prime Minister! *More drink.*

To sweet peas! Well, I don't think they did that one, actually.

The Brits can hold their liquor quite well but the Yank is sloshed.

Then from out of nowhere, I hear, "And now Lt. Ed Feldman would like to say a few words."

Did I just hear "Ed Feldman?" I may have been drunk but I knew my own name.

So I went to the podium and here's what I said (and I can only tell you this because I listened to the tape later):

"Little did I dream when I was a boy in New York listening on the radio in my bedroom about the heroism of the people of Dover, England. Who despite all the attacks by the Nazis and their hurling of buzz bombs recklessly into Dover. And the Dover people who would not move away from their homes. Nobody was going to push them out. Little did I dream that I ever would have the honor of standing in this place, as I am today, and listening to the strains of that immortal song, 'There'll be bluebirds over . . . the White Cliffs of Dover.'"

And the place went crazy. Cheering, applause.

Afterwards, the C.O. of the nearby U.S. air base at Manston came up to me. "Lieutenant, you didn't really mean what you just said, did you?"

"Of course I meant what I said. This is a great honor." In truth, I was so drunk I didn't know where I was.

"Well, Lieutenant, I ask because it was the biggest pile of bullshit I ever heard in my life."

But one man's manure is another man's fertilizer.

The Times of London reported my visit to the festival. When I returned home, I spoke to every Woman's Club in the state. I wrote a five-day series for the *Wilmington Journal-Every Evening*. I was a hero.

Now the end of my two-year air force stint is approaching. And wouldn't you know it . . . *Col. Gideon is actually promoted to general.*

"You're a goddam miracle worker. I want to shake your hand, Lieutenant. Well done, sir. Well done, indeed."

"Thank you, *General Gideon*." We shook hands. And I saluted sharply, turned, and exited Gideon's office.

The power of publicity. Never underestimate it.

As I rush headlong into the end of the 1950s, I realize I'm going nowhere. After my tour in the air force, Fox welcomed me home. Gave me my old job back and raised my salary to the level it would have been if I hadn't been called up to active duty. But in 1959, after almost ten years at Fox, I'm making $200 a week and I've got a wife and two children.

It was funny at Fox back then. They wouldn't give you much of a salary, but you could pad your expenses like the devil. They didn't care if you made $200 a week and you charged $400 a week in expenses as long as you could justify it somehow. Abe Weiler was the entertainment editor of the *New York Times,* and you could put him on your expense account once a week. In fact, one of the studios did a check once and found that on one particular day, Abe Weiler had eleven lunches.

Abe Weiler was the kind of guy who said "Don't thank me, send money" as a joke. The *New York Times* was always very strict about that sort of thing. But Weiler and I were such close friends that one day I put fifty one-dollar bills in an envelope and sent it to him, after he said send money. *So I sent money.* Well, by chance he opens my envelope when the executive editor is in his office. Bills fall out. Weiler calls me on the phone and he's berserk: "Ed, you sorry S.O.B. I'll get you!"

In 1959, I had decided I needed more opportunity for advancement. The thing about the forty-eight-cent profit on the soda—there was a lot of money in the movie business. To make that forty-eight-cent profit, the theater owners had to offer films the public wanted to see—to bring people into the theater where they would buy the soda—and the studios would be well paid to provide those movies. But the money wasn't flowing in my direction—I had basically "maxed out" at Fox. Going nowhere at a rapid clip.

I get a call one day from Harold Rand, a buddy of mine who went over to Paramount as head of publicity. He offers me my choice of two publicity jobs—the Marlon Brando picture *One-Eyed Jacks* or *The World of Suzie Wong*, a film to be made in Hong Kong by a new producer, Ray Stark. Either of the jobs would extricate me from the Fox rat race and give me a bigger paycheck.

It's funny how you look back over your past and realize that just a few decisions, some seemingly small, shaped the course of your life for years afterward, maybe forever. Here's one of those decisions—I picked *Suzie Wong* because *I wanted to go to Hong Kong*. And there I worked closely with Ray Stark. Eventually, this relationship would indirectly lead to my career in producing. Of course, I didn't know that then. I just wanted to see Hong Kong.

Ray Stark was called the Electric Rabbit. People thought it was because he had seemingly unbounded energy and perseverance. But in truth, he was first given this moniker by his mother-in-law, the legendary performer Fanny Brice. She simply thought he looked like a rabbit because of his small stature and prominent teeth. And he did have the energy of a rabbit connected to a wall socket. Sort of an early version of the Energizer Bunny from the commercials. He kept on going and going and going . . .

It's impossible to talk about Ray Stark without referring to Fanny Brice because much of his original power and capital came from her. Many years later, Brice was the subject of one of Stark's biggest hits: the Broadway musical, and then movie, *Funny Girl* with Barbra Streisand. Today, there is little recollection of the real Fanny Brice—she died an untimely death in 1951. If older people do remember her, it's probably because of her characterization of Baby Snooks on the radio. She was still playing the part at the time of her death. But Brice was a hugely talented and famous comedienne and singer in the 1920s and 1930s, notably with the Ziegfeld Follies.

Ray Stark's early life is somewhat shrouded in mystery. There was even doubt about his age. Most stories pick up the life of Ray Stark in 1939 when he married Brice's daughter, Fran. Stark was working at the time in the publicity department of Warner Bros. Supposedly, he had attended law school at NYU (and simultaneously worked as a copy boy at the *New York Journal-American*) but dropped out to make his way to Hollywood.

I happen to know that Stark grew up somewhere in the East Bronx, not too far from where I grew up on Harrison Avenue, West Bronx, but years earlier. He was always embarrassed about his old neighborhood and I never could get him to tell me exactly where he had lived. I used to say that Ray Stark was born in the Bronx and spent the rest of his life trying to make people forget it.

Stark became an agent in 1940 and he had power even back then. During World War II, he was in the navy but he would attend to his military duties only in the morning. In the afternoon, he would work at the agency in his sailor uniform. Not your typical wartime military service.

Over the years, he represented big movie stars for Charles K. Feldman's agency. Starting in the early 1950s, Stark began dabbling in moviemaking, investing in John Huston's *Moulin Rouge,* among other projects. But in 1956, Stark decided to make the formal move to production. He partnered with Eliot Hyman in forming Seven Arts Productions (originally, Associated Artists Productions) with capital provided by the Canadian financier Lou Chesler. But Stark was more interested in films and Hyman was more interested in television, so Stark branched out by forming his own production company. I came on the scene in 1960 when Paramount and Stark put me in charge of worldwide publicity for *The World of Suzie Wong.*

After my many years working publicity at Fox headquarters in New York, *Suzie Wong* was a welcome change. The plan was that I would be stationed in Hong Kong during the shoot there, about five weeks, then travel with the company to London, where the interiors would be shot at MGM Elstree Studios. Then I would head back to Paramount's offices in New York and complete my *Suzie Wong* publicity work. All told, I would be with the picture for about a year.

Before I was hired, I met with Stark for what was basically a job interview. My immediate impression of him was that he was very, very funny. A pleasant, engaging personality. We liked each other instantly. It wouldn't be long, though, before that changed 180 degrees.

Within weeks, we wanted to murder each other.

"Ed, no one knows about this picture. There's no publicity out there. It's invisible. You've got to get to work with the publicity. Put us on the map. Get going, will you, before it's too late."

Stark was very upset with me. But he was dead wrong. *The World of Suzie Wong* was one of the best-publicized pictures of its day. No question at all. We were doing a bang-up job. But first-time producer Stark was in a panic and there was no talking him out of it.

I must say, I had terrific raw material on this project. *The World of Suzie Wong* was based on a hit Broadway play of the same name. It starred American heartthrob William Holden and France Nuyen, who was hot off the film version of *South Pacific* and had starred in the New York production of *Suzie Wong*. It told the sizzling story of an American expatriate architect-turned-painter and his love affair with a beautiful Asian prostitute. And it had exotic Hong Kong locales.

My job was to get recognition for the picture worldwide before it opened. So, much of my work would happen during the Hong Kong shoot. Here's the sort of thing I did:

I came up with the idea of having Holden and Nuyen, and the set, blessed by a Buddhist priest on the first day of filming. Fine. Now where can I find a Buddhist priest? Somebody suggests the Yellow Pages. So I thumb through and find a number of listings for Buddhist temples. I call one that seems promising. I explain that we need a Buddhist priest at 10 A.M. on Wednesday at Kowloon Star Ferry. And the man on the other end asks about the stipend. I offer a hundred U.S. dollars. I didn't know at the time that this was a fortune in Hong Kong. We were paying extras only $3 per day.

So Wednesday arrives and I've arranged for a huge celebration. I have a fireworks barge ready. There are newsreel and still photographers standing by. And up walks this somber Buddhist priest with an assistant, who is carrying a beautiful valise. The robe the priest is wearing is very drab and I'm feeling a little disappointed. But this is a holy man—I can't expect him to be too ostentatious. The assistant opens the valise and inside is a blue robe, a white robe, a red robe, a black robe, and a green robe. The priest looks at the robes and then at me, and says in perfect English, "What are we shooting today—black and white, or color?"

So against the background of the resplendent fireworks over Hong Kong harbor, I'll have Holden and Nuyen kneeling, being blessed by the Buddhist priest. I explain this to Holden and he says, "Ed, you really want me to kneel here? I don't think I want to do that."

"Bill, you've got to do it. Please. For me."

Holden pauses for a few beats, then whispers, "Ed, only you could get me to kneel down before a Buddhist priest." And he kneels.

He smiles up at me, "But I'll get you if it's the last thing I ever do."

Well, the story broke worldwide. Everybody covered it. Big news. But Stark wasn't happy.

"Where the hell is our publicity, Ed?" It became his mantra.

We would fly editors and writers into Hong Kong from all over the world to cover the *Suzie Wong* shoot. I arranged to have *Esquire* magazine do a big photo story on the "Girls of *Suzie Wong*." We brought the editor, Clay Felker, and the celebrated New York fashion photographer Bert Stern to Hong Kong for the piece. (They had to come back in a few months, though, and redo much of it. I'll explain why shortly.)

I had a clipping service monitoring the *Suzie Wong* press coverage worldwide, and I'll tell you, those clippings would have filled Stark's office.

Still he wasn't happy. "Where the hell is our publicity, Ed?" he chanted.

Want a nervous, insecure, hypercritical, micromanaging, never-satisfied producer? Open the Yellow Pages and look under "Stark, Ray."

Finally by the end of the Hong Kong leg of my assignment, I'm fed up with Ray Stark. I'm going to bolt . . . and soon.

With all my Stark problems, I must say, I really enjoyed being around Bill Holden. He was a delightful, charming man. And at that time, he was in his physical prime.

Ask a woman of a certain age about William Holden today, and she will say something like, "Oh, I adored him in *Love Is a Many-Splendored Thing* with Jennifer Jones. The way they just *looked at each other.*"

Or "I'll never forget the way he danced with Kim Novak in *Picnic*."

Remember, that was fifty years ago. You would think they had just seen him at today's matinee at the Cineplex.

One night, Holden and I are having dinner at a nice candlelit restaurant in Kowloon. Wherever he went, if there was a live orchestra, they would strike up the theme from *Love Is a Many-Splendored Thing*. And they proceed to do that here. As the romantic music is playing, I'm sitting there looking over at Holden in the candle's glow. Impulsively, I get up, go over to him and plant a kiss on his cheek, and return to my seat. Holden is amazed. "What the hell did you do that for?"

"Bill, I did that for all the women in the world—who would *dream* of being where I am *right now*."

I knew I had to leave Stark and *Suzie Wong*. But there was a little problem. The timing. Lorraine was set to fly into London and spend a week with me there, and then we would spend a few days in Paris. From there, we would return to New York City.

I considered leaving *Suzie Wong* after Hong Kong, but I didn't want to ruin Lorraine's first trip abroad. So I remained on the picture during much of the London shoot.

The company was housed at the staid old Connaught Hotel in London's Mayfair district. Management didn't seem to know what to do with the Ping-Pong table in the hall, where Ray Stark would take on all comers.

Then all of a sudden, Stark fires France Nuyen and the director, Jean Negulesco. Although Nuyen had been a success in the Broadway production, things hadn't worked out well on the film. For one thing, she seemed depressed all the time, and she was gaining weight. Her costumes—mostly tiny, tight-fitting *cheong-sams*—were bursting at the seams. Supposedly, she had had an unhappy affair with Marlon Brando and maybe this was taking its toll. The people risk rides again.

I had known Nuyen since I worked publicity on the film of *South Pacific* for Fox. She spoke very little English back then and was very poor. I remember taking her to department stores to buy stockings and underwear, which I paid for out of my own pocket. After her success on Broadway with *Suzie Wong,* Nuyen changed. No longer the inno-cent and grateful young woman, she told me a couple of months after *Suzie Wong* opened: "Ed, if you want to talk to me in the future, call my agent."

So Nuyen was gone and so was the director. Although Negulesco was an established director of films like *Three Coins in the Fountain,* nei-ther Paramount nor Stark was happy with the Hong Kong and London footage. Negulesco was replaced by Richard Quine, an old buddy of Stark from his agent days.

Stark replaced Nuyen with an unknown twenty-year-old actress, Nancy Kwan, who was touring with *Suzie Wong* back in the United States and Canada, understudying the lead role. Stark had auditioned Kwan much earlier for the film but had passed on her then because she was unproven as an actress. But he recognized her potential and signed her to a seven-year contract at a starting salary of $300 per week. In the interim, Kwan had taken acting lessons at Stark's behest and now she was ready for her proverbial close-up.

I always suspected that Stark cast Kwan partly to build up her stature, so he could loan her out to other producers at a nice profit. By fall of 1960, with *Suzie Wong* about to open, Kwan had become a cog in the Hollywood publicity machine, appearing on the cover of *Life* magazine and just about everywhere else.

Stark was willing to cast Kwan in almost any part. For the movie *The Wild Affair,* she was the daughter of very British, very Cockney—of the "What say, gov'ner?" ilk—parents. I thought this was absurd and I told Stark so: "Ray, you cannot get away with her having two Cockney par-ents. She's Chinese."

He says, "That's your trouble, Ed. You continue to believe she's Chi-nese."

Actually, she was Eurasian—Chinese father, English mother.

After *Suzie Wong,* Stark loaned her out to Universal to star in *Flower Drum Song,* which was a huge hit. Eventually, she bought out her contract—and her freedom—from Stark, well before its expiration.

Replacing the female lead in the picture meant all of Nuyen's com-pleted scenes had to be reshot, and that meant going back to Hong Kong for another month. Also, all of the unpublished publicity we had done in Hong Kong had to be redone, including the *Esquire* shoot. Now, this sort of thing is enormously expensive, but not for Stark—for Paramount, who was bankrolling the picture. But Paramount didn't balk. Whatever Stark wanted was just fine. Even on his first picture, Ray Stark was a powerful man.

But he wasn't powerful enough to get me to stay on *Suzie Wong*.

Stark and I had a big, big fight in London the night before Lorraine arrived. A massive fight. Over the same old thing: "Where the hell is our publicity, Ed?"

Except now it had evolved into shouting: "WHERE THE HELL IS OUR PUBLICITY, ED?"

Stark behaved like an abusive husband. That night, he screams at me. The next day, he's making up. He had my room at the Connaught filled with fresh flowers for Lorraine's arrival. I mean, *filled*. In today's money, a couple of thousand dollars' worth.

Dr. Jekyll-Stark and Mr. Ray Hyde.

Lorraine and I had a wonderful time in London and Paris. I was very relaxed and jovial because I didn't think I'd see Stark again. My plan was to tender my resignation to Paramount as soon as I hit New York. Let *them* tell Stark.

I figured the chances of the team of Stark and Feldman being reunited was like reuniting a split hydrogen atom after the explosion.

But here we go again with that "Life Is Funny" business.

I was dead wrong.

Back at Paramount headquarters, I haven't resigned yet, but things are easy without Stark around. No sense being out of work. I'll just coast until I find something.

I suddenly get a call from Eddie Solomon, a friend of mine from my Fox days. And he says, "Ed, are you happy with what you're doing?"

"Not really," I say.

He was with Joseph E. Levine's Embassy Pictures and they needed someone to head up advertising and publicity. At this point, Levine and

Embassy are pretty small time, but it's got to be better than the next Stark tirade, which was coming any day now.

So I submit my resignation to Paramount and tell them I'm going with Levine. Martin Davis, the head of the publicity department who later became president of the company, commiserates with me. "Ed, I understand that it's a tough gig. I want to wish you all the luck. I mean it."

Then twenty-four hours later, Davis calls me back into his office and says, "Forget what I said before. You are absolutely doing the most immoral, unethical thing that we have ever heard of. Leaving the picture in the middle. I will personally make sure that you will never work again in this business!"

I knew this was Stark's doing.

Then Davis calls Levine on the phone and tries to get me fired from my new job. But to no avail.

Now go forward almost two years and I'm nervous about staying any longer with Levine. I'll give you the details in the next chapter.

Who could have predicted this? I'm sitting in my office on the date of my wedding anniversary, and I get a call from . . . Ray Stark. Even with our tempestuous relationship on *Suzie Wong,* now he wants me back. "Ed, I miss you," he says. "Come back."

"Ray, why do you want me? We hated each other every day we ever worked together."

"Because not only do I miss you, Ed, I made a *big mistake.* People like Jerry Wald have been telling me that for two years. You are an excellent publicist; one of the best. Come back."

I sensed that Stark had matured as a filmmaker and had mellowed. The old insecurities on *Suzie Wong* had disappeared. He seemed ready to accept me as a colleague rather than as an underling.

Plus he was offering me something that, to my knowledge, no other publicity executive had ever received before—*stock options.*

So I said, what the hell. We all deserve a second chance.

You're probably thinking that things turned out disastrously with Stark for a second time.

Surprise! We got along *great. Great!*

Stark was like a different person.

I worked on some of the most interesting projects of my career at Seven Arts with Stark and his partner, Eliot Hyman. Seven Arts, for a pretty small company, had its hands in some very big-time things. Eventually, Seven Arts even bought Warner Bros. My stock options were like gold.

Let me tell you that Eliot Hyman was an entertainment industry pioneer and visionary. And he had an interesting history. Back in the 1920s, he was a tire distributor and made bulletproof tires for the gangster Dutch Schultz. During World War II, he made a fortune in microfilm. But his real coup happened almost by accident. In the late 1940s, he used to play gin with a group of movie industry types in New York. One game included Steve Broidy, who was head of Monogram Pictures in Los Angeles.

Hyman asked Broidy why he was in New York. Broidy explained that Monogram was having financial problems and he was there trying to sell the television rights to a package of their old movies.

Hyman asks, "How many movies ya got?"

"Hundred and ninety-nine."

"How much you think you can get for them?"

"Oh, probably three thousand dollars apiece. About six hundred grand total."

"Tell you what, Steve. I'll give you a check right now for an option on the television rights."

Now, Hyman didn't know anything about the movie or television business, but he schedules a meeting with an NBC vice president to try to peddle this package of pictures for television.

These weren't exactly the classic movies of all time. Mostly B movies from the 1930s and 1940s. Things like Bowery Boys comedies. But they weren't that bad either. They were entertaining and watchable.

Hyman makes his pitch to the NBC executive, and this is the answer he gets: "Mr. Hyman, you don't understand. Television is going to be like radio. Jack Benny will be Jack Benny. Fred Allen will be Fred Allen.

People watch to see their favorite personalities. *We're never going to show movies on television.*"

Now those were words destined to be made into a sandwich and swallowed whole.

So Hyman calls up Channel 13, Newark, owned at the time by the Cheeseborough Manufacturing Company, which made products like Vaseline and Ponds face cream. And he goes and sells the metropolitan New York television rights for $80,000.

Eventually, that package of old B movies from Monogram made $13 million from television rights. Hyman had struck the mother lode. He used that deal to acquire other, better libraries. His crowning glory, though, was buying the pre-1948 Warner Bros. library, including remake and sequel rights, for $21 million in 1956. Movies made before 1948 were especially valuable because they didn't require the payment of residuals to creative talent.

The purchase included the 850 feature films and about 1,500 shorts and cartoons Warners had made since 1912, even before the studio was officially formed. This deal was probably the worst business decision in Jack L. Warner's long and storied career in Hollywood. The company needed the money at the time, but I hear he really based the deal on bad tax advice.

Hyman believed anything with sprocket holes was worth something, no matter how old. And he built up a fortune on that premise.

Those film libraries he assembled were the cornerstone of the Seven Arts enterprise. In 1962, the future for Hyman, Stark, and company looked very bright indeed.

I was their advertising and publicity man. I had my stock options. And I was ready to roll.

My first project at Seven Arts was the film everyone thought was unmakeable—*Lolita,* the scandalous story of a middle-aged man who falls for a teenager. It was based on the 1955 novel by the esteemed Vladimir Nabokov and was directed by Stanley Kubrick. It starred the distinguished actors James Mason and Peter Sellers. The film was classy but the story was unsavory.

By the way, I became pretty good friends with Peter Sellers when I was with Warner Bros. I'll talk about that later.

We came up with the tagline "How did they ever make a film of *Lolita*?" which we matched up with a picture of Sue Lyon, our Lolita, innocently sucking on a lollipop. (The heart-shaped sunglasses she wore in the ad became a national icon. They were bought in a Long Island five-and-dime store right before the photo shoot by the legendary Bert Stern.)

Back then, the Catholic Legion of Decency was very formidable. The group published a list that assigned a "moral estimate" to feature films. The list was broken down by category, starting with "Unobjectionable for All" down to "Condemned." This is like the MPAA's current system of "G" down to "NC-17." Well, they wanted to slap a Condemned rating on *Lolita*. This would have been a real problem for us. Our contract with the distributor, MGM, specified that the film could not have a Condemned rating. Plus MGM was a very conservative company. They didn't want to have any trouble with the Legion of Decency.

Howard Strickling, the famous publicity chief at MGM, put together an innocuous ad campaign that was along the lines of *Gidget goes middle age*. I told him, "Howard, this is ridiculous." So he tells me to make up my own campaign, and he would let the head of MGM and Eliot Hyman make the decision jointly.

They went with my raucous, saucy approach.

When I met with the Legion of Decency, I brought two ads with me to show them: the one we ended up using, with the lollipop, and another, especially juicy one. It showed Sue Lyon cuddling up to James Mason with the tagline, a quote from the film, "If Mother finds out, she'll divorce you and strangle me."

My strategy worked. I agreed not to use the second ad, and they agreed to move *Lolita* from "Condemned" to a new "Special" category if we would enforce a rule of not admitting anyone under the age of eighteen to the theater.

Now it's time for the New York premiere. I have James Mason and Sue Lyon arrive at Loew's State Theater together in a limousine and then walk up the red carpet, arm-in-arm, to emphasize the middle-aged man–teenage girl angle. Lyon was dressed to the nines in a virginal white outfit designed by Jackie Kennedy's couturier, Oleg Cassini.

I sidle up to the theater manager. "You know, that girl's not eighteen. You can't let her in." And I pointed to the sign, No One Under 18 Admitted.

So with cameras flashing, the manager stops her at the door of the theater and says, "I'm terribly sorry, Miss Lyon, but you're not old enough to attend this movie."

My assistant, Dick Brooks, took her to sit at the counter at Rumplemeyer's on Central Park South and have an ice cream soda during the premiere.

The pictures of Sue Lyon being refused admittance to her own movie and then sipping an ice cream soda during the screening broke in almost every major newspaper in the world.

I spent a lot of time with Stanley Kubrick on *Lolita.* Ironically, Kubrick grew up in the Bronx in a house almost directly across Harrison Avenue from me. I didn't really know him then because he was a little older, but Lorraine was friends with his younger sister.

Kubrick's father was a doctor with a general practice. The Kubricks and the Feldmans both lived in modest, middle-class surroundings. But years later, the columnist Dorothy Kilgallen wrote in the *New York Journal-American,* "Stanley Kubrick and Ed Feldman grew up together in tenements across the street from each other in the Bronx." To me, that was just show business.

But my mother was apoplectic. "We don't live in a tenement! We have a very nice place. *Tenement!* I could show that Dorothy Kilgallen person a *tenement!*" She fumed about it for two years.

Stanley Kubrick was truly a prodigy. At age seventeen, he became a photographer for *Look* magazine. Four years later, he made a short film that he sold to RKO about a day in the life of a boxer, called *The Day of the Fight.* The gritty black-and-white documentary won several awards and holds up even by today's standards. It prefigures filmmaking techniques used by Kubrick in his later feature films.

After our teenage years on Harrison Avenue, I didn't see Kubrick again until we walked into a *Lolita* advertising and publicity meeting together at Seven Arts some fifteen years later.

Stanley Kubrick was interesting to deal with. He was very intense and spoke in a low key. He would give you a look—he would raise those magnetic, hooded eyes of his. He tended to be solemn. And he was surprisingly straitlaced. Kubrick thought his partner, James Harris, had a thing for Sue Lyon. In real life, the director of *Lolita* thought it was incomprehensible that an older man would have even a passing interest in a teenage girl.

Kubrick lovers may be amazed by this: Of all the directors I have worked with, the erudite and sophisticated Kubrick was the most hands-on with the promotion of his movie.

Kubrick would call me at home almost every night to get an update on the *Lolita* advertising and publicity. We would talk for about thirty minutes. His questions were very direct: "What are they doing with this . . . ? What are we gonna do with that . . . ? How's the campaign coming?"

And he demanded answers. You couldn't bluff him.

He had met Lorraine before, but if she answered the phone, he would never acknowledge her. Just a terse, "Is Ed there?" Not even, "Hello."

After a few weeks of this, Lorraine finally says to him, "Stanley, you know I'm not the telephone operator here."

"Oh, yes, how are you, Lorraine?"

Kubrick was so absorbed in the advertising and publicity that he would actually check up on the studio. On *Lolita,* he purchased the newspapers from the top twenty markets at a newsstand for a solid week, then measured the advertising column-inches for the picture with a ruler. He discovered that MGM had come up short on their contractual advertising coverage.

I told MGM, "Our director has found that you shorted us on the advertising." They were embarrassed and we never had that problem again.

Kubrick was so particular and exacting, he looked at one reel from *every print* the MGM lab made of *Lolita.*

The last time I saw Stanley Kubrick was when I visited him on the stage of *2001: A Space Odyssey* at MGM Elstree studio in London. "Hi, Ed," he said, in his matter of fact way. But he was very gracious and showed me exactly what they were doing. Actually, he was much more gracious and personable than in the earlier years. What I saw that day was breathtaking and would set the standard for special effects films to come.

Kubrick became more and more insular over time. He moved to England and rarely traveled—he was terrified of flying.

Kubrick remained a brilliant filmmaker throughout his entire career, but working with him could be a strange experience. Keith Hatcher, our location manager on *102 Dalmatians,* had been an early location manager on *Eyes Wide Shut,* Kubrick's last film. Hatcher never met Kubrick face to face. Kubrick instructed him to leave the location photos on the back steps of his house and then Kubrick would retrieve them after Hatcher had gone.

The Night of the Iguana was a publicist's dream. It was directed by the colorful John Huston, as part of his five-picture deal with Seven Arts. It starred Richard Burton as a randy, drunken defrocked minister. Burton was hot as fire then because of his love affair with Elizabeth Taylor, which started during *Cleopatra* the year before. It also had Ava Gardner, Deborah Kerr, and . . . seventeen-year-old Sue Lyon, newly famous after her *Lolita* ice cream soda.

But just as important, we were making *Iguana* principally in Mismaloya, Mexico, a tiny place accessible only by boat from Puerto Vallarta. This did two things. It gave us a very exotic locale, perfect for this steamy Tennessee Williams opus. Plus it allowed us to restrict the press's access to the set. You didn't play ball with us, you didn't get taken to Mismaloya. And because of this, the London Express Worldwide News Service guaranteed me five major consecutive stories to be written by Peter Evans on the making of the picture. In return for an exclusive, *Life* magazine did a huge story on the filming, which resulted in some of the most striking movie-set photographs of the era.

Ray Stark originally wanted his old buddy Kirk Douglas for the Burton role. Back when the picture was being cast, I told Stark, "Here's a great idea. Why don't we get Richard Burton to play the lead?"

"Burton? No, he's all wrong for the role. It's Kirk Douglas. Douglas loves the part and he's perfect."

So a few minutes later, Stark is on the phone with the head of our distributor, MGM. "Listen, I've got great news. Kirk Douglas wants to play the lead."

Silence. Stark's expression grows cloudy. Then brightens.

"Well, if you don't like Kirk Douglas, I can also get . . . Richard Burton."

It's a deal.

In *Iguana,* there is the part of an elderly poet. I suggested to Stark that we get Robert Frost to play the role. Frost, at the time, was the poet laureate of the United States and very visible.

Stark says, "Ed, that's a great idea! Have him in my office Tuesday at ten o'clock."

"Ray, we're talking about the poet laureate of the United States. You can't just summon him to your office. He's probably busy writing poems."

Frost declined the part, but for a month after I'm writing all my memos to Stark in rhyme.

Things like that endeared me to Stark. We were getting along famously. I was becoming an important adviser and confidant.

But back on the set, it was very hot in Mismaloya, so we would shoot from six in the morning to three in the afternoon. We built a bar on the beach, and after the day's shooting everyone would convene around the bar—Huston, Burton, Elizabeth Taylor, Ava Gardner, Deborah Kerr, and her writer husband, Peter Viertel. I had a ball.

Tennessee Williams showed up for a few days, and because of the limited accommodations, he and I had to share a room. And I must say, in my whole life, I never thought I would ever call out: "*Oh, Tennessee,* may I borrow your toothpaste, please?"

We worked out a deal to have *The Night of the Iguana* featured on the premiere episode of David L. Wolper's primetime NBC series, *Hollywood and the Stars.* Naturally, we used Elizabeth Taylor in the show. She was the biggest celebrity there was, right then, and her services were very valuable. So her lawyer, Mickey Rudin, calls me up the day after the show airs and says, "Ed, may I ask you what right you had to use Elizabeth's likeness in that show?" He couldn't believe this highly paid celebrity was appearing on a sponsored TV show for free.

And I say, "Well, I thought she would want to help her boyfriend's career."

And he says, "That is so *outrageous* that I'm not even going to get mad. And I'm not even going to pursue it any further."

I knew better—I should have gotten Taylor's approval. But so I was a little outrageous. I was a *publicist,* right?

Elizabeth Taylor would arrive by boat every day at the set around noon, looking fresh and fabulous. The rest of us were wilted from the heat. We concocted a little story and fed it to the news-hungry press that Taylor was worried that Burton had a yen for Sue Lyon and would pair off with her if he got the chance. In truth, Burton barely acknowledged Lyon's presence because he stayed pretty loaded. Until one day when he's called on to do a love scene with Lyon. Well, they're going at it. After a while, they take a break and Burton comments, "My God, she's got a tongue like a snake."

In actuality, we all believed Taylor was worried about Ava Gardner. I suspected that Gardner was the real reason she showed up on the set every day. And Burton did seem to have a thing for Gardner. Our unit publicist, Greg Morrison, is sitting in her dressing room one day and Gardner is getting a rubdown, with just a towel covering her. Burton saunters in, surveys the situation, and walks over and peeks under Gardner's towel.

"My God," he says, "it winked at me."

Ray Stark had always wanted to make a musical of the life of his mother-in-law, Fanny Brice. Originally, back in the late 1940s, it was going to be an MGM musical with Judy Garland. But things just didn't come together.

Brice's story was compelling, primarily because of her relationship with her husband, Nick Arnstein. True, Brice was a major star in the first half of the twentieth century and her life had a terrific rags-to-riches angle. But it was the Arnstein side of her story that added drama and heartbreak.

Anyone who has seen *Funny Girl* remembers the bittersweet Brice-Arnstein romance. Brice was a young, fresh, but somewhat homely theatrical performer, and Arnstein was the handsome, lovable rogue—gambler, roué, cad. It was a story destined to be told.

Actually, it had been told already, in 1939, by the unauthorized picture *Rose of Washington Square* with Alice Faye and Tyrone Power in the thinly disguised Brice and Arnstein roles. Brice sued over that film and won $30,000, although she had asked for $750,000.

Finally, after fifteen years, things began to gel in the early 1960s for Stark's Fanny Brice project. He hired Isobel Lennart, who had been attached to the project back in the MGM days, to write the book; Jule Styne to write the music; Bob Merrill for the lyrics; and Garson Kanin to direct. All top-notch professionals.

For the leads, he selected Sydney Chaplin, the son of Charlie Chaplin and a big Broadway star in his own right, and a promising newcomer, Barbra Streisand.

Stark wanted me to work on advertising and publicity for the show. I was a Seven Arts employee, so Stark worked out a deal where Seven Arts would loan me to the show as a consultant. My name even appears in the original *Playbill* with that title. I would work on my regular Seven Arts movie projects but would be heavily involved in *Funny Girl*.

This was just fine with me. I grew up in New York and loved the theater, especially musical theater. I saw all the classic shows growing up and couldn't get enough of it.

I was getting along with Stark famously then, but he could still be difficult. Originally, he was going to coproduce *Funny Girl* with David Merrick, who was an established Broadway musical-theater producer with a string of hits under his belt. He was developing *Hello, Dolly!* at the same time Stark was developing *Funny Girl*.

Stark finally found someone who was as difficult as he was. Merrick and Stark lasted about a month. At one point, they wouldn't talk to each other. And they're sitting there in meetings at a table, talking through me or our publicist, Frank Goodman.

"Please, tell Mr. Merrick this . . ."

"You tell Mr. Stark that . . ."

And they're sitting right across from each other!

You reflect on *Funny Girl* now and it's perfect. Great songs, great script, great characters. How could it fail?

Well, it almost did. Things did not go at all well during our out-of-town tryouts. The show was not coming together.

We tried working with the score. In Philadelphia, the director felt we didn't have enough going on in the first act. So Styne and Merrill leave the room, and in an hour and a half, return with the seduction song, "You Are Woman," an instant classic with the immortal line, "Would a convent take a Jewish girl?"

Jule Styne was a great composer but he was also like a Damon Runyan character. He was into the bookies very heavily—several hundred thousand dollars. I knew that this was like a cycle for him. He'd gamble hard, get into the bookies for a lot of money, and then pay them back when a show opened. Luckily for him, the shows were usually hits.

I'd get mysterious calls from men who were obviously his bookies: "Mr. Feldman, I'm a business associate of Jule Styne. I was just wondering, how's the show looking?"

Things were looking grim, actually, but I wanted our composer intact and breathing, so I lied: "The show is looking great. I'm sure you'll get your money back."

They would tinker around with the show, changing dialogue, adding songs, cutting songs. But in my opinion, the real problem with the show was the director, Garson Kanin. Remember that Barbra Streisand then was a young, inexperienced performer. Kanin had a theory that if the actors did their role enough times, they would do it right. The truth of the matter is, she needed someone to take hold of her and make her performance perfect. So while we were still in Philly, Stark fires Kanin and hires Jerome Robbins. He lets Kanin keep the director credit and gives Robbins a "Production Supervised by . . ." credit. With Robbins, the show begins to fly.

By the time we opened at the Winter Garden Theater on Broadway, it was just about perfect. Streisand received a dozen curtain calls and was an instant star.

I knew how great she was during the very first public performance of *Funny Girl*—out of town in Boston—when she sings, "I'm the greatest star!" I thought to myself, this girl will be a big star for decades.

I was in charge of the opening night gala for *Funny Girl*. It was my idea to take over the newly renovated Rainbow Room at the top of the RCA Building at Rockefeller Center. Now it's the afternoon of the event and I'm at the Rainbow Room with Fran Stark, Ray's wife, setting things up. Fran leads me to the middle of the room and says, "Ed, see these three tables? I want a sign on them that says, 'Reserved for the Personal Guests of Ray Stark.'"

I say, "Fran, all five hundred people invited for tonight were invited by Ray Stark. He even signed the invitations personally. They all consider themselves a personal guest of Ray Stark. You're going to have a problem."

"Would you please do what I've asked you to, Ed."

Fine.

So that night, I'm working the door and Fran rushes up to me in a dither. "Come with me."

We walk over to a vantage point and she points at one of the three Reserved tables. "Do you see those two men there? I want them removed immediately. They don't belong at our table. There's no room for our friends."

I look at the two men.

"Fran, I'll do almost anything for you. But I cannot go over there and throw out the United States Senator from New York, Jacob Javits, and the Undersecretary of the United Nations, Ralph Bunche. The publicity would be awful."

So she leaves my side in a huff.

Now I'm back working the door. And I begin to hear the orchestra playing a familiar tune. It was pleasant and I begin humming along, preoccupied with my work. Then I'm softly singing along. "Dolly'll never go away again."

Wait just a damn minute! The orchestra at the opening night party of *Funny Girl* is playing the theme song of our biggest competitor, David Merrick's *Hello, Dolly!*

Well, it turned out that Merrick's press agent, Lee Solters, had slipped the orchestra leader a few bucks to play a medley of tunes from *Hello, Dolly!* at our opening night party. Funny joke, considering Stark and Merrick had partnered on *Funny Girl* for about ten minutes.

Stark's apartment on East Fifty-seventh Street was robbed a couple of nights earlier and the burglars took a lot of Fran's jewelry. The papers call me up, wanting to know the value of the stolen jewelry. How should I know? So I just invented a number I thought was reasonable: $80,000.

Well, this number appears in the papers. I get a call from Stark. "Ed, where's your imagination? A lousy eighty thousand dollars. Why in God's name didn't you say *a half-million?*"

Funny Girl was a huge hit. We sold out every performance. Somebody said, "Ed, you could put your kids through college if you'd sell house seats under the table."

Martin Davis at Paramount, who said I'd never work in the business again, called me for house seats. I'm not one to hold grudges, so I get him a pair on the third row.

Here is the ungrateful so-and-so's response, "Ed, we'd really prefer to be on the fourth row."

Orchestra tickets for Broadway musicals today run upwards of $100 each. Back then, we were charging $12.50. Scalpers were getting $70. We proposed to raise the price to $15. The Shubert people, who owned the Winter Garden, went crazy. "You are destroying the New York theater."

The advertising and publicity on *Funny Girl* went well. Back then, they would never include songs from musicals in spots because they would have had to pay a hefty royalty to the musicians union. But I went ahead and developed a thirty-second radio spot that featured twenty seconds of Streisand singing "People" and concluded with an announcer saying, "People who see *Funny Girl* are the luckiest people in the world" right after Streisand sings ". . . are the luckiest people in the world." It was very successful.

The reviews for *Funny Girl* were pretty lackluster except for the two that really counted: the *New York Times* and the *New York Herald Tribune.* But God always seemed to shine down on Ray Stark.

I'm standing with Henry Grunwald, a senior editor of *Time* magazine, at the opening-night party, talking up the show and Streisand. "She's great, isn't she?"

Grunwald replies, "She's fantastic." Then he turns to his associates and says, "I want Streisand on the cover of the next issue."

Barbra Streisand has the reputation nowadays of being very difficult. Back then, she could be difficult but nothing like what they say today. I thought she was particularly unpleasant during the opening of the show. We were running interviews of people on the radio in connection with the opening. So I decided to give her a little zing. I set up a live radio interview with Streisand's divorced mother, who says the following: "Her looks she got from her father. Her talent she got from me."

But I'll have to say, Streisand was a real trouper during *Funny Girl.* She was there every performance, sick or not. This may have been a product of insecurity; I don't know.

But one Tuesday morning, the stage manager gets word that Streisand is very ill and will not make the evening performance. So we tell her standby, Lainie Kazan, to get ready to go on.

Lainie Kazan became famous later, but then she was in the chorus and totally unknown. Kazan makes the mistake of getting her agent to contact the press so they will turn out to see her as Fanny Brice.

So, while Kazan is warming up to sing "People," the word gets back to Streisand about Kazan's PR efforts. Now Streisand must have been nervous about Kazan already because she was talented and aggressive, and had all the makings of a big-time operator. That night, Streisand drags herself to the theater and goes on. She made it through the performance but she wasn't up to par. She really was sick.

The next day, Wednesday, is a matinee day and she will have to perform twice. I say, "Listen, Barbra, you're gonna kill yourself. Why don't you let Lainie go on for the matinee? You rest up, and do the evening."

She agrees that's a good idea.

The matinee audience hears the announcement, "At this performance, the role of Fanny Brice will be played by Lainie Kazan."

With a loud collective groan, half of the audience gets up to go claim a refund. That was unfortunate. Kazan was very talented and did a nice job. As far as I know, that was the only time she went on for Streisand.

Sydney Chaplin played Nick Arnstein for a little over a year, then left. It was probably mutual. Although he received equal billing with Streisand, he was really in her shadow and he didn't much like it. It got so bad that Chaplin would sometimes actually walk off stage during "People" and smoke a cigarette. In his defense, he told me, "Ed, do you think anyone in the world notices me when Barbra Streisand is singing 'People'?"

We learned from David Merrick's people not to advertise the show in print with the names of the stars. That way, you're advertising the show, not the actors. When they inevitably leave, it's not so noticeable. Still, this was *Funny Girl,* and when Streisand was leaving to open the show in London, Stark thinks he'll close the Broadway production on her last night.

We said, "Ray, the show is selling tickets. Don't close it down."

Stark listened, and the show played for another year and a half with Mimi Hines as Fanny Brice.

When it's time to do the movie version, everyone assumes that Streisand will star. But Stark drove a hard bargain. For the privilege of starring in the film of *Funny Girl,* Stark demanded that Streisand sign a five-picture deal. This was vintage Ray Stark. Remember Nancy Kwan's indentured servitude at $300 a week? Naturally, Streisand was resisting making such a commitment. Her managers said Stark was only bluffing. He wouldn't dare cast anyone else.

Stark says to me, "What can we do about this, Ed?"

I say, "Let me try something."

The names of some other actresses had been floating around in the press for the part. But no one paid much attention to the speculation—everyone assumed Streisand was a shoo-in.

So I get word to the columnist Dorothy Kilgallen, and the next day, a six-column headline blares out from the *New York Journal-American*:

Shirley MacLaine to Play Fanny Brice?

We heard that Streisand's agent, David Begelman, told her not to believe what "Ray Stark puts in the paper."

But she wouldn't take the chance. Soon word got back that Streisand was telling Begelman: "I don't want anyone else to play Fanny Brice. Let's sign whatever he wants." So she was stuck with Ray Stark for five pictures and she must have resented the hell out of it ever since.

But one of the pictures was the hit film, *The Way We Were*. And she won the Academy Award for *Funny Girl* (tying with Katharine Hepburn) . . . and that's not chopped liver!

Streisand had her first meeting with William Wyler, the director of the film of *Funny Girl,* in London. Wyler was deaf in one ear and Streisand didn't know this. She's talking to him on the side of his bad ear and he says, "Barbra, could you talk to me on the other side. Can't hear out of that ear."

Later, Streisand said, "That's great! Ray sends me a director to make a musical and he's *deaf!*"

On the first anniversary of *Funny Girl* on Broadway, I suggested to Stark that we bring the real Nick Arnstein out from California for the occasion. I knew we would get a lot of press over it. Stark had actually been supporting Arnstein in a retirement home for years. Stark says, "Ed, I love the idea but my marriage would be over."

Fran Stark, Arnstein's daughter, would have nothing to do with her father. She had never spoken with him in her adult life. She didn't even want him being portrayed in the show (but it wouldn't have been much of a show).

The Nick Arnstein of *Funny Girl* is the sanitized version. The real Nick Arnstein was much more of a scoundrel. He was an inveterate womanizer and adulterer. He went to prison twice, Sing Sing in 1915 and Leavenworth federal penitentiary in 1924. The play makes it look like he was basically a gentleman gambler who swindled some people reluctantly, then fully owned up to his actions and willingly and nobly went to jail. The real Arnstein masterminded a $5 million bond theft, jumped bail for two months, and fought the charges with his wife's money, almost breaking her financially and emotionally.

The Ray Starks—Fran and Ray—had a very unusual relationship. When Stark was home in Los Angeles, they were "Mr. and Mrs. Ray Stark." When Stark was away, and that was often, they led separate lives. Fran valued her social standing and cultivated duchesses and countesses the world over. She was active in charity work in L.A. She was part of that Holmby Hills social set that figured so prominently in Ronald Reagan's political rise. Her social status at least partly explains why she didn't want to be linked in any way with her father, the ex-con Nick Arnstein.

It was no secret that Ray Stark, when he was out of town, was a chaser. Stark and I were in London one time when Laurence Harvey was starring in the West End production of *My Fair Lady*. After the curtain, we're meeting him with some other people for dinner at a Chinese restaurant in Soho. Harvey arrives with two beautiful chorus girls from the show. Stark pairs off with one of the girls and another member of our group takes the other one. After dinner, he tells me quietly, "Ed, I'm going to take this girl home. She lives in Brighton." This meant he would see me in the morning.

"Ray, Brighton's a long way away. Fifty or sixty miles. And it's not a very good road. It's not the Long Island Expressway, you know."

"Ed, it's not such a long trip." He gives me a wink and a nudge. And off he goes, arm-in-arm with the girl toward his chauffeured car. She was about a half-foot taller than he was.

Fran died in 1992 at the age of seventy-two. Stark was devastated. For months afterward, he would get very emotional about her. Even with all the running around and the distance between them emotionally and physically, he really did love her and he missed her very much.

Stark told me: "Ed, Fran and I were married fifty-two years. Every single night of those fifty-two years, no matter where on earth we were, no matter what I was doing—I would go quietly to the next room, and call Fran."

In greyhound racing, they encourage the dogs to run around the track at breakneck speed by sending a mechanical, electric-powered rabbit along a rail positioned next to the track at the infield. The greyhounds run and run, but they never catch the rabbit because a man sitting in a control booth adjusts the speed of the rabbit to keep the dogs going. If they look like they're gaining on the rabbit, the man powers up the rabbit and he zips ahead. If the dogs start slowing down, he powers the rabbit down to let them get closer, then gooses the rabbit again.

Now, these are experienced greyhounds. They know the drill. Race after race, they chase that electric rabbit something fierce. He looks awfully tasty but they never catch him. Still they run and run and run, until they retire to a little farm in Florida somewhere, I suppose. All run out.

I was beginning to feel like one of those greyhounds. I was chasing a rabbit and I worried that it was an electric one. Maybe sometimes I was chasing after Ray Stark, the official Electric Rabbit. For a time, I was chasing after my share of the forty-eight cents. But later, my rabbit was a career as a movie producer. There were plenty of people out there chasing that same rabbit. Even if you catch that particular rabbit, there's no guarantee it will be good for you. Because it may be an electric rabbit.

Ray Stark, the Electric Rabbit himself, had his own electric rabbit. Her name was Ulla. He chased her and chased her, but he could never catch her.

I was in London on Seven Arts business with my assistant, Dick Brooks. We decided to take off for a long weekend and go to Copenhagen, Denmark, with our London-based publicist, Mike Baumohl. Now Baumohl was a hustler—he always had a deal going. Either he opened the first motel in Denmark or he opened the first Laundromat in Sweden or he was the first one to sell lighted Jesus pictures in Catholic countries. Always something.

So Brooks, Baumohl, and I go to Copenhagen. Baumohl stays at his motel, and Brooks and I check into the Royal Viking Hotel. We're sharing a suite. Brooks goes down to the lobby for awhile and returns with this stunning brunette Swedish woman named Ulla. She is tall, gorgeous, and twenty-two years old. And she has her luggage with her.

I order up a daybed for the living room. I figure Ulla and Brooks will be taking over the bedroom.

We all go to a big party that night. They're filming the *Christine Keeler Story,* and Brooks and I know some people on the picture.

We have a great time and return to the suite very late. I sit down on the daybed and start taking off my shoes. Ulla comes over and says, "Ed, you're sitting on my bed."

I go in the bedroom and Brooks is having a hissy—he wants to throw Ulla out, bag and baggage, because she won't sleep with him. I say, "Calm down, Dick. It's just as well. I'm a married man. I don't need an affair going on here."

So Brooks and I sleep in the bedroom. All night long, he's muttering, "I'm gonna throw her out the window. I'm gonna throw her out the window."

The next morning, we're all having breakfast in the living room. I come up with a bright idea. "Ulla," I say, "how would you like to go to London?"

"Oh, I'd like that very much, Ed."

"I am going to propose something to you. I have a friend in London named Ray Stark, and I am going to give you a round-trip ticket to London. I am going to pay in advance for seven days at the Dorchester Hotel. And I'm going to give you five-hundred dollars to play around with."

In those days, $500 was a lot of money.

"And the only catch is this: I'm going to introduce you to Ray Stark, and no matter what Ray Stark promises you, you are to say no."

And she says, "I can say 'no' in four languages."

I then call Stark up in London, and I say, "Ray, I've found the wildest nymphomaniac I ever met in my life. A Swedish girl named Ulla. And instead of bringing you some chocolate from Copenhagen, I'm bringing you her."

And he says, "Terrific, terrific, terrific."

"Now, Ray, a warning. She's so crazy I had to pull her off the hotel manager this morning."

And he says, "Great, great, great. I tell you, Ed, Sunday night I've got dinner with Jack Clayton, the director, but I'll come over and meet you at ten-thirty at Trader Vic's at the Hilton Hotel. Clayton and I should be finished by then."

We fly back to London late on Sunday and take a cab to Trader Vic's. Ulla, Brooks, and I sit at a table near the entrance. Brooks and I are like two giddy schoolboys. Stark arrives and he trots down the stairs toward us with a jaunty little spring in his step. Then he sees this gorgeous girl sitting there and the normally glib Ray Stark gets brain-lock. I thought he was going to faint. The first thing out of his mouth is, "My dear, why don't you come up to my suite and hear the music from the new Fanny Brice show."

He was talking about *Funny Girl*.

And she looks at him and says, "Who's Fanny Brice?"

She wasn't putting him on, either. Why would a Swedish girl know about Fanny Brice?

Now Stark is captivated with Ulla. For three days, he's wooing her. He promised her a contract with Seven Arts. He promised her a six-month contract with the Eileen Ford Model Agency. He promised her the moon, the stars, whatever.

And she keeps saying, "No." In four different languages.

By Wednesday, he's very frustrated. Then he smells a rat. "Ed," he says, "are you putting something over on me with this girl? Is she a setup?"

And I say, "Ray, it cost thirteen-hundred dollars to bring her down by airplane. It's costing two-thousand dollars for a week at the Dorchester Hotel. You think I would spend three or four thousand dollars on a *practical joke?*"

"You're right, Ed. I'm sorry. But that Ulla is just so *gorgeous*."

Anyway, by Thursday he is so frustrated, he runs off to Paris. Before he leaves, he tells me, "Listen, there's an executive coming in from MGM, a friend of mine. Red Silverstein. Introduce her to him. Maybe he'll have better luck than I've had."

So I bring Silverstein into the deal. He doesn't even meet Ulla but on Friday morning, I have him call up Stark at his hotel in Paris. He says, "Ray, Ed Feldman deserves a ten-thousand dollar bonus. Last night, he introduced me to the wildest nymphomaniac I have ever met in my life. I'm exhausted."

Ulla kept her end of the bargain and no one ever told Stark the truth.

But he never forgot her.

Remember that breakfast at Stark's mansion, when he talked to Robert Redford on the phone? Later on, during that same breakfast, we had been reminiscing about the old days. Then Stark stops talking for a moment and gazes off wistfully. Finally, he says, "Remember Ulla, Ed? She was so beautiful."

When Stark died in early 2004, I thought a lot about our relationship, and I'll have to admit I had very mixed feelings. For many years, he had been wonderful to me and advanced my career immeasurably. Yet early in our time together, he treated me very cruelly.

Stark had many friends in the business and he had a good share of detractors. But when all is said and done, it remains that Stark was a rare personality in Hollywood—an individualist, a creator, a pioneer.

And with the exception of my family, he is one of the most important people who ever entered my life.

4

THERE ISSA NO
STRONGA LURE

I LOOKED AT JOE LEVINE AND THEN AT THE HOOKER SITTING
over on the sofa. My God, she was ugly. Here we are in Rome, home to
some of the most beautiful women on earth, but he has trolled the
hooker lake bottom. And happy about his catch.

I turned back to Levine.

"Joe, I forgot to tell you but I've got a date. Can't join you for dinner. I'm sorry."

I didn't have a date. But in the land of Sophia Loren and Gina Lollobrigida, this woman was about as appetizing as a plate of clams and
mussels left out in the sun next to the Via Veneto for a week.

I grabbed my hat and coat, muttered good-bye, and was through the
door in a flash.

Oh, and I forgot to mention something else. Levine was on crutches,
recuperating from double knee surgery. He could just barely hobble
around.

Joseph E. Levine.

Now I've worked with some characters in my life but Levine is
Character Hall of Fame material. I was director of publicity for Levine's
Embassy Pictures. In the two years I was in that job, Levine was lifted
from a little-known importer of B movies (*Hercules Unchained* with

Steve Reeves) to a well-known importer of distinguished dramatic films (*Two Women* with Sophia Loren). I even landed him a major story in *Time* magazine where he was feted as the man to jolt the film industry out of its slump. (Levine, with his ego, fantasized that he would be on the cover. I said, "Not unless you're Patrice Lumumba." Lumumba was the Congolese political leader who had just been assassinated.)

But back in Rome, I've now had dinner by myself and killed some time before returning to Levine's massive corner suite on the second floor of the Hotel Excelsior. I used to refer to it as the "Mussolini Suite" because Levine would stand out on the balcony overlooking the Via Veneto in an *Il Duce* pose.

Although the suite had two bedrooms with a big sitting room between them, making them seem about a half mile apart, I didn't want to encounter Levine and the woman together in any way, shape, or form.

I put my key in the lock and opened the door quietly and cautiously, then peered in. Whew. Nobody in the sitting room. And the only real light was coming from a small table lamp. It was midnight, so I figured Levine had already turned in alone, or was entertaining the woman in his bedroom.

I took off my jacket as I made my way into my bedroom. Then I stopped and turned around. Something was funny. The sitting room was exactly as I had left it a few hours earlier, and Levine's bedroom door was slightly ajar and a faint light was coming through, probably from his bathroom.

It was as if the suite was empty. But I couldn't imagine Levine wouldn't bring the woman back here after dinner. And I thought it's pretty unlikely Levine would go out nightclubbing while hobbling around on crutches.

I crept over to Levine's door and cocked my head to listen for any sounds. Nothing. I opened the door and looked in. The room was not only empty, but it was obvious Levine's bed hadn't been used since the maid turned it down hours ago. The little mints were even still on the pillow.

This was odd. I checked his bathroom, my bedroom, then the closets, back of the curtains, under the beds. No Joe Levine.

In my mind, he had gone to dinner with the woman and hadn't come back. I checked the front desk for messages. None. I asked the clerk if he had seen Mr. Levine return this evening. The clerk said he had seen him leave with a lady friend but he hadn't returned.

It's now 1 A.M. and I'm very tired so I turn in. Joe's a big boy, he can take care of himself.

At 6 A.M., I'm jolted awake by the phone ringing. It's Joe De Blasio, our production manager in Rome. De Blasio had bad news: Levine is in the hospital.

Right away, I thought the worst—

Tripped on his crutches, fallen in the street, and run over by a taxi. Or a bus. Leaving Levine on life support. How would I break the news to his family? Or . . .

The woman's pimp robbed him at knifepoint and left him bleeding in a dark alley. Joe pleading for his life. Or . . .

Mugged by a bum and beaten over the head with his own crutches while try-ing to protect the woman. Joe didn't deserve that. A brave, brave man.

Why didn't I stay with him last night? I could have kept this from happening. Sure he's flamboyant and self-centered, but he's a good man at heart and a helluva showman. Please, God, protect Joe.

But back to De Blasio. "Joe, what happened?" I said.

"Well, you remember that girl. She wouldn't do him at the Excelsior. So she talked him into going downstairs . . . on his crutches in the ho-tel and getting into her Fiat.

"So they drive across Rome to her apartment, in the Fiat. Now she lives on the fourth floor and there's no elevator. He's on crutches, re-member. So he makes it up the first flight, slowly, one step at a time . . . one step at a time. And he stops to rest on the landing. Then he goes up the second flight, one step at a time . . . one step at a time. So he stops to rest again.

"But this time, Ed, he passes out. Boom. Just like that. Down. Un-conscious. He doesn't move."

"Heart attack, Joe?"

"Oh, no, he's fine. Just needed a little bed rest and to get off those crutches for awhile. They'll release him a little later today."

"Wait a minute, Joe. You're telling me Levine got on his crutches, hobbled out to this woman's car, squeezed into her little Fiat, rode across town, hobbled into her building, climbed two flights of stairs with another flight to go, one step at a time. And the woman's no prize.

"You're telling me Levine did all that and in his weak condition. Why would he do such a thing, Joe?"

"Ed," he says, switching to an exaggerated Italian accent, *"There issa no stronga lure in the world."*

Levine's behavior was incredibly risky that night—consider how many corporate executives or public figures have been humiliated by this kind of thing. The list of name actors found in compromising positions is like a celebrity *Who's Who*. And one film executive even took the extreme step of issuing a press release stating that he was *not* on Hollywood Madam Heidi Fleiss's infamous list of "clients" even before anyone accused him. (And he never was accused.)

Now, bad behavior seemed to enjoy a very long run in actress Shelley Winters's showbiz family. Consider this.

Shelley and I worked together on *What's the Matter with Helen?* in 1970, which, by the way, was the very first picture I actually produced. One night on the set, Shelley is chatting with my wife, Lorraine, between takes. And she starts showing Lorraine her jewelry. She says, "You know, Lorraine, I had a couple of husbands who were big-time philanderers. And every time I caught one of them, he'd give me a major piece of jewelry. This is my Anthony Franciosa watch, this is my Vittorio Gassman ring." Et cetera. (Then Shelley asked Lorraine if she had any guys for her to meet!)

Poor Lorraine has had to rely on birthdays and anniversaries for *her* jewelry.

The entertainment industry has more than its share of temptations, sexual and otherwise. You are routinely working with some of the most attractive people in the world, famous or unknown. The massive amount of dollars involved almost guarantees that expensive drugs or pricey women will be readily available for the taking. Many people, even seasoned professionals, find it very hard to resist these temptations.

I produced *My Father the Hero* for Disney with Gérard Depardieu

starring. Katherine Heigl, then a teenage unknown but later made famous in the TV show *Roswell,* was playing Depardieu's daughter. Part
of the humor of the film was that the daughter was very pretty and
looked older than her years. At the start of filming, I took the unusual
step of making it known to the crew that any attempted funny business
with Heigl and they were off the picture, *that day.*

"There issa no stronga lure" begets what I would call The Risk of
the Lure. In filmmaking, it's always there and it can be very expensive
and disruptive. Movie sets are highly charged environments with enormous pressures. But the risk is manageable.

Consider this a rule of producing for the short list:

The risk of the lure is strong: Manage it like it could cost you millions.

(I'll give you its number on the list later—I need to think about it.)

But there was another strong lure for Joseph E. Levine. He hired me in
1960 at what I then considered a pretty handsome salary to put him on
the map. He wanted to be famous and he wanted to be considered a
big-time movie producer. In short, he wanted to be a big shot in films.
And I must say, he was pretty damn successful with it. And considering
the B movies he was churning out, he was almost scarily successful.

Remember, I joined Levine and Embassy Pictures after that very
tough stint with Ray Stark on *The World of Suzie Wong* for Paramount
Pictures. And remember also I had been with 20th Century Fox for
nine years prior to this.

So when I told my mother of my new job with Embassy Pictures,
she says, "Edward, what's an Embassy Pictures? I've never heard of Embassy Pictures. Everyone's heard of 20th Century Fox and Paramount.
Nobody has heard of Embassy Pictures. How can I tell my friends that
you work at Embassy Pictures and they've never heard of Embassy Pictures?"

Mother and her friends weren't the only ones who had never heard
of Embassy Pictures. She was right—few had.

But that was to change quickly.

"Ed, I've got a problem here. The lion is getting very, very edgy."

I could see from his expression that the lion tamer wasn't kidding. Nope, definitely not a kidder. I went to the door and slowly opened it. I looked through the crack, careful not to extend any valuable body parts outside. Yep, that lion out on Forty-eighth Street, Manhattan, New York, was indeed *very* edgy. But not only edgy. Looked hungry *and* edgy to me. But what do I know about lions?

I begin backing away from the door and as I do, I call to the lion tamer, "Stu, just make sure you keep him outside. Just keep him outside."

It's the premiere party of *Hercules Unchained,* my first big event for Joe Levine. And he's given me a blank check. We called the premiere party "A Night with the Gods." Has any truly awful B movie *ever* had a bigger premiere than this? Not in this solar system.

But we weren't just launching third-rate cinema, we were launching Joseph E. Levine right along with it.

Actually, this was the East Coast premiere of *Hercules Unchained*. Six nights earlier, we had thrown the West Coast premiere, also "A Night with the Gods." It was at the Beverly Hills Hotel and we turned all the poolside cabanas into private dining rooms. One for Louella Parsons, one for Hedda Hopper, one for Clark Gable.

Clark Gable?

Yes, Clark Gable. I was surprised just like you. I saw him coming down the steps into the Beverly Hills Hotel pool area and I almost fainted.

And how did Clark Gable like Hercules Unchained, *Ed?*

Well, we didn't actually show *Hercules Unchained* at the premiere but we threw a heck of a party. I had nubile maidens swimming in the pool among garlands of flowers, their diaphanous outfits shimmering in the light.

I placed an ice statue of Hercules in the garden adjacent to the pool with Chanel No. 5 spritz coming out every thirty seconds. Pfft. Pfft. But I forgot it was hot out here in L.A. Hercules was eight feet tall at six o'clock, he was seven feet tall at seven o'clock. Hercules is melting as I watch.

Then came the New York premiere at the Forum of the Twelve Caesars restaurant—a midnight Roman soirée with live centerpieces, like a human Hercules, gilded and standing motionless for two and a half hours. (No more ice Hercules—I'd learned my lesson.) Gourmet food! Glitz and glamour! Big celebrities! And that lion on Forty-eighth Street, hungry and edgy. Just like me. Hungry and edgy, hungry and edgy.

We were rolling, rolling, rolling.

And how did the New York premiere audience like Hercules Unchained, *Ed?*

Don't know. We didn't show it there either.

But you never saw such a party!

You know, I work in a funny business. I throw two big premieres for this forgettable movie, complete with ice sculptures and Chanel No. 5 spritz and Clark Gable and a hungry lion, for chrissake. And I don't show the movie. And I don't parade the movie's stars around. Not only that, I even told Steve Reeves emphatically not to come from Italy for the premiere parties—mainly because his real voice didn't measure up to his brawny physique. (His studly voice in the picture was dubbed by a very young, nebbish-looking electrical engineer.)

And Levine is *thrilled.*

And then later I get one of Levine's pictures, a serious and disturbing drama with Sophia Loren, a film that is a very difficult sell, a seventeen-page spread in *Life* magazine. And then Levine won't talk to me for three weeks.

But I'll come back to this.

For the two years I worked as publicity chief for Embassy Pictures and Joe Levine, I had essentially two jobs: promote Embassy's slate of pictures and promote Joseph E. Levine. Because of this second responsibility, Levine gave me carte blanche to spend what I wanted. I've told you about the *Time* magazine story on Levine and "A Night with the Gods." In fact, that New York party convinced editor Clay Felker to run a huge story in *Esquire,* written by Gay Talese, entitled "Joe Levine Unchained."

Levine had always been big on publicity. Even before I got there, he would throw a luncheon for distributors and theater owners and, in the middle of the ballroom, bring out a million dollars in cash surrounded by armed guards to show how much he was going to spend promoting the picture. Corny but effective.

During my tenure with Levine, I had one publicist, Dick Brooks, and a prominent nonexclusive column-planter, Mike Hall, on payroll, and we all worked our fannies off. We went on a big five-day, five-city tour (New York, Atlanta, Chicago, Dallas, and L.A.) to promote three of our releases at one time, *The Wonders of Aladdin, The Thief of Bagdad,* and *Morgan the Pirate.* I even had a hat constructed that I could turn into a pirate's hat, then a sultan's hat, then Aladdin's hat while I was talking about how we were moving from picture to picture.

The legendary actor/comedian George Jessel, on retainer with Levine, traveled with us as toastmaster and as the guy who made funny. One night in Dallas, I'm awakened at 2:30 A.M., and there is Jessel standing there with his hairpiece gone and in a ratty old bathrobe. He says, "Ed, I need fifty bucks right away." He had a hooker in his room and he was short the cash. There's that bad old lure again.

(But Jessel would sometimes try to score it for free from flight attendants—by telling them to call Ed Feldman to arrange their Hollywood screen tests. Never worked though.)

On another picture, at Levine's direction, we engaged Artkraft Strauss, the famous theater marquee builder, to construct a movie theater front, which we shipped by plane to Rome. It was set up in Levine's hotel suite to make it look like the opening night of our upcoming epic, *The Last Days of Sodom and Gomorrah.* (The hotel's Italian employees referred to us as the "American Lunatics" behind our backs.) This display was for the benefit of the J. Arthur Rank Organisation, our foreign distributor, and to make Levine look like Showman of the Year in Rank's eyes.

So in walk the four senior Rank executives, the theater lights are blinking, and Levine is giving them a long-winded speech about this movie and what we've done and the promotion. Then they say, "But Joe, with all this, when do we see the movie?"

Levine says, "We'll show it to you but I don't know if you'll understand it because its in rough cut. Do you have any experience with rough cuts?" Now he's saying this to the head of production at Rank and his associates, who were viewing rough cuts when Levine was still doing independent distribution in Boston.

Things went downhill from there. With Levine, the Rank executives had found the perfect pigeon to hate. That night, some unfortunate anti-Semitic remarks were made over dinner. I finally just got up and went back to the hotel by myself.

I said before that Levine was a character. Here's a little more evidence. Levine would expect everybody in the office to chip in and present him with a very expensive birthday gift—a major gift. And then he would have his secretary call the store, say Tiffany, and find out how much it cost. God forbid if we didn't buy him an expensive-enough gift.

When his lawyer gave him a gift one time and he found out it cost $500—a lot of money in those days—he's telling me what a cheap sonofabitch his lawyer is. He would check the value of every single gift and measure the giver's affection accordingly.

I hired Yousuf Karsh, one of the preeminent portrait photographers of the twentieth century, to shoot publicity photos for us for *Sodom and Gomorrah*. "Karsh of Ottawa" had taken the classic *Life* magazine cover photo of a tough-looking Winston Churchill in 1941, right after Churchill had delivered his famous "some chicken, some neck" speech to the Canadian Parliament. Some people have credited this one photograph, which was syndicated worldwide, with energizing the Allied war effort in Europe and helping bring eventual victory.

I was able to get Karsh because his beloved wife had just died and he was looking for a project, plus we were willing to pay his rather hefty fee. Levine winced when I told him how much, but I reminded him that this was the man who photographed Roosevelt, Stalin, Churchill, Hemingway, the pope. So Levine agreed to Karsh but only if the photo subjects included *Joe Levine* in addition to the *Sodom and Gomorrah* coverage. "This is worth a lot of money to me," he said.

I figured having a Karsh photo spread on *Sodom and Gomorrah* would do wonders for our publicity effort. And I was right.

So Karsh and his assistant go to Ouarzazate, Morocco, the most out-of-the-way place you can imagine. He's working in the desert, it's 110 degrees, and he's wearing a black suit with a tie and a white shirt. He is doing a splendid job and everyone is cooperative—Pier Angeli, Anouk Aimée, Stanley Baker. All is fine until Karsh tackles Stewart Granger, the star of the movie. He gets Granger into the gallery for headshots. Now, Granger had very little respect for anyone except Stewart Granger. During the shoot, he was petulant and made derisive comments like "get on with your clickety-click-click," treating Karsh like some hack local photographer. And here was Karsh, a diminutive, polite, soft-spoken man who had taken some of the most famous portrait photographs of the previous twenty years.

Finally, Karsh gets the work done. Then Karsh looks at Granger and says in his Armenian accent, "Mr. Granger, in my life I have photographed many of the great personalities of the world. Einstein and Gertrude Stein. Hemingway and Churchill. Roosevelt and the pope. All very fine people. But you, Mr. Granger . . . without a question, you are the biggest *prick* I ever met!"

Sodom and Gomorrah was the only motion picture project of Yousuf Karsh's long and distinguished career. And it was possible only because we included a stop-off in New York to photograph Joe Levine. The photograph had him in a docile, pensive pose with his hands folded in front of him, just as Levine wanted. He had gotten his wish—Karsh had made him look like Pope Pius XII.

The beginning-of-the-end between Ed Feldman and Joe Levine began with a phone call from Maurice "Red" Silverstein, head of MGM International. Levine and I were in Rome, and Silverstein asked us to come over to the screening room at Titanus Films and see a picture called *Two Women,* starring Sophia Loren and directed by the esteemed Vittorio De Sica. Levine and I watched the film, which was in Italian and in rough cut, but was readily understandable with its striking visual imagery.

Two Women is a very tough film about a woman and her teenage daughter in wartime Italy. To survive, mother and daughter must make their way through the countryside, trying to elude soldiers of both sides. The film contains a very brutal rape scene, and Loren spends much of the picture disheveled and grimy, very much at odds with her glamorous image.

Silverstein explains that MGM will distribute *Two Women* in foreign markets but not in the United States. MGM's president back home doesn't believe anyone in America wants to see an Italian-language picture with Sophia Loren "looking like that." But Carlo Ponti, the film's producer and Loren's husband, doesn't want to sell the rights piecemeal. So we put up a record $350,000 for the U.S. and Canadian rights.

It is clear from the start that this will be a difficult film to promote. But I showed the film to *Life,* the premiere magazine in the country then. And they wound up doing a seventeen-page cover story on the rebirth of Sophia Loren. I couldn't have been happier. But Levine wasn't. Remember my mission was to promote films *and* Levine.

So the layout appears and Levine is flipping through, looking for *his* picture. And he can't find it. Now I'm not the one to tell *Life* magazine what to print. I thought Levine would be thrilled from just a straight business perspective, especially given the big money he had advanced on the movie. But he wasn't. "How could you leave my picture out?" he scolded.

But put this in perspective. When Levine went away, all he would want when he got back was to see the articles and column plants that appeared while he was gone—to see his name and picture. It got so that if things were a little light with the publicity, we'd put old clippings in his folder and he never noticed it. He was looking only for his name and picture, and never once checked the date of the clip.

So after the *Life* spread, Levine gave me the silent treatment. For a solid three weeks, he wouldn't talk to me at all.

Now I was getting very nervous because I realized no matter what I did, it was only about *Joe Levine.* I told Lorraine, "It's time for me to leave."

Earlier, I told you about my surprising call from Ray Stark on my wedding anniversary, inviting me back.

So I left Levine and went back to work with Ray Stark, this time as vice president of advertising and publicity for Seven Arts, the company he comanaged with Eliot Hyman.

(By the way, in those days, the word *marketing* was never mentioned.)

When I went in to tell Levine I was leaving and to give six weeks' notice, he was cordial and wished me well. But I go back to my office, and the office manager says, "Ed, Levine wants you out of here by five o'clock today."

Like a chump, for three hours I dictate notes on everything we had in the pipeline, so my successor could get up to speed quickly. As if Levine gave a flip. I'm surprised he didn't have armed guards escort me out.

Two Women turned out to be a real jewel in Levine's crown. Sophia Loren won the Academy Award for Best Actress (the first for a foreign-language performance) and the Cannes Film Festival Best Actress award. The picture won the Golden Globe as Best Foreign Language Film.

By the time I left Embassy, Joe Levine's name and picture were everywhere. And his films were becoming more respectable. Out with Steve Reeves, in with Kim Novak (*Boys' Night Out*) and Katharine Hepburn (*Lion in Winter*). *Hercules Unchained* morphed to *Long Day's Journey into Night* and then to *The Graduate* by way of *Two Women*. Joe Levine in the 1960s was easily one of the most important and visible single individuals in the industry.

As I look back on my tenure with Levine, I think I really did a good job for him, probably some of the best publicity work of my career. What most people don't know about Levine, and certainly didn't know then, is that he could barely read. He was a terrific showman and had a real knack for being a movie executive, in addition to having one of the biggest egos in the Western or any other Hemisphere. But the image created for Levine in the early 1960s was, to a large extent, an illusion. You might argue that eventually he grew into the image, that he was something of a film industry statesman by the time of *Carnal Knowledge* and *A Bridge Too Far.* But when I worked for him, he was a product of good publicity.

There is a time-honored quote attributed to Joe Levine in reference books. This quote describes very nicely my stint with him: "You can fool all the people all the time if the advertising is right and the budget is big enough."

Here's a postscript on Joe Levine. When I was moving to California in the late 1960s, my friends and colleagues threw a big going-away party for me at Gallagher's Steak House on Fifty-second Street, New York. People from all over the business were there. All of us had entirely too much to drink, though. So I'm in a fog when I get up to speak near the end of the evening. And I proceed to say the following: "I just wish Joe Levine could be here tonight. But unfortunately he's in Mt. Sinai Hospital, having his taste buds removed."

All you aspiring producers out there, don't ever get drunk and say something like that. It's a terribly stupid thing to do. You'll never shake it.

A few weeks later, when I'm based in California, I'm flying to Las Vegas with Lorraine and some others on Frank Sinatra's private plane. And I'm reading the sixtieth-anniversary issue of the weekly *Variety*. In this issue, they did a special feature on "sometimes *Variety* goes where it's not welcome." As an example, they quote "film executive" Ed Feldman, who said Joe Levine had his taste buds removed at Mt. Sinai.

Of all the fifty thousand things they could have run, they publish my drunken Levine joke.

So now I'm feeling really bad about it and I write a note to Levine in apology. I hear nothing. Then I'm invited to a preview of *The Graduate* by its producer, Larry Turman. And Levine hits the ceiling, almost breaking up his business relationship with Turman because I'm invited to the screening.

Finally, about a year later, I see Levine at a function and I say to him, "Joe, I must tell you I am truly apologetic for what I said. Please forgive me."

Levine stares at me, then finally says, "Not after what you said about me." And he walks off.

I was with Joe Levine for two years, which is about the same length of time I worked with one of the film industry's icons, Jack L. Warner. In fact, we can use these two in a sort of compare-and-contrast way. I'll talk about Jack Warner at length later but I wanted to introduce him here.

Jack Warner and three brothers formed the Warner Bros. Studios in the 1920s after several false starts in the entertainment business. They hit the big time with the first talking film, *The Jazz Singer,* in 1927. Over the years, Jack ran the studio and established himself as a shrewd but capricious movie mogul.

I worked with Jack Warner from 1967 to 1969, after my employer, Seven Arts, acquired Warner Bros. and moved me to California as the assistant head of production. (That was the move we were celebrating at Gallagher's.) Jack stayed on at the studio in his old office, and my New York bosses assigned me to keep him happy.

One day, I'm sitting at lunch in the Warner executive dining room with Ken Hyman, Warner's head of production, and Norman Lear, a producer-director who would eventually create with Bud Yorkin the landmark TV show *All in the Family,* among others. We're just sitting around, chatting, finishing our lunch when in walks Jack Warner. I'll have to say, for a man in his late seventies, Warner looked fantastic. Trim, well groomed, dapper, fastidiously dressed. Warner glides by and our eyes follow him.

Finally I speak up, "Just look at that man. Look how he keeps himself for a man of his age." Hyman and Lear nod in agreement.

Then Hyman says, "Well, fellas, I know what his secret is."

Lear and I look at Hyman, waiting for the revelation. A few beats go by.

"I hear he's got a young girlfriend in Palm Springs. *And* that he's got a very active sex life. A *very* active sex life."

Lear looks at me and we nod in unison. We understand perfectly.

A few beats go by.

Lear speaks up, "Fellas, you know what *I* hear?"

Hyman and I wait—a few more beats go by.

"I hear . . . *he cums dust.*"

Joe Levine and Jack Warner—one a Hollywood nouveau, up from the depths of B-moviedom, barely literate, and the other, a Hollywood pioneer with his name on a major studio. So seemingly different, but finally brothers under the skin. Truly—

There issa no stronga lure!

DUKE, THE KID, AND
THE COLONEL

JUST AS I REACH FOR THE LAST BITE OF MY SANDWICH, A MAS-sive hand appears over my plate, clutching a newspaper. But not really *clutching* it, more like waving it, brandishing it. Very agitated. My eyes follow the animated newspaper for a couple of seconds. I recognize it.

A gruff, gravely voice booms out, "Ya read this, Kid?"

Only one man in the civilized world could belong to that voice—John Wayne. The Duke. Mega-movie star. National icon. And right now, he was mad as a hornet.

I look up.

"Hello, Duke. Yeah, I read it."

I think probably half of the Warner Studio had read it. That news-paper had published a scathing review of Wayne's new movie, *The Green Berets.* They ripped it up one side, down the other, out the door, around the block, first this way, then that way . . . If that newspaper were a dog, then *The Green Berets* was a chewed-up rag doll on the floor, its ears and limbs mangled or missing with a long thread stretching to the kitchen.

"Well, Kid, what are you going to do about it?"

If Rich Little were doing this scene, Wayne would be saying some-thing like, "Pilgrim, now listen and listen tight. We're gonna put to-gether a small team of crack commandos. Under cover of nightfall, we're gonna parachute into that rag's compound and we're gonna set those Commies straight. Ya got me?"

But this is real life. Same voice but different words:

"I tell you what I want you to do, Kid. I want you to reprint this review. I want it reprinted in every major newspaper in the country."

I look at Wayne blankly. Oh, God. Now what do I do?

John Wayne is one of Warners' biggest stars; his movie is about to open; and he wants me to plaster the country with this red-hot-poker-up-the-kazoom review.

"Red?" Did I say *Red*? That newspaper was Red all right—it was none other than that Communist tome, the *Daily Worker*. (Actually, it was by now called *The Worker*, but it was still the *Daily Worker* to us.) Now, this wasn't fancy-pants, Park Avenue dilettante Communist. Not that "Workers unite. And Beulah, will you mix me another martini" brand of communism. No, sir. This was the real stuff. The Marx-Lenin-Trotsky-Stalin variety. Hard core. Mother Russia Communism.

And those SOB's had just torn up Wayne's flag-waving melodrama of the Vietnam War.

The *Daily Worker* wasn't the only publication panning *The Green Berets*. Almost everyone was. But those Commies at the *Daily Worker* were the ones in Wayne's sights.

Now how did I come to be mixed up in this?

Well, it's 1968, I'm the assistant head of production at Warners . . . and all the other senior executives are out of town. I'm the ranking suit around the studio for a few days.

It's all up to you, Feldman.

I glance around the lunch table. Wayne's son, Michael—the picture's producer—looks at me expectantly. My other lunch companions have that bemused "how-ya-gonna-get-out-of-this-one-Feldman" expression.

OK, here goes.

"Duke, the *Daily Worker* is read by three thousand people every day. You want to set up this review so that it reaches *millions* of people? What kind of an *American* are you?"

I could hear a little gasp from the lunch table and could sense they were shooting each other glances. If nothing else, John Wayne is Super

Patriot. If they put movie stars on Mount Rushmore, there he'd be, touching shoulders with Teddy Roosevelt.

John Wayne: "My country, right or . . . *right.*"

Wayne looks down at me. His anger has slowly given way to incredulity. He continues to stare at me. Now incredulity gives way to exasperation.

"What kind of an American am I? What kind of an American am I?"

He shakes his head, turns to the door, and stomps out, muttering to himself, "What kind of an American am I? What kind of an American am I?"

All eyes are trained on the door, Wayne's voice trailing off.

Things are quiet for a moment, then Michael Wayne says to me, "How could you question my father on what kind of an American he is?"

And I give him one of my patented what-else-could-I-do expressions.

I really liked John Wayne. I hadn't had much contact with him before the *Daily Worker* episode. But after that, Wayne and I spent a lot of time together in connection with the promotion of *The Green Berets.* I'll tell you about that in a little while.

I was at Warner Bros. in California for about two years, from 1967 to 1969. As I mentioned before, my employer in New York, Seven Arts, acquired Warners and moved me to L.A., where I began my first job in actually making movies. I had always worked in publicity and advertising before, so this was a huge career milestone for me.

At Warners, I worked under the new head of production, Ken Hyman, the son of Eliot Hyman, who was the president of Seven Arts. Ken had just produced *The Dirty Dozen,* which was a huge hit; and this had made him one of the hottest producers in town. Being involved in the changing of the guard at Warners, one of the old "studio system" operations, and bringing it into more modern times was a tremendous opportunity for me. And it gave me the chance to learn the production end of the business while rubbing elbows with some real living legends. Two of the most colorful of these were John Wayne and Jack Warner, the Duke and the Colonel.

I talked with you about Jack Warner earlier. Jack and three brothers had founded Warner Bros. studio in the 1920s. The company had prospered over the years and produced and distributed many classic films. But in the mid-1960s, the venerable old Warner studio had fallen on hard times and was losing money. Jack Warner, the only remaining Warner brother, was still in charge. Although healthy and alert for his years, Warner was Old Hollywood and having trouble releasing the reins of studio management to more forward thinkers, the new generation of moviemakers.

My employer, Seven Arts Ltd., purchased Warner Bros. in 1967 for around $90 million, a high price at the time. Apparently Seven Arts had always intended to cash out of the Warner investment quickly, but I didn't know this when I moved to California. As it happened, Seven Arts sold Warners just a year and a half later to Kinney National Services.

When Ken Hyman and I arrived at Warners, we found a number of terrific projects in process—Paul Newman in *Cool Hand Luke,* Warren Beatty and Faye Dunaway in *Bonnie and Clyde,* Julie Christie and George C. Scott in *Petulia.* In the archives, we even found an unused Cole Porter score, written for a project called *Mississippi Gambler*—couldn't use it though, far too old-fashioned.

We also found *The Green Berets.*

In 1967, the Vietnam War was in full swing. And Warners was in full swing shooting John Wayne's *The Green Berets,* based on a book of the same name and taking inspiration from the 1966 hit song "The Ballad of the Green Berets." We had inherited this project from the Jack Warner era. And I can say the new Seven Arts regime at Warners would never have green-lighted it. Many around the studio found it simplistic and jingoist. Strongly prowar when many people, including me, were conflicted about the heavy casualties and questionable rationale of Vietnam. It wouldn't have taken much to have pulled the plug on Mr. Wayne's opus.

For one thing, the footage we were looking at was terrible. Wayne had directed *The Alamo* eight years earlier and it was passable. But on *The Green Berets,* we were getting interminable shots of men standing around talking with their arms folded. Wayne had cast some of his actor buddies in key roles and a few, like Aldo Ray, were awful. A mediocre script was unfolding as a stinker of a movie, politics aside.

We had to do something. We finally elected to have Mervyn LeRoy take over for Wayne as director. LeRoy was a prominent and established director—*Thirty Seconds Over Tokyo, Madame Curie, Quo Vadis.* LeRoy was under contract to Warners and he was available. Plus he had the Old-Hollywood stature—he had even been married to Jack Warner's niece for awhile—to assume Wayne's directoral duties without Wayne's going ballistic. Wayne ended up being surprisingly pleasant—maybe even relieved—about the whole thing. I think he knew he was in over his head trying to act and direct in the film. So LeRoy heads east to the North Carolina set and almost immediately the footage is much better.

The Green Berets didn't end up too bad after all. The critics hated it but it was popular with the public. LeRoy had insisted that he go uncredited as director, a decision he later regretted—considering *Green Berets'* surprising success.

It's probably some sort of poetic justice that *Green Berets* contains one of the great gaffes in movie history—right up there with the boy holding his ears *before* the surprise gunshot in Hitchcock's *North by Northwest.*

At the film's conclusion, Wayne is in a dramatic, heartrending scene with a small Vietnamese orphan boy on a beach. And the sun slowly sets . . . in the *east.*

Now it's time for the world premiere of *The Green Berets.* We agree that I'll be the studio executive to accompany Wayne to the event in Atlanta. (Ever the publicist, I had suggested having it on the hugely anti-war Berkeley campus, but no one took me seriously.) It's timed to coincide with a massive patriotic parade held each year in Atlanta on the Fourth of July called "Salute 2 America." There would be three hundred thousand people on the line of march. Wayne was the grand marshal and also included were David Janssen from the movie and Victor Jory, the last living male star of *Gone with the Wind.* This being Atlanta and it being *GWTW,* Jory's status was just shy of deity. Following the parade would be the world premiere event at the Fox Theater in downtown Atlanta. Now I must tell you, the Fox Theater seats about five thousand people and at the time was probably the largest theater in the United States. This was going to be a very big deal.

As the parade was assembling, I could see that the police had snipers positioned all along the parade route: on the top of each building, around this and that. It's scary. Frankly, they were worried about liberal crazies—*Green Berets* wasn't exactly the favorite movie of the antiwar group. As grand marshal, Wayne would be riding in an open car. And he said, "Come on, Kid, you ride with me."

And I said, "Not on your life, Duke. Someone will shoot at you, and miss you and hit me." I know about open cars: I've seen the Zapruder film of the Kennedy motorcade.

But everything went fine, and Wayne was charismatic and charming as usual. The crowd was ecstatic. Now we get to the theater (I arrive in an unmarked hardtop), file in, and the place is packed.

The first speaker introduced before the movie starts is Victor Jory, and he says dramatically and passionately, "America, Atlanta, today I saw you wave the American flag and I beg you from the bottom of my heart to never stop waving that flag as long as you live."

And the crowd went crazy. Crazy! Screaming with delight.

Then Wayne is introduced. And in a voice full of gravel and conviction, he says, "I want to tell you something. There's a hell of a lot right with America."

And he gets cheers, applause, and it's deafening.

And out of nowhere, I hear, "And now, representing the Warner Studio, executive Ed Feldman from Los Angeles."

Did I just hear "Ed Feldman?" I'm not on the program. I look around and people are motioning me to go out on the stage.

The announcer repeats, "And now, Ed Feldman!"

I peer out at the audience—five thousand of the most patriotic, whipped-up mass of humanity I'd ever seen and Deep Southerners, all the way. I see a familiar face off to the side. It's our publicity field man in Atlanta, Gerald Rafshoon, who would go on to become Jimmy Carter's communications director ten years later. With a sly grin, trying to rattle me, Rafshoon says in a way-too-loud voice, "You're a Jewish man, aren't you?" (Rafshoon is Jewish too.)

And so I go out there—the token Hollywood Jew—wondering if I'm going to make it out of the theater alive.

The crowd is screaming, stomping their feet, waving flags. And I begin to speak, "It's a privilege to be here in Atlanta on such a day. That of all the places in America, I never saw such patriotism expressed by so many people. God bless America!"

And the place explodes! More flag-waving, cheering.

After I'm off, Wayne comes over, puts his hand on my shoulder, and gives me a big grin. "Kid, not bad for a city boy. Not bad at all."

With a wink and nod, he strides off.

John Wayne died in 1979. His star is so huge that twenty years later, in the Jackie Chan comedy Western, *Shanghai Noon,* Chan's character is named Chon Wang—and everybody gets the joke, even kids.

I got to know John Wayne very well during our promotion of *The Green Berets.* And I will tell you he was basically the most honorable man I ever met in the business. If he gave you his word, you never had to question it.

Once one of his associates made a mildly anti-Semitic remark to me. And Wayne growls at him, "You better shut your mouth or I'll throw you over that balcony."

If a crew member's wife came on a movie set, he would pay attention to her because in his mind, you must have respect for a man's wife. It was the old code of the West.

They don't make them like the Duke anymore.

They don't make them like Jack Warner anymore either. And there are those who would reply, "Thank God."

One of my big responsibilities at Warners, in addition to actually working on movies, was managing Jack Warner—the *Colonel.* (I had figured him for a "Kentucky Colonel," but it turns out he was commissioned a lieutenant colonel in the air force during World War II for getting a series of military short films produced.) After Seven Arts bought his company, Warner remained on the lot in his old office with basically a production deal ("indie prod" for independent producer). The brass in New York told me to keep him happy . . . within reason.

Having Warner stay on after the ownership change was sometimes a bit of a problem. He had been accustomed to holding court in the private executive dining room at Warners for years. He had hired the chef from the luxury liner *France* and required every producer, director, and writer, as well as the Warner executives, to eat there. They didn't have to show up but he charged them anyway, whether they were there or not. It cost only $3 per day and the meals were sumptuous, but the imperiousness of it still rankled.

Warner would sit at the head of the table—the food was served ranch style—and regale the others with stories and jokes. No one could ever sit in his chair, even when he was away. And when he was away, the table would be packed, every seat but his taken.

Things occasionally got contentious around the lunch table. Once a producer and a director got into a heated exchange with Warner over something or other. Very brave of them: I was impressed. Words are flying back and forth when Warner says, "You dare argue with the man whose name is on the water tower?"

Later, when we were getting ready to paint the water tower, these two guys offered to pay for the paint job—if we would put *their* names up there for a week.

I found out later that Warner had been using that water tower bit to win arguments for years.

I shut down the executive dining room not long after. It was losing a lot of money. I think it hit Warner pretty hard—another reminder, in his own mind, that he shouldn't have sold the company.

Jack was still left at Warner Bros. because he had basically tricked his brothers when they sold out a little over ten years earlier. There were three living then—Jack, Harry, and Abe—with Harry, the president, and Jack, the head of production. The relationship between Harry and

Jack had been difficult for years and everyone knew it. But then how could they miss it: One day, a pretty old Harry ran through the Warner lot chasing Jack and swinging an iron pipe, yelling obscenities. They ran past actors, messengers, extras, grips. When he finally realized he couldn't catch Jack (Harry was eleven years older), Harry threw the pipe at him but missed.

In 1956, Abe wanted to cash out and was pressuring his brothers to sell. Harry was worn out (I guess so, with all that running and throwing) but had resisted retiring because he didn't want Jack to replace him as president. So the brothers ended up selling the company with the proviso that all would retire from the business. To make a long story short, Jack had a secret side deal with the new owners to buy back his stock. And suddenly Jack was the new president, in Harry's old job, and was the largest single shareholder of Warner Bros.

Harry learned of this chicanery when he picked up *Variety* one morning, then suffered a stroke with the newspaper still in his hands. Harry recovered but the bad blood continued until Harry's death. Jack even refused to come back from Europe to attend the funeral, which was being held up pending his arrival. Ironically, fours days later, Jack had a near-fatal car crash near his villa outside Cannes while driving under the influence.

The Warner brothers as their own Greek tragedy.

Jack Warner was the most eccentric man I've ever met. Here he had helped build up a major powerhouse movie studio yet he often came across as crude, insensitive, and embarrassing.

We were putting together a film called *Hell in the Pacific* to star Lee Marvin and the Japanese actor Toshiro Mifune. Now Mifune was internationally known and regarded as one of the world's great actors. In his homeland, he had worked extensively with the legendary director Akira Kurosawa. *Hell in the Pacific* would be his first U.S. picture.

We wanted to give Mifune a dramatic welcome to Hollywood, so we arranged an elegant dinner party upstairs at The Bistro in Beverly Hills. The guest list was star-studded: Elia Kazan, Joe Mankiewicz, Clint Eastwood, Lee Marvin. And Jack Warner was there. As the host for the evening, I shepherded Mifune and his wife around the room, introducing them to the other guests.

At one point, Warner walks up and I proceed to introduce him to the Mifunes.

"Mr. and Mrs. Mifune, I have the honor of introducing Mr. Jack L. Warner, the president and founder of Warner Bros."

And of course they bow, and Warner looks them over. Then he says to Mifune, "Didn't we meet at Pearl Harbor?"

Mifune replies cooly, "I don't think so." And unbelievably, there was no other reaction at all from him. Yes, a very good actor.

Hell in the Pacific, by the way, ended up at another studio.

On another occasion, Warner was asked to deliver an important speech. He's rattling on at the podium, when out of the blue he announces, "Excuse me. I gotta take a leak."

So he strides off the stage, goes into the back, and reappears a couple of minutes later and resumes the speech. And never acknowledges he'd been gone.

He was the man who said upon meeting Madame Chiang Kai-shek, the famous wife of the Chinese general and first president of Taiwan, "I forgot my laundry."

He was the man who told Albert Einstein, "I had a theory of relatives too. Don't hire 'em." (Reportedly Einstein didn't get the joke.)

He was the man described famously by actress Simone Signoret: "He bore no grudge against those he had wronged."

I'm sitting in my office one day and the phone rings. "Kid, could you come over?" It was Jack Warner. (Yes, he called me Kid too.)

I walked across the hall. We had left Warner in his old office even though he had no title or official responsibilities with the company. And he says to me, "Kid, I want you to buy me a book." It was a novel by the famous writer Howard Fast.

I had been told by the New York office, don't argue with him. Whatever he wants you to do, do it.

So I go back to my office and I call the William Morris Agency, who was representing the book, and I said, "Look, a check's coming over for $50,000. You'll have it by two this afternoon."

"You own it, Ed. Give Mr. Warner our regards."

After lunch, I go back to his office and tell him we own the book. He says, "Well, Kid, who can we get to write this mother?"

One of the big controversies of his life had been Jack Warner's participation with the House Un-American Activities Committee back in the late 1940s. The committee, chaired then by J. Parnell Thomas (with the later Senate effort led by Joe McCarthy), was on a Communist witch-hunt through the ranks of Hollywood studios. Warner had made a picture in 1943, *Mission to Moscow,* that was very pro-Soviet. Did that make Warner a pinko? Hardly. The Soviets were American allies then and besides, President Roosevelt had asked Warner to make the film. Still, *Mission to Moscow* gave the committee leverage over Warner and he quickly caved in, naming names to the committee. One outcome of this was that a whole group of top Hollywood screenwriters was blacklisted by the studios for a long time. Some even went to jail.

Howard Fast was a well-known member of the American Communist Party in that era and one of the best novelists of his time. He was jailed in 1950 for refusing to cooperate with the committee.

So in response to Warner's question "Who can we get to write this mother?" I suggested Michael Wilson, Dalton Trumbo, or Abe Polonsky, all screenwriters Warner had helped get blacklisted. Trumbo's screenplay of Fast's novel, *Spartacus,* helped lift the blacklist. I said this to get Warner's goat a little but he thought I was serious.

And Warner says, "You're right. Those guys are great writers. But what would the town think after what I accused them of? I don't think I could face that."

So we wind up with Nunnally Johnson, one of the most famous screenwriters who ever lived. A man who had written screenplays for *The Grapes of Wrath, The Man in the Gray Flannel Suit,* and *The Dirty Dozen.* He had done an extraordinary number of very fine movies.

We're now meeting in Warner's office. It's Jack Warner, Nunnally Johnson, Curtis Kenyon, our story editor, and I. But first I excuse myself to use Warner's private bathroom. I could have gone before I got there but I was just so damned impressed with the bathroom, I couldn't resist. He had a black marble commode and sink, and pure gold fixtures. My God, you could have sold the gold handle right off the toilet. And sitting there on Warner's private throne, I felt like I was in the epicenter of show business.

So back in the meeting with Johnson, I'm waiting for words of wisdom to come out of Jack Warner's mouth. He reclines in his chair and thinks for a moment. Then he leans forward and this is what he says to one of Hollywood's top writers of all time: "Nunnally, I really don't give a shit what you write . . . as long as you open with a map."

Now, if you think back on many of the old Warner pictures—especially Westerns—they'd open with a crawl (a title moving slowly across the screen giving information) or a map. Something like, "As the pioneers reach Silver City, Colorado . . . ," and you'd see a map of Colorado with the route tracing in. The flaming map at the beginning of *Bonanza* on TV was a takeoff on Warner Bros. *Star Wars* had the most famous crawl of all time: "In a galaxy far, far away . . ."

Think about the beginning of *Casablanca,* a Warner picture and one of the great screen classics, and how efficiently it sets the film up:

With the coming of the Second World War, many eyes in imprisoned Europe turned hopefully, or desperately, toward the freedom of the Americas. Lisbon became the great embarkation point but . . . not everybody could get to Lisbon directly. And so a tortuous roundabout refugee trail sprang up. Paris to Marseilles . . . across the Mediterranean to Oran . . . then by train or auto or foot across the rim of Africa to Casablanca in French Morocco. Here, the fortunate ones, through money, or influence, or luck, might obtain exit visas and scurry to Lisbon and from Lisbon to the New World. But the others wait in Casablanca . . . and wait . . . and wait . . . and wait.

And then, boom, the action begins immediately. The map and narration run for sixty-six seconds.

I asked Warner about this one time and he believed that the audience found the first fifteen minutes of exposition to be boring. The shorter, the better. Warner movies usually ran around ninety minutes and very few exceeded one hundred minutes.

But that really wasn't the reason. I found out later that if he didn't have to shoot the first fifteen or twenty minutes of each picture—the exposition—he would save enough money to make three or four additional pictures a year.

Warner was that crafty and that clever.

Nunnally Johnson finished the script but the film was never made. The New York brass had said keep him happy but not *that* happy. They had no intention of making any Jack L. Warner pictures.

They had put Warner into "indie prod" purgatory—a place I would find myself before too long.

The Ken Hyman regime at Warners did pretty well for our year and a half. In addition to finishing up pictures started by our predecessors, we made Sam Peckinpah's *The Wild Bunch,* one of the greatest Westerns ever; *Bullitt* with Steve McQueen, directed by Peter Yates, containing one of the greatest car-chase sequences in film history; and Francis Ford Coppola's studio-picture debut, *Finian's Rainbow.*

Ken Hyman had found Sam Peckinpah two years earlier. Or I should say Peckinpah found him. After the premiere screening of Hyman's film *The Hill,* starring Sean Connery, at the Cannes Film Festival, Peckinpah came up to Hyman, introduced himself, and complimented the picture. Hyman had been so taken with Peckinpah in their brief chat that he screened Peckinpah's *Ride the High Country* shortly after and was very impressed. Impressed enough to hire him later at Warners.

Hyman thought Peckinpah was a genius, but Peckinpah was a heavy drinker and, to some people, a little bit crazy. I remember when he would sit in his office, drinking and rolling the chamber on a loaded revolver. It was a nervous thing with him. One day I said, "Look, I'm not coming into your office if you're going to roll the chamber. I don't play with guns."

The Wild Bunch was a tough picture because we always worried about Peckinpah. He was not someone you could manage. You didn't tell *him* what to do. He told *you* what to do.

Now, he had a wonderful cameraman, Lucien Ballard. Suddenly the dailies came back with a yellow tinge on them. And the yellowness was fantastic. It was as if you could feel the heat coming off the film. But we're sitting in dailies and the head of postproduction at Warners then was a Teutonic editor named Rudi Fehr, and he said, "Don't worry, Ed, we'll get it out in the lab."

But I said, "You don't understand. This is genius, whoever did this."

He said, "But it's not clear. It looks like the heat is coming off the ground."

I said, "That's what they're trying to do."

We realized we were making a great movie. *The Wild Bunch* was the beginning of the extended slow-motion, very bloody gunfight sequences that would be copied ever since. What Peckinpah wanted to show, basically, was that dying was not glorious and people getting shot was not heroic. And he brought that quality to the picture.

But with Peckinpah, you always had to take the good with the bad. On his second picture with us, *The Ballad of Cable Hogue,* I get a call on a Sunday night from one of the big Las Vegas casinos. Peckinpah is shooting in the desert near Las Vegas. He and the film's star, Jason Robards, appeared at this casino, drunk, and proceeded to urinate on one of the crap tables. They were taken to the jailhouse and I had to hire a Las Vegas attorney to spring them. The casino also wanted us to cover the economic damages. The crap table had to be recovered and so it wasn't generating income for the two hours *that* took.

Those two got off lightly. If they hadn't been Peckinpah and Robards, and we hadn't been Warner Bros., they probably would have had their legs broken.

Peter Sellers worked for us on the comedy *I Love You, Alice B. Toklas,* during this time. I had met him on *Lolita* a few years earlier and had kept up with him since. After one of his pictures would open, I'd call him to say how funny he was. He was always charming and gracious. With the *Toklas* picture shooting on the Warner lot, Sellers and I became chummy.

Later on, I used to run into him in London. He was spending more and more time there, and I went over frequently on business.

I worked quite a bit with Mike Baumohl, a publicist based in London. (You may remember he figured prominently in the "Ulla" caper I described before—Ulla, the Swedish bombshell who could say no in four languages.) Well, Baumohl was known as a sort of London way-station for meeting women. He would throw nice parties in some visitor's honor and invite twenty men and twenty attractive women. Have Harrod's do the catering. The parties were sort of a "mixer" for lonely travelers. But they always sounded better—and juicier—than they really were. They became legendary in film circles.

Well, Baumohl and I are having dinner with Sellers, and he mentions the parties: "It sounds truly fascinating. How about having a party *for me*—in my honor?"

Baumohl and I look at each other; he gives me a wink and says, "Peter, that's a great idea. We'll set it up."

So Baumohl plans the party. He invites sixteen women; Harrod's does the catering, as usual; and he tells Sellers to show up at such and such a time and place. Except Baumohl and I have a little surprise for him.

Now, Sellers has been looking forward to this party for weeks. He fancied himself a ladies man and had imagined an evening surrounded by beautiful, adoring women.

On the big night, he walks in, all hot to trot, and greets us with a wide grin. "Mike, Ed, this is wonderful. Thank you." And he begins surveying the scene. Slowly, his grin begins to fade. Baumohl and I exchange amused looks.

The women Sellers was expecting were tall, blond, and beautiful. The women we gave him were short, frumpy, and ethnic.

"Where are all the gorgeous girls?"

"Peter, this is the best we could drum up."

He stays for a little while, mingles a bit, then leaves in a funk. He didn't talk to us again for a year.

Now Baumohl and I are feeling a little bad for the women, so we take a few of them to dinner at the White Elephant, then one of London's trendiest restaurants. As we're sitting there at our table, Peter O'Toole comes over, takes a look, then says to me in a stage whisper, "Ed, is this some kind of a Hadassah meeting?"

I believe that Peter Sellers was one of the finest actors of his generation. His performance in *Being There,* as Chance the gardener who becomes Chauncey Gardiner, is a masterpiece. But following his near death in 1964, he became very eccentric. One day, I get a call from the production manager on *Alice B. Toklas*: "Ed, you'd better come over right away."

I arrive on the set a few minutes later to find Sellers in a fit, almost hysterical. "Ed, get her off the set." And he points to the script supervisor, who's wearing a purple dress.

"She has to change her clothes. That color. It's not in the stars. It's very bad karma."

So we send the poor woman—who is naturally a little bewildered and upset—over to the wardrobe department for a dress that will put all things right in the universe.

I was particularly happy about *Bullitt* and its director. The script had a very elaborate and intricate car chase through the streets of San Francisco. I had seen an English film, *Robbery,* that had a fabulous chase sequence. So I encouraged Ken Hyman and *Bullitt*'s producer, Phil D'Antoni, to hire *Robbery*'s director, Peter Yates, to come to America to direct *Bullitt*. Yates quickly rose to the ranks of A-List Hollywood directors after his stunning work on *Bullitt*.

Steve McQueen was a big star when we made *Bullitt*. He was pretty easy to get along with except once. A Warner lawyer was trying to save us some money, so he set up the insurance coverage on the production of the picture to include the provision that McQueen could not ride motorcycles during the shoot. Now riding motorcycles—his bikes— was one of his great passions.

So we're two days away from the start date and I get a call from McQueen: "Look, Man, there are only two things in life that are important to me. My balls and my bikes."

Not his wife and his children but his balls and his bikes.

". . . and I'm not showing up for the picture unless I can ride my bikes."

I said, "Well I've got a problem. Tomorrow is Washington's Birthday and every insurance company in the country is closed. I'll take care of it on the next day. I'll get it done."

"That's not good enough, Man. I want you to guarantee me right now that I can ride my bikes on this picture."

"*Man,* I can't take that responsibility. But I will take care of it."

"Well then, Man, I'm going to Monterey tomorrow and go fishing. And I may not be there for the start of the picture."

So I said, "Well, Man, you do what you have to do and the Studio will do what it has to do."

I didn't want to threaten Steve McQueen but I wanted him to know he'd better be there. Looking back now over my experience of many years, I know that actors may bluster and bluff and carry on. But they always show up because not showing up is a breach of contract.

And McQueen came, he showed up.

He was very good on the movie and the shoot was uneventful except for one thing—he rejected some day player because he was taller than the star.

Yes, things were progressing nicely for Ed Feldman's plunge into the world of moviemaking.

A little *too* nicely.

During my first year at Warners, word started circulating that National General, the big theater chain, was putting together a deal to buy the company. I got a call from Joyce Haber, a columnist for the *Los Angeles Times* who was a very close friend of mine. She says, "Ed, what can you tell me about the National General buy?"

I said, "Not very much, Joyce . . . except I've been promised the candy concession at the Bruin Theater in Westwood." (The Bruin was a National General theater.)

It was a joke but she printed it. She shouldn't have, but she did.

So I get a call from Eliot Hyman, my boss of bosses, and he took me out to the woodshed. "Ed, don't do that again. Don't be a wiseass."

I was chastened but that buyout story and later ones were true. Warners was for sale again. In 1969, Kinney National Services, a conglomerate with interests in car rentals, parking lots, building maintenance, and funeral homes (no relation to National General), purchased the company for some $400 million. Seven Arts had made some other acquisitions, notably Atlantic Records, and the price included the original Seven Arts assets. So the difference between the $400 million and the $90 million purchase price for Warners was not all profit.

Kinney, under the leadership of Steve Ross, had begun buying leisure-related properties: movie camera manufacturer Panavision, the Ashley Famous talent agency, and various publishers including D.C. Comics. Warners fit right into that equation.

Ross installed Ted Ashley as the chief of Warners and we were all out. Ashley brought in his own team, led by John Calley.

I wasn't "out" right away. It was a gradual process. I was put into "indie prod"—made an independent producer to be housed on the Warner lot. There's an old joke in Hollywood that you know when your contract is expiring and you're on your way out because your office keeps getting moved closer and closer to the studio gate.

I'm here to tell you that the joke is absolutely right. Closer, closer, and then you feel the gate bump your behind as you exit.

Fast forward about twenty-five years and I'm attending a memorial service for Ted Ashley, who died of leukemia at age eighty. Now Ashley had been a tremendous success at Warners. Through his leadership, Ashley built on our modest accomplishments and transformed Warners into a genuine industry leader.

I respected Ashley but let's face it, he ended my career at Warner Bros. Still, I felt compelled to pay my respects to an industry giant. So when the invitation arrived, I accepted.

Now I'm at the service held on the Warner lot, listening to poignant, humorous, inspiring words delivered by Ashley's friends and associates—people like John Calley, Terry Semel, and Bob Daly. I'm standing there in my reverie when out of nowhere I hear: "And now Ed Feldman would like to say a few words."

Did he say, "Ed Feldman?" Nah, he must mean some other Feldman. I looked around.

One of the men standing in front of me turns and says, "Ed, you're on." I'm on *what?*

I make my way up to the podium. What should I say? An angel sits on one shoulder, a devil on the other.

Ted Ashley was a great man, Ed.

Ted Ashley fired you, Ed.

Then I remember the words of Eliot Hyman: "Ed, don't be a wiseass." Eliot was right.

Be the Duke, not the Colonel.

So here I go. "Ted Ashley is the man who put spirit back into Warner Bros. A man who was ahead of his time. Just took a company that was in a morass and made it into a giant corporation."

I went on like that for three or four minutes. And I'm glad I did.

Ted Ashley *was* a great man. And in the end, he probably helped me. I'm not sure I was cut out to be a studio executive. As I look back over my career, what I did after Warners suited me just fine.

You know, after I returned to my place at the Ashley service, I could swear I heard the voice of the Duke in my head:

"Not bad for a city boy, Kid. Not bad at all."

6

PIVOTING ON DIVAS
AND LEMMON

MY SECRETARY BUZZED ME: "BETTE DAVIS IS ON LINE TWO."

Now, Bette Davis has one of the most distinctive voices in the world, so she really didn't need an introduction. Plus one of the most famous faces in the world. Her peepers were even the improbable subject of a megahit pop song later on, in 1981, "Bette Davis Eyes." (*All the boys / Think she's a spy / She's got / Bette Davis eyes.*)

I could figure out the timing of Davis's call before picking up the receiver. It's 1963 and she has just been nominated for Best Actress in the Academy Awards for her role in a film produced by my employer, Seven Arts, called *What Ever Happened to Baby Jane?* I'm the head of advertising and publicity at Seven Arts, and I had felt a particular affinity for this project, which I'll explain later, even though I wasn't directly involved in its production.

Baby Jane starred Davis and another screen diva, Joan Crawford, as two sisters both washed up in show business. Davis's character had had a career as a child star named Baby Jane and, in the picture, has turned into a deranged old woman who revels in mentally and physically torturing her crippled sister, Blanche, Crawford's character. Her feelings are compounded by guilt over accidentally causing Blanche's crippling accident (she thinks) and jealousy over Blanche's successful career as a film actress before the accident.

Now, Davis and Crawford were close to the same age, mid-fiftyish, even though they seemed much older in the movie. They had both enjoyed long, star-studded careers under the old studio system, chiefly at Warner Bros. and, for Crawford, early in her career at MGM. But in the early 1960s, Davis and Crawford were basically has-beens who also happened to be bitter rivals.

This rivalry was probably heightened by the fact that Crawford was the widow of a rich business executive, Al Steele, who had been head of Pepsi-Cola (Crawford was even on the Pepsi board of directors), and Davis was flat broke. *Baby Jane* was to be the come-back picture for both of them. In Davis's case, she desperately needed the money.

So I pick up the receiver to congratulate Davis on her nomination. Before I can get the words out, Davis snaps into the phone with that staccato voice of hers, always seeming to be tinged with imaginary booze and cigarettes, "Ed, just listen to this telegram I received from Joan."

Oh, boy, I thought, this is going to be good. Davis has been nominated for Best Actress and Crawford hasn't been nominated for anything.

I say, "Please, Bette, I would love to hear Joan's telegram." Now *that* was an understatement. I couldn't *wait* to hear Joan's telegram.

"Listen to this, Ed—

"Congratulations, Bette. I'm sure this has made up for the ten dark years which have just passed."

People always seem to be interested in the path I took to becoming a movie producer, which is a very unconventional one. So unconventional that Harrison Ford made a joke out of it at an award ceremony and got a good laugh.

I arrived at producing through the advertising and publicity route. Before I started at Warner Bros. as the assistant head of production in 1967, I had never been directly involved in the production of a movie.

Now, I had worked on plenty of advertising and publicity campaigns but I had no hands-on moviemaking experience.

But I did know the business very well and I believed I had a good sense of what works in the movie theater, both essential traits for a producer.

At Warners, as I told you earlier, I had supervised some big films, including *Bullitt* and *The Wild Bunch*. But supervising movies as a studio executive isn't *producing* movies yourself. I still wasn't there. It would take one more move—to Filmways in 1969.

There were three pivotal films in my journey to movie producer. The first is *What Ever Happened to Baby Jane?,* made while I was head of advertising and publicity at Seven Arts, a relatively small movie and TV production/distribution company.

The other two pivotal films are *What's the Matter with Helen?* and *Save the Tiger,* both produced by me at Filmways in the early 1970s. *Helen,* starring two more divas, Debbie Reynolds and Shelley Winters, was the very first picture I produced. And *Save the Tiger,* starring Jack Lemmon in an Oscar-winning performance, was the first high-quality, artistically significant picture I produced. *Save the Tiger,* released in 1973, established me as a producer of substance in Hollywood and took me to a whole different plateau of moviemaking.

To start at the beginning, let's go back to the year before Bette Davis's phone call. I was working for Joseph E. Levine and his Embassy Pictures in 1962, as director of publicity. Remember that Levine, producer of *Hercules Unchained,* was the man on crutches who collapsed in a faint while making his way up three flights of steps to visit a hooker in Rome.

Levine is approached by director Robert Aldrich to make a film based on a novel by Henry Farrell titled *What Ever Happened to Baby Jane?* Aldrich had been developing this project for quite a while, and the script was in good shape. He already had Bette Davis and Joan Crawford attached. Evidently, Aldrich had intended *Baby Jane* as a Broadway play with Davis and Crawford, then decided later to go the feature-film route.

Aldrich had been shopping the project all over town. I knew this without anyone telling me because in the early 1960s, Levine and Embassy were usually near-to-the-last stop for a producer with a decent movie project.

Aldrich had just finished directing *The Last Days of Sodom and Gomorrah* for Levine, and that's how I knew him.

So Levine meets with Aldrich and his attorney, Isadore Prinzmetal, in Levine's office to discuss *Baby Jane*. Now understand, Levine is very, very difficult to deal with. Things deteriorate quickly until finally Aldrich and Prinzmetal come storming out of Levine's office, headed for the front door.

I'm standing in the hallway, observing this scene. Aldrich says to me as he exits, "Forget it, Ed. This is not going to happen. Levine's impossible."

So I rush into Levine's office and say to him, "Joe, run after them, apologize, and let's make this movie. We could make a fortune. *Then* never talk to Aldrich again."

Levine says, "I don't give a shit. Let them go."

Now, here's why I consider *Baby Jane* pivotal to my path to producing. The picture had been turned down by almost every studio in the business. The prevailing wisdom was, who wants to see those old washed-up broads in a picture? But coming from advertising and publicity, this package was dynamite. Davis and Crawford were very famous and very accomplished: major, major stars; they were willing to work for practically nothing up front; the story was compelling and fascinating; and I knew I could sell the hell out of it.

Still no takers. A tremendous missed opportunity for Levine and all the other studios that had passed.

Flying totally in the face of the prevailing wisdom, I became *the* champion for the project.

And I was dead right about *Baby Jane*.

As luck would have it, about a month later I had finally had it with Joe Levine and moved over to Seven Arts as head of advertising and publicity. One of the first things I did was talk up the *Baby Jane* project. "Let's grab this thing. We've really got something here." Coincidentally, Ken Hyman had found the project also and was considering it for Seven Arts.

Eliot Hyman, Ken's father and the head of Seven Arts, strategized a deal wherein Seven Arts would retain 25 percent of the project; the distributor, which eventually was Warner Bros., would have 25 percent; Aldrich would have 25 percent as producer and director; and Davis and Crawford would split the remaining 25 percent. Now this was going to be a very low-budget movie. Seven Arts budgeted *Baby Jane* at $980,000, well below the going rate for a feature film then. That figure included up-front payments for Davis and Crawford of $50,000 each against their share in the profits.

We were able to make the movie for that low budget mainly because we had a shooting schedule of thirty-four days, almost unheard of for a feature film; and we were filming in black and white. Even though Warners was distributing, we couldn't even afford to shoot on the Warner lot. We ended up at a small facility across the street from Paramount that is now known as the Raleigh Studios.

We were going to have *Baby Jane* in theaters one hundred days from the start of shooting—thirty-four days of filming, then sixty-six days for post-production and making of prints and distributing them to theaters. And this was going to be a very wide release. Back then, a typical studio release might be a few hundred screens. We were going onto a multiple of that number.

Even at Seven Arts, there was dissension, though. Ray Stark, Eliot Hyman's partner in the company, said, "I'm going on record as being against this movie."

Well, Stark was wrong.

For a big-time movie buff like me, working on *Baby Jane* was heaven. Bette Davis and Joan Crawford were two of my movie star idols from my younger days and I couldn't get enough. Although I wasn't actually involved in the production of the movie, I *was* responsible for the marketing of it. And I never missed an opportunity to visit the set and hang out with Davis and Crawford.

Let me tell you, those two were about as eccentric as you could imagine, even on top of their long-standing rivalry. One day, the set would be freezing cold because Crawford believed the cold tightened her skin for the camera. The next day, the set would be hot because Davis had some sort of respiratory condition. Hot-cold. Hot-cold.

Early on, Crawford, being a Pepsi board member, had a Pepsi machine delivered to the set. The next day—you guessed it—Davis had a Coca-Cola machine delivered to the set.

I visited Crawford several times in her Manhattan apartment about the publicity for the picture. When you entered, you encountered this bright white carpeting and she insisted you remove your shoes, which I did. So I'm discussing the marketing of the film with Joan Crawford, sitting there in my stocking feet, hoping my toes weren't poking through, on a sofa covered in protective clear plastic. All of her living room furniture was covered that way.

Crawford's business-mogul husband, Al Steele, had died about three years earlier. I used to joke that he died taking his shoes off.

Before the movie opened, we scheduled a big late-afternoon party at '21' Club in Manhattan to introduce Davis and Crawford to the editors and publishers of major newspapers and magazines based in New York. There were probably 150 people in attendance. This was their first joint appearance and the level of anticipation was high. I don't think this group could have been any more excited if Marilyn Monroe and Jackie Kennedy were going to appear together.

Well, Davis and Crawford make their big entrance, arm-in-arm with Bob Aldrich, to a tremendous ovation. We escort them around the party and introduce them to the press. But then later, Davis decides to make a little speech. She stands up on a chair and says to the group, "It is such a pleasure to see all of you here this wonderful afternoon. I want to thank you from the bottom of my heart for coming to . . . *my party*."

With that, Crawford turns to Aldrich and me, and mutters, "That cunt." Then she turns on her heels and storms out of '21' Club.

But with all their eccentricity and off-set rivalry, those two were consummate professionals on set. Remember that their careers had been built up under the old studio system. Now people may criticize the old bosses—Mayer, Warner, Zanuck—but they were all-business. If you wanted to be a star in their regimes, you'd better show up on time, ready to work, performances ready, following instructions. No nonsense. No star temperament. Otherwise you were out.

I'm convinced Davis and Crawford were so capable they could have done their roles in *Baby Jane* whether director Aldrich had been there or not.

We were able to turn out a picture as good as *Baby Jane* in only thirty-four days because of Davis and Crawford, and the professionalism and talent they brought to the project.

Davis had serious money problems and I tried to help her out later. We were doing a remake of *Of Human Bondage* with Kim Novak in the lead role, which Davis had portrayed so brilliantly in the 1934 version. (She had been a write-in nominee for a Best Actress Academy Award.) I thought it would be a clever publicity gimmick to feature Bette Davis in the remake in the part of the old crone. Studios do this sort of thing a lot nowadays with remakes—bring back one of the original stars— but in those days, it was rare.

So I told Davis, "Look, Bette, we're filming in Europe. We'll pay you twenty-five thousand dollars for one or two day's work. We'll pay your travel. Take your daughter. Whatever you want."

Do you know what she said? She said, "Ed, thank you but I can't do it. I can't spit on my fans." She felt she would be doing her loyal fans a disservice by being used, basically, as a publicity stunt for the new movie. Davis had a lot of class.

The nephew of my boss, Eliot Hyman, married Davis's daughter. He used to say, "Ed, you can't believe it. I get home and there sitting in my living room is Bette Davis, having a drink and smoking a cigarette, and saying in that staccato voice of hers, 'What are you doing with my daughter?' Nobody else has Bette Davis as a mother-in-law. It's like living in a Warner picture."

I always knew that *Baby Jane* would be a press machine picture, and that was my specialty. Our angle—we had these two divas and they'd like to kill each other in real life. We played it to the hilt.

So now the picture is complete and we preview it in Long Beach, below L.A., and it plays very, very well. Then we arrange a preview at the RKO 86th Street Theater in New York. We picked a helluva night. It was October 20, 1962, a date well known to students of American history. At 8:00 P.M., our theater was empty because everyone was home in front of the TVs watching President Kennedy give his famous address on the Cuban Missile Crisis.

But by 8:30 P.M., the theater is full and everyone is in a surprisingly festive mood, considering the possibility of imminent nuclear war. I must say, the attendance at this screening was skewed very gay. But that shouldn't have been surprising. Davis and Crawford were goddesses in the gay community.

So I'm sitting in the loge with Crawford, watching the screening. Davis isn't there. And the audience is howling at the eccentricity of Davis's character. The picture played like gangbusters. Crawford and I are walking out and she turns to me, and says with the straightest of faces, "Ed, isn't it a shame the way they all laughed at Bette?"

To provide a variation on a famous expression, "Rivals all the way to the bank."

Seven Arts had a major hit with *Baby Jane*—critical and financial. I have to say that the advertising and publicity department did a masterful job. But a lot of people in the business just didn't get this project and probably never would.

Based on the success of the RKO 86th Street screening, I came up with the idea of taking Davis around to the various New York theaters and bringing her up on stage after the showing to greet her fans. Well, Ben Kalmenson, the number-two man at Warner Bros., calls Eliot Hyman and says, "Eliot, that cocksucking publicist of yours (meaning me) wants to trot that old bag Bette Davis around New York to meet the fans." We did it anyway and it was a huge success. The Ben Kalmensons of the world would never understand.

This little low-budget feature of ours, with the two old washed-up broads, was nominated for five Academy Awards—Bette Davis for Best Actress, Victor Buono for Best Supporting Actor, Best Sound, Best

Black-and-White Cinematography, and we won for Best Costumes in a black-and-white picture.

The movie made a lot of money for Warner Bros. and Seven Arts. Davis and Crawford made what would probably be today's equivalent of about $2 million each.

And this was the picture nobody wanted.

Here's a little postscript on the Davis-Crawford rivalry. After Crawford sent Davis her "ten dark years" telegram, she also secretly arranged to accept the actual Best Actress Academy Award for the winner if she wasn't there at the ceremony. Back then, it was permissible for a previous winner to accept for a no-show winner. So Crawford was lined up to walk up on stage and accept the Academy Award on behalf of either of the three nominees who weren't able to attend. (She had won previously for *Mildred Pierce* in 1945.) If things went in her favor (and the odds seemed to be three to two), Crawford would have had the ultimate last laugh on Davis.

Anne Bancroft was the winner for *The Miracle Worker,* and Crawford dutifully accepted for her. But because nominees were seated backstage in that era, Davis could seethe in peace, out of the public eye.

Now go forward a few years—to the late 1960s. I'm sitting in my office at Warner Bros., just a stone's throw from the front gate, contemplating my pending unemployment. It's almost the end of my contract. I was a casualty of the regime change at Warners when Kinney National bought the studio and installed new management. I was old management and they put me in "indie prod" until my contract was up. And that day was fast approaching.

I'm just basically pushing papers now. Although Warners was supposed to provide the means for me to develop and produce feature films during this period, it wasn't going to happen. There would be no Ed Feldman productions. They were just running my contract out and I knew it.

Now I'm getting pretty nervous. I had moved my family to L.A. to take the Warner job—a production job, my first—and I have no prospects for my next one. I had a great track record in advertising and publicity in New York, but in production I'm still a neophyte and not that well known in L.A. filmmaking circles.

Then the phone rings. It's Martin Ransohoff, head of Filmways. I had met Ransohoff when I worked for Joe Levine. Ransohoff had produced a light comedy for us called *Boys' Night Out,* with Kim Novak and James Garner, and I was responsible for advertising and publicity on the film. The picture did very well and Ransohoff was delighted with my work. We had remained friendly over the years and saw each other socially.

So now Ransohoff wants me to work directly under him in the movie department at Filmways. Ransohoff had founded the company in the early 1960s and had been enormously successful. On TV, Filmways had *The Beverly Hillbillies, Green Acres,* and assorted other cash cows. The movie effort, headed up by Ransohoff himself, had a string of big, profitable films. But with all the growth, he needed help in the movie department and I was his man. Plus I would sit on Filmways' board of directors.

So I go to work at Filmways and I'm all set to finally produce a movie.

Debbie Reynolds was going to do a Filmways TV series for NBC, and part of the deal had NBC financing a feature film that she would star in. This was going to be my first project at Filmways.

So I find a script called *What's the Matter with Helen?* And before you know it, I'm in the thick of producing my first picture. United Artists is set to distribute.

Maybe subconsciously, I was trying to capture the same lightning in a bottle we did with *Baby Jane.* A suspense thriller about the relationship between two older women, one crazy as a loon. Debbie Reynolds was the sane one and we signed Shelley Winters for the crazy one. (This was really good casting, as you'll see.) In the picture, these two women were brought together because their sons have just been convicted of a brutal "thrill" murder, and they want to start a new life away from the notoriety.

But I wasn't the only one trying to capture that *two-older-women, one-*

crazy lightning. After we did *Baby Jane* at Seven Arts, and it was an enormous hit, there was a whole string of these types of movies. Bette Davis even did another one with Aldrich called *Hush, Hush, Sweet Charlotte,* costarring Olivia de Havilland.

In the late 1960s, TV was hitting the film business hard and some really good people were available to work on this fairly low-budget *Helen* project. We had the famous Lucien Ballard as our cameraman; William Reynolds was the editor; Sydney Guilaroff on hair; William Tuttle, makeup; Morton Haack, costumes. Top people—best in the business.

I'm producing this movie and I'm learning how to produce on the job. But I seem to have everything under control, I think.

Now it's the night before shooting begins, and I'm tossing and turning in a nervous, fitful sleep, having a very bad anxiety dream. In my dream, all of these big-time people are assembled on set. The director has the actors in place. The camera is ready to roll for our first take. Then Ballard, the cameraman, turns to the director, Curtis Harrington, and says, "We have no film."

The director looks puzzled. "We have no film?"

"No. No film. None at all."

"Well, where's the film?"

People are looking at each other and shrugging their shoulders.

The director turns to me. "Ed, did you remember to buy film?"

Oh my God. I didn't know I was supposed to buy the film. No one told me that. I could have stopped off for some on my way over.

Now the word is traveling around the set like wildfire. "Feldman forgot to buy the film."

"Doesn't he know we need film to make a movie!"

"What a schmuck!"

I wake up in a sweat and I can't go back to sleep. Where *do* we get the film?

Not to worry, Mr. Producer. The camera best boy picks up the film at Eastman Kodak on his way to the set. Everyone knows that.

I sidle up to Ballard first thing the next morning. "Got plenty of film?" I say.

Ballard shoots me a puzzled look. "Sure, Ed. More than enough."

John Huston – The ultimate Man's Man. He played God and Noah in *The Bible*. But could he tame Elizabeth Taylor? (1966) *Personal collection*

Eleanor Roosevelt – The woman I admired most. Here with me buying the first ticket for *The Diary of Anne Frank*. (1959) *Paul Schumach*

The fabulous Edward G. Robinson. At the farewell dinner for Jack Warner. (1969) *Personal collection*

On the set of *The World of Suzie Wong* with Bill Holden. (1960) *Personal collection*

Shelley Winters sticks it to me on the set of
What's the Matter with Helen? (1970)   *Personal collection*

Harrison Ford as John Book in *Witness* – on
the set in Pennsylvania with Lorraine. (1984)
Josh Weiner

With Burt Reynolds on the set of Fuzz.
No matter what he says, I wasn't his type. (1971)
Personal collection

Taking direction from Peter Weir on *Green Card*,
on location in New York City. (1989)
Robert Marshak

On the set of *Forever Young*, Mel Gibson's
first picture through his Icon production
company. (1991)   *Personal collection*

On the set of 102 Dalmatians in London with Glenn Close
as Cruella DeVil. Glenn is one of the great actresses of our time
and a world class woman. (2000)   *Clive Coote*

The producer and a stellar cast on the set of *The Truman Show*
– Natascha McElhone, Noah Emmerich, Laura Linney and Jim Carrey.
(1997)   *Melinda Sue Gordon*

With Emma Thompson and
Gérard Depardieu on
My Father The Hero
in New York. (1993)
John Seakwood

I show Jason Scott Lee (as
Mowgli) one of my patented
action moves. On the set of
The Jungle Book. (1994)
Frank Connor

The power of the producer. NOW that *Jungle Book* tiger is a pussycat. (1994) *Frank Connor*

Talking with the legendary Walter Wanger, producer of the ill-fated *Cleopatra*. Wanger was also famous for firing a shot heard 'round the world – at the privates of his wife's lover. (1968) *Personal collection*

"Welcome to India, sahib," said the camel. Much nicer than the elephant's noisy and odorous greeting. Our first day of shooting on *The Jungle Book*. (1994) *Frank Connor*

With Natalie Wood and George Segal on *The Last Married Couple in America*, my first film as an independent producer. Sadly, this was Natalie's next to the last film before her untimely death in 1981. (1980) *Personal collection*

Howard Hughes calling. I'm at the premiere he asked me to set up for Gina Lollobrigida. The movie was so bad I had to invent a fake charity to sponsor the night. (1958) *Paul Schumach*

Air-kissing Kim Novak at the premiere of *The Great Bank Robbery*. (1969)   *Personal collection*

"Snow don't go," they used to say. Oh yes it does. On the Mammoth, California, location of our hit movie, *The Other Side of the Mountain*, with star Marilyn Hassett and director Larry Peerce. (1974) *Personal collection*

With director Peter Weir on the set of *The Truman Show*. Pretty great to do a third film with Peter. (1997)
Melinda Sue Gordon

On the set of the TV-movie *Valentine* in North Lake Tahoe. From left to right, Lorraine, Jack Albertson, our son Richard, and Mary Martin. This was Mary's first film in 34 years. (1979)   *Personal collection*

With Christine Lahti, our leading lady in *The Doctor*. (1990)
Richard Foreman

Harrison Ford flew in from Wyoming to present me with the Producer of the Year award at the Hollywood Film Festival. (2001)
Lee Salem

"It's not my fault. You can't shoot me because the picture's bad!"
I protest to the Lone Ranger (John Hart) and Tonto (Jay Silverheels)
at the premiere of *The Phynx*. (1970)   *Personal collection*

With President Clinton at the U.S.
Embassy in London during the
shooting of *101 Dalmatians*. (1996)
Personal collection

With Charles and Diana at the
Royal Wedding? Nope. Just actors
(Caroline Bliss and David Robb)
on the set of the TV-movie
Charles & Diana: A Royal Love Story.
(1982)   *Personal collection*

Just checking, I thought. Just checking.

"Ed, you better get down here. There's a problem with Shelley."

I rush down to the studio and find Shelley Winters in her dressing room surrounded by a group of people: the director; Guilaroff; Tuttle; Haack; Winters's agent, Jack Gilardi. I enter the dressing room and Winters points at me. "There he is. There's the SOB who sends my costumes to cheap cleaners!"

We're a few days into shooting and Winters's weight has ballooned up so that her costumes are very tight on her. She's blaming the dry cleaners and we weren't even sending the costumes to the dry cleaners.

Debbie Reynolds, looking very svelte in her wardrobe, was a stark contrast to Winters's appearance, and Winters knew it. She even sent over to Western Costumes for her wardrobe from a Roger Corman picture she had done. But that didn't work. The era was off by about ten years and they were still too small. So finally she had thrown a fit and refused to come out of her dressing room.

Guilaroff, the hair stylist, tries to use flattery. "Shelley," he says, "I think you look wonderful."

She shoots back, "You old faggot. What do you know?"

Then her agent, Gilardi, steps into the fray. "You know, I think Shelley has a point. Her costumes really aren't very flattering."

Gilardi is married at the time to former Mouseketeer Annette Funicello. So I retort, "Well, Jack, I don't like what your *wife* wears a lot of the time."

Things are now rapidly deteriorating and we're getting nowhere. Finally I order everyone out, leaving just Winters and me. I close the door.

I walk over and stare her straight in the eye. "Now listen to me, Shelley. I want you on set in exactly fifteen minutes, in costume, ready to shoot.

"If you're not out there in costume, ready to shoot in fifteen minutes, I'm shutting down the production. When we resume, day after tomorrow, Geraldine Page will be wearing those costumes. And I assure you, *she* will be ready to shoot."

And I left the dressing room, went outside, and began checking my watch.

Now, I was bluffing. I didn't have Geraldine Page or anyone else lined up. I had never even met her.

The clock ticks and ticks. After exactly nine hundred ticks, Winters emerges from the dressing room, in costume, ready to shoot.

I found out later that two actresses Shelley Winters seriously disliked were Lee Grant and . . . yep, Geraldine Page.

Debbie Reynolds, like Joan Crawford and Bette Davis, was a product of the old studio system, mainly at MGM. She might bluster and complain a bit off-set, but on-set, she was a professional. I never had any problems with her.

Even though she was a two-time Academy Award winner, Shelley Winters was another matter. For one thing, she drank a lot, even on the set—nerves, I guess—and that made her erratic and undependable.

One morning, she leaves her house on Santa Monica Boulevard in Beverly Hills and forgets her car keys. They're locked in the house. So she goes to the street and sticks her thumb out. A truck driver stops and gives her a lift, not having any idea who she is.

He takes her within two blocks of the studio and lets her out. She walks the rest of the way. Feldman's first picture and the star hitchhikes to work.

And her temper was legendary, as you've probably guessed by now. I come back from lunch one day and she is on the set, berating her assistant something fierce. She's yelling and carrying on. The poor girl is crying, looking at the floor, enduring the tirade. I walk up and put my arm around the assistant. "Shelley, stop this. Don't you know this is a *human being*?"

She looks at me for a beat and then says, "That's your big mistake, Feldman. She is *not* a human being."

Our cameraman, Lucien Ballard, had been married to the legendary screen beauty Merle Oberon. In the 1930s, Oberon had a very serious car accident that left scarring on her face. Ballard devised a special light that would sit by the camera lens and wash out Oberon's facial scars. The light became known as an "Obie."

Well, Winters would say to Ballard, "Make me look like Merle."

Fat chance. No light that powerful.

We finish *Helen* and it actually turns out pretty well and makes a tidy profit for Filmways. Shelley Winters may have been a pill to work with, but she really was a very good actress and did some nice work on the picture, as did Debbie Reynolds.

We even received an Academy Award nomination—Morton Haack for Best Costumes, ironically enough, considering the flap over Shelley Winters's costumes.

My next project was the Burt Reynolds film *Fuzz*. Then along comes one of my best films, *Save the Tiger*, starring Jack Lemmon.

My writer friend Steve Shagan and I had sons about the same age, so we would get together on weekends, the boys would play, and Shagan and I would talk shop.

One day, he brings out a screenplay he's written called *Save the Tiger* and wants to see if we would consider it at Filmways. Now Shagan was employed by Cinema Center, the feature-film unit of CBS, but he had written this script on his own time.

I read the script and it's terrific. But I say to Shagan, "I can't take it because you're under contract to CBS."

Shagan says, "Aw, they don't care."

"Steve, you need to check with your lawyer because I'm telling you they have right of first refusal."

I was correct. They did. And before long, CBS was planning to put *Save the Tiger* into production with Sydney Pollack directing and Jack Lemmon starring. Plus a budget of $4.5 million, a lot back then.

Shagan kept me abreast of the progress of the picture during our weekly outings with our sons. The budget is growing and the shooting schedule is up to around sixty-five days. Finally I tell Shagan, "Steve, they're going to put you in turnaround." No inside information; I just didn't believe CBS was going to invest that kind of money in a dark, dramatic piece whose commercial prospects were very iffy.

Shagan says, "Ed, they would never do that to Jack Lemmon."

They would and they did. The next week, CBS dropped *Save the Tiger.*

Which meant I could now produce it for Filmways. But not at $4.5 million and a sixty-five-day shooting schedule. We had to get very, very realistic.

For starters, I knew we couldn't afford Sydney Pollack. So as great a director as he is, Pollack was out. We whittled the schedule down to thirty-five days. And very important we got Jack Lemmon to work for *scale*—all of $485 per week against a share of the gross receipts.

You see, Lemmon desperately wanted to do this movie. He was known primarily for light comedy and he could do all those films he wished. But he wanted to do serious dramatic acting also, and those parts were rare for Lemmon at the time, even with his Oscar nomination for *Days of Wine and Roses* in 1964.

I need a distributor to finance the picture, so I trot down Canon Drive to the office of Bob Evans, head of production at Paramount. (The Paramount production offices were on Canon Drive for a couple of years, not on the studio lot.)

Bob Evans came from the clothing industry—the "garment" business. He and his brother started the clothier Evan Picone, but I knew him from his acting days when he was in *Best of Everything* at Fox and I was working publicity.

I tell Evans, "Bob, by God, a garment picture for you. I can make it for million-two or -three. And I've got Jack Lemmon."

Evans says, "You got a deal, Ed."

Now we set out to find an affordable director. I had admired the small independent movie *Joe* and its director, John Avildsen. So Shagan and I trek to Florida to meet Avildsen and discuss the picture with him. At the time, Avildsen was directing an ultra-low-budget Jackie Mason movie on Miami Beach.

Shagan and I were very impressed with Avildsen. He was decidedly counterculture—bandana and all—but he was passionate about *Save the Tiger,* and Shagan and I felt very good in entrusting this valuable project to him.

I did run into one snag though. Avildsen had always operated his own camera during production and he wanted to do this on *Save the Tiger.* I was pessimistic about our prospects for this happening. After all, this was a Paramount release and therefore "union" all the way. I seriously doubted if we could get the union to go along. But I wanted to be supportive of Avildsen, so I helped him argue the case anyway.

Not surprisingly, the head of the union turned him down flat: "Mr. Avildsen, for years you've been toiling in the minor leagues. And now you've been brought up to the majors. We do things differently here."

As we are leaving union headquarters, Avildsen says, "You know, Ed, I'm not sure I want to do this picture if I can't operate the camera. I've always worked that way."

I turn to him. "Now wait a minute, John. I went in there and we argued your case to the union. I did everything I could but I'm not the union. You've always worked on small independent films before but this is the big time. I want you to tell me right now if you're on this picture or not."

Avildsen pauses a moment and says, "I'm in, Ed. I'm in."

Save the Tiger is about Harry Stoner, the owner of a clothing manufacturing company, and two critical days in his life. For the first time in his career, it looks like he can't make payroll, and he is seriously considering hiring a professional arsonist to burn down a little-used facility for the insurance money. His relationship with his wife is rocky. His friend and business manager at the company, Phil, is aghast that Harry would consider arson. His big fashion show for the buyers is starting, and his future and the company's future are riding on the outcome.

All the pressure is causing Harry to hallucinate and see visions of dead World War II comrades from the Battle of Anzio. He is coming apart at the seams. And all the while, he dreams of a much simpler, nobler time, when he would stand for the national anthem even when no one else was in the room, and ball players would play on grass, not plastic, and come sliding into base with their spikes high in the air. Now they're just "antiseptic kids," he says. When asked what it is he wants, Harry replies plaintively, "Just another season."

There was very little money on this shoot, not even for costumes, and Harry was a garment manufacturer. We spent our meager costume budget on three identical silk suits that Lemmon, as Harry, wears for most of the picture. It's sort of a running gag because people he meets, even strangers, will comment, "Nice suit." To make it work, the suit had to be *very* nice.

We had no more money to make costumes, so we borrowed clothes from the big department store chain Joseph Magnin, in exchange for a prominent credit on the film. When we finished principal photography, the Magnin people came by and picked up all the borrowed costumes, including stockings and underwear. We couldn't do reshoots even if we had to.

Jack Lemmon was one of the nicest, most cooperative, and professional actors I've worked with. One time, we were shooting a conversation between Harry and Phil—Lemmon and the great New York stage actor Jack Gilford. The first night, the camera was to be trained on Lemmon, and Gilford would deliver his lines from off-camera. Then the next night, the camera would be trained on Gilford, and Lemmon would deliver the off-camera lines. Well, after the first night, Lemmon came down with a bad case of the flu. We told him to stay home and get well; we would bring an actor in to read his lines for Gilford. Lemmon would have none of that. "Oh, no," he said, "Jack Gilford fed *me* the lines. I'll do the same for him. It wouldn't be fair otherwise."

The part of Harry Stoner was a tour de force for Lemmon. He nailed the character of Harry head on and won an Academy Award for his effort—his only Best Actor win in seven nominations. By the way, Lemmon was very smart to work for scale against a percentage of the gross receipts. He walked away with several million dollars for *Save the Tiger*.

Jack Gilford was nominated for Best Supporting Actor for Phil. Steve Shagan was nominated for Best Original Screenplay and won the Writers Guild Award for Best Original Dramatic Screenplay.

Avildsen did a tremendous job directing *Save the Tiger*. He brought the picture in on time and on budget, never working past 6:30 P.M., even though we were filming in a real garment factory with real garment workers as extras. Avildsen went on to win an Academy Award for *Rocky* in 1977 and had commercial success in many films including the *Karate Kid* series.

My boss, Marty Ransohoff, didn't like *Save the Tiger* at all, however, and said so to Paramount—just in case the picture bombed. I thought Jack Lemmon would kill him. But that didn't stop Ransohoff from calling Lemmon the day of the Academy Awards and asking him to mention *his, Ransohoff's, name* in the event Lemmon won. On stage that night, Lemmon duly thanked Ransohoff but, in the excitement, forgot to thank the film's producer and champion . . . me.

Ransohoff left Filmways not long afterward, and I was elevated to the top spot in the movie department.

So there you have it. With the help of four divas and Jack Lemmon, I am now a card-carrying, full-fledged . . . *Hollywood Movie Producer.*

"Uh, Ed, could you hold on for a second. Now we're all adults here. Are you saying that you became a real, honest-to-goodness movie producer and you never had to deal with the problem of . . .

The Girlfriend?"

I don't know what you mean. I never had a girlfriend then, much less a girlfriend problem.

"No, not *your* girlfriend. Your boss's girlfriend. You know, the one who has no talent but wants to be a *star.*"

Oh, that. Well, I must have skipped over it. You're not interested in that, are you?

"That's the part we've been waiting for. Now get on with it, mister."

OK, OK.

I'm producing *Fuzz,* my second picture at Filmways. It was written by the famous crime author Ed McBain under his real name, Evan Hunter. The picture stars Burt Reynolds in one of his first major movie roles. (We came out right before *Deliverance.*) The villain is being played by Yul Brynner. Well, the villain has a girlfriend and we envisioned that she would have a sultry look to complement Brynner's shaved-head, exotic persona, and that she would be in her twenties.

My boss, Marty Ransohoff, had other ideas. He thought the part would be ideal for a girlfriend of his. We took a look at her. Very pretty, great figure. But I tell Ransohoff, "She's too old."

"Ed, she's twenty-nine."

"Marty, she danced at the same place in London Julie Andrews danced at when she was a child. That place closed in 1946. She's got to be at least forty."

So we hire a young black model, Tamara Dobson, for the role. Ransohoff says to me, "You mean you're not going to use my girlfriend?"

"Marty, if you're ordering me to put her in the picture, she's in the picture. If you're asking me to put her in the picture, she's not in the picture."

"After all I've done for you, Ed. This?"

"Marty, this has to do with the business."

So we use Dobson, not Ransohoff's girlfriend.

It's several months later, and we're in the middle of shooting *Fuzz*. Ransohoff and I are at the studio, outside the set, having a conversation, when Tamara Dobson comes up to me, puts her arms around me, kisses me on the cheek, and squeals, "Ed, you are just so cute!"

Then she gives me a little wave and a big smile as she wriggles away.

Ransohoff stares at her as she walks out of sight, then turns back to me. "Well, goddammit, Feldman, *your* girlfriend can be in the picture but *mine* can't!" And he stomps off.

Now, I'm just standing there with a bewildered look.

Then I hear some suppressed giggles nearby that rapidly turn into guffaws. I look around and spy Burt Reynolds and a buddy. Reynolds is pointing at me and heehawing. He had put Dobson up to it.

"Hey, Ed, can *my* girlfriend be in your movie?"

And the buddy says, "How about *my* girlfriend, Ed?"

"Very funny, guys. Ya got me."

And *now* I'm a full-fledged . . .

Hollywood Movie Producer

FORGET CRUISE! FORGET PENN!
GET ME ZELJKO IVANEK!

"ED, DO YOU THINK MY BREASTS LOOK TOO LARGE?" THAT'S Kathryn Harrold speaking. She's starring in my science-fiction horror film for Paramount, *The Sender,* in the early 1980s.

About once a week, Harrold would question me about her breasts. "I think my breasts are too big on screen. What do you think, Ed?"

My answer was always the same: "Kathryn, no one is going to fight you over that."

Kathryn Harrold was a beauty and as far as I could tell, her breasts were just right. But show me an actor without insecurities, and I'll show you an actor lying in his casket. And even then, I'm not so sure.

Roger Christian is directing *The Sender* for me. This was his first feature film as a director, but he had directed two short subjects before, one of which received the Academy Award.

Christian had won the Academy Award for Art Decoration–Set Direction on *Star Wars,* and had been nominated for *Alien.* One lesson that Hollywood seems to keep relearning over and over is that success in one area of filmmaking does not automatically guarantee success in another.

I should have suspected something when he refused to talk to me at all during *The Sender,* once we had our "go" from Paramount.

The Sender is the story of a troubled young man with telepathic powers. He subconsciously projects his anxieties so that others around him will believe his imaginings are real. And many of them are terrifying, depicting death and destruction. Kathryn Harrold plays his doctor and Shirley Knight is his mother.

As far as I can tell, *The Sender* was one of the first films to feature an imaginary character that people in the movie *and* the audience think is real. Now it's fairly commonplace with pictures like *A Beautiful Mind* and *The Sixth Sense*.

Our film had some fairly elaborate special effects for its day. They were all done in the camera—no outside special effects house was used. Well, some of Christian's special effects looked pretty bad. So I get Paramount to give us an extra $300,000 to redo them. Now most directors would welcome having the money for a second chance—but not Roger Christian. He said the effects were perfect as they were.

So I take an assistant cameraman and one of the special effects people, and we redo some of the less-convincing effects and make them much better.

But for me, this takes the cake—

The role of the troubled young man was a juicy one. His performance carries much of the picture. We wanted to cast it right. We had the choice narrowed down to three young actors, none very well known at the time—

Tom Cruise, Sean Penn, and another actor.

We might have had any of them in *The Sender*. Well, Christian makes his choice and defends it vigorously. I didn't agree with him but I thought, what the hell? I'll let Paramount fight this battle. They'll never go along with him.

Surprise! They did.

For posterity, *The Sender*—which could have starred Tom Cruise or Sean Penn, eventually two of the biggest stars of their generation—actually starred an actor named—

Zeljko Ivanek!

I've worked on a lot of films in my career. Most of the shoots went well, the pictures turned out fine, and then I went to the next one. Some of the films were my projects that I initiated and the others were projects that I was hired to produce.

But there are some constants in the producing business. One is that you will always encounter the unexpected. No matter how well you plan, you can't allow for every possibility. But you do your best. I'll show you examples here.

Another constant is that you can never predict exactly how things will turn out. A movie you thought was weak will make money. And a movie you thought was terrific tanks.

"Snow don't go."

That was the conventional wisdom in Hollywood.

People don't want to see pictures taking place in snow. Where did that notion come from? I have no idea. Could a heavily snowbound movie make money? Absolutely. From *Dr. Zhivago* to *Fargo* to *Dumb and Dumber.* Snow *can* go.

Like a lot of the conventional Hollywood wisdom, "Snow don't go" didn't really mean you couldn't have a lot of snow in a movie. It meant that it was considered a very tough sell. Doable but difficult.

If you think snow is a tough sell, try "quadriplegic in the snow."

It's 1972 and my son Mark is a student at the Beverly Hills Hawthorne School. We're having dinner one night and Mark speaks up, "Dad, you should make a movie about my teacher, Jill Kinmont. There's a great movie there."

Mark explained that Kinmont had been a young Olympic skiing hopeful in the 1950s. During a race, she had a terrible accident that almost killed her and left her paralyzed from the neck down: a quadriplegic. Kinmont's story is very inspirational as she deals with her tragic condition yet finds love and fulfillment in life.

Amazingly, people confined to wheelchairs back then were not allowed to teach in the Los Angeles public schools. So she was employed at Mark's school, which was in the Beverly Hills school system.

A lot of people have great ideas for movies, so I didn't pay much attention to Jill Kinmont's story. Until a few month's later, when I open *Life* magazine and there is a double-page photograph of her in a wheelchair. A smaller picture catches my eye—she is looking up at a cottonwood tree with the headline, "Jill Kinmont's Winning Battle." The issue, which came out in August 1972, was one of *Life*'s last regular issues before it folded as a weekly publication. The pictures were accompanied by a huge story about Kinmont and her inspirational struggles, entitled, "A Broken Life Made Whole."

I was the head of motion pictures at Filmways and I decided Mark was right—Kinmont's story really was an excellent basis for a movie. It was summer and school was out, so I drove up to her house at Pacific Palisades. Because of that meeting, I purchased the rights to her life story for $5,000 and commissioned a little-known writer, David Seltzer, to do the screenplay.

It just so happened that before Seltzer finished his first draft, a Writers Guild strike began. Now, he couldn't turn in the screenplay to me because he would be expelled from the union. So he just kept on writing. Rewrite after rewrite. When the sixteen-week strike finally ended, the script Seltzer submitted is just about perfect. We ended up shooting about 98 percent of it—that's how good it was.

Was Jill Kinmont's story a tough sell to Filmways?

Not really. Filmways would produce the picture but the money would be put up by the studio distributing the picture. *That* would be the tough sell. But on this count, I got lucky.

Lorraine and I had dinner one night with the director, Sidney Furie and his wife, and a producer friend, Mort Engelberg, and guest. Furie was hot right then. He had done *The Ipcress File* and movies with Frank Sinatra and Robert Redford, and had just finished *Lady Sings the Blues* with Diana Ross.

Engelberg says, "Ed, tell Sidney about your musical—the one about the crippled girl and skiing." So I describe the movie to Furie and he sounds very interested. The next day, I send him a copy of the script.

Later in the week, I glance out of a second-story window at home and see this Talmudic-looking person walking up the driveway. Dark clothing, head bowed. He could have been mistaken for a rabbi on his way to Saturday morning services. It's Sidney Furie. It turns out he's read the script and wants to direct the movie. And most important, he will direct it for $75,000. Furie normally earned several hundred thousand a film. You know, it's easy for people to say, "I'm in your corner." And then it comes to money and they're not in your corner. Well, Furie was *in my corner.*

Furie had worked with Paramount exclusively for several pictures, and Universal was eager to do a picture with him again. So my film got me introduced to Ned Tanen, head of production at Universal.

I had never worked with Universal before and, like a lot of people, considered it kind of a scary and intimidating place. It may have had something to do with their high-rise office headquarters, generally referred to as the Black Tower. After I started working with them on projects, the legendary Lew Wasserman, Universal's CEO, would scare the hell out of me. You'd go into his office and his black desk was completely clear—he never had anything on it. One time, I showed up at the executive floor of the Black Tower in a sport jacket I had just bought on sale at Carroll & Co., the well-known Beverly Hills clothing store. It wasn't very loud, just a little checkered number. Wasserman walks up to me, feels the lapel of the jacket, and says, "Ed, you going to the track this afternoon?" I was so chagrined that I never wore the jacket again and finally gave it to the gardener.

With Furie aboard, we had a green light at Universal. But one day, I get a call from Ned Tanen, asking me to come over. Tanen proceeds to tell me that Furie's current picture, with Paramount, is going over schedule in New York, and Tanen thinks we will be delayed long enough to miss the snow season. Forget conventional-wisdom sayings. With this picture, it's a fact: "No snow, no go."

I figured we were dead but Tanen says, "I love this project. I'll give you two or three weeks to find a new director. But the director has to work for this same kind of money."

Now Larry Peerce was a good friend of mine. We had just done a TV movie for ABC called *The Stranger Who Looks Like Me.* Peerce had directed some good features in the past, notably *Goodbye, Columbus* with Richard Benjamin and Ali MacGraw.

I gave Peerce the script and then had dinner with him to talk over the project. He tells me right off, "Ed, I can't do your picture. I cannot deal with crippled people."

And I said, "OK. Let's finish dinner and let's stay friends."

I come home despondent because I realize it's going to be hard to find a major director for $75,000. The next morning I get a call from Peerce's agent at William Morris and he says, "Ed, Larry wants to do the movie now." And with Peerce signed on, we get a go at Universal. Our budget is $1.2 million—for Universal, it's almost a free picture.

Casting Jill Kinmont was critical to the film. Marilyn Hassett showed up at the audition, fresh-faced and eager but pretty inexperienced. Yet she had a magic smile and fit the part well. We took a chance.

Later on, after rehearsals and just as we're set to begin the shoot in the snow country at Squaw Valley, California, Peerce comes into my suite, pours himself a Scotch, plops down in a chair, and exclaims, "Ed, Marilyn can't act!"

Now, this is a Universal picture and I'm scared of Universal, remember? (And their spooky Black Tower.) We're not replacing the leading lady at this late date. So I tell Peerce, "I don't care if she can't walk. She's your choice. You make her act, Larry. She's starring in the movie."

As it turned out, we had to post-synchronize nearly every one of her lines in post-production. I'm sitting there on the mixing stage one day while Hassett dubs her lines with Peerce standing next to her. I notice his hand patting her on the behind. Now *that's* news! Peerce and Hassett ended up being a couple for almost eight years, and they did three more movies together, two of them with me.

The *Other Side of the Mountain* shoot went well. Peerce and I had worked with Beau Bridges on that ABC TV movie, and he played the romantic lead for us on this picture: a dashing if somewhat reckless young man who falls in love with wheelchair-bound Jill Kinmont.

I thought the dailies looked terrific but I never heard anything from Ned Tanen at Universal. I began to worry.

Finally, I called Tanen on some pretext and asked what he thought of the dailies. He said, "They're great! Ed, if I didn't like them, I would've called you. Right?"

We finish the picture, and Peerce and I show it to Tanen. He walks in wearing sunglasses, sits down for the hour-and-forty-minute running time, then gets up and says, "Thank you very much," and walks out. I figure we're finished. It's over. The picture stinks, we're done. The Black Tower has swallowed another victim.

The next day I get a call from Tanen. "Can you and Larry come over at noon?" And I figure we're going to be removed from the picture. We make our way to his office. Looking very serious, Tanen gets up and closes and locks the door. He stares at Peerce and me. I'm sure our expressions were the same ones worn by the wives of Henry VIII right before the axes fell.

"Before I show the picture to the big executives here, I want you to know how I feel about this movie. You guys have made a fabulous picture. And I don't care what Lew says or Sid Sheinberg or Jules Stein or anybody. I think it's a terrific movie."

Another "Well, I'll be damned" moment in the life of Ed Feldman.

Peerce and I danced and hugged each other in the elevator going down.

A couple of days later, we're walking along in the studio commissary when Lew Wasserman comes over, pats my head, and walks on. And everybody sees this. It's like God touching you.

Peerce and I are having lunch after that when Jules Stein—the founder of MCA, which subsequently bought Universal, and a more celestial personage even than Wasserman—comes over to our table and says, "Are you Larry Peerce and Ed Feldman?" We say yes.

"I saw your movie last night. It was one of the proudest moments in my life at this company."

The Other Side of the Mountain is an example of a movie that builds business by word of mouth. One of the early showings was in Tampa, Florida, where my mother, my brother, and his wife lived. We all went to see it opening night there on a Friday. The theater was almost empty. I return to L.A. the next day, and that night my brother calls me. "Ed, we went back tonight and it was sold out." This scenario was played out all over the country.

In Denver, we played for twenty-four weeks—almost half a year.

Universal was curious about why the picture had done so well. Their research yielded this conclusion: young women were absolutely hysterical over the movie. They said they had sex in their lives but very little love. They couldn't stop crying over a story that showed a man willing to commit his life to marrying a quadriplegic. We had sewn up the woman's audience without even realizing it. Today they use the expression "chick flick."

"Snow don't go . . . until it does!"

Here's a postscript—

We did a sequel. The Beau Bridges character had died in a plane crash at the end of the first movie, so he was out. Where the first movie was actually based on Jill Kinmont's life, I basically made up the sequel story and hired Douglas Day Stewart to write the script. But how do I finish it?

I'm sitting in my office at Universal, reflecting on this dilemma, when Providence shines down once more.

The phone rings and it's Jill Kinmont. "Ed, I'm getting married."

So I ended the movie with Marilyn Hassett as Jill Kinmont getting married under the shadow of the mountain at dawn. She's dressed in a Victorian wedding dress and sitting in her wheelchair, while the minister intones the ending. The sun comes up, illuminating the *other side* of the mountain.

And it was gorgeous.

"I think I deserve a twenty-five-thousand-dollar bonus. Look what the picture did."

"Ed, you know we don't give executive bonuses here at Filmways." That was Richard Bloch, the president of the company and a former owner of the Phoenix Suns of the NBA.

I'm pretty damn mad right now. Under my direction, Filmways had spent $22,000 to develop *The Other Side of the Mountain* and had already made $5 million on it. I thought I deserved a bonus.

Now I was making in the neighborhood of $150,000 a year as head of the motion picture department of Filmways—good money—but like many men in early middle age, I was worried about the future. I had a nice house in Beverly Hills, with a mortgage, and hefty college expenses, current and future.

I may have been a movie producer but I was on straight salary. I had little downside but no upside. But I should clarify. I had no downside, right then. I could envision a time when I'd walk in and they'd have some thirty-year-old moving his things into my office and my stuff would be out on the sidewalk. I want to head that off.

So I say to Bloch: "Then I guess Filmways is not a company for me. I see no future here."

One of my heroic moments. I quit Filmways while I'm on top.

But I'll have to say that Dick Bloch did me a favor by forcing me out.

I wasn't unemployed long. Gil Cates, the director, immediately puts me on as producer for his movie *The Last Married Couple in America,* with George Segal and Natalie Wood. This was Natalie Wood's next-to-the-last movie before her sad untimely death. The picture turned out well. I guess I really can make a living as an independent producer.

I'm fifty years old and for the first time in my working life, I'm not a salaried employee of a pretty big company. From now on, my yearly income will be a direct result of my success as a movie producer.

"So what are you doing, Ed?"

I look at Francis Ford Coppola. The beard looks good. I encouraged him to grow a beard when I was head of publicity at Seven Arts and he was working for us as a staff writer. He was just about to make his move to directing. I thought a beard would make him look more avant-garde and part of the "in" crowd.

"Francis, I have this little romantic picture . . ."

"Wonderful. I'm looking for a little picture."

Francis Ford Coppola has just come off of *Apocalypse Now,* one of the most troubled movies in history, and he's looking for something small and simple.

Attention: Students of Film History—

When Francis Ford Coppola finds a small and simple picture, what do you think it becomes?

Right. It becomes *One from the Heart,* the picture so big, troubled, and out of control that it bankrupted Coppola's American Zoetrope studio. I could have staked a claim as a creditor for $140,000 from that fiasco, but I wrote it off years ago.

One from the Heart really did start out small and simple. The script was written by Armyan Bernstein, and we brought it to MGM as part of my first-look development deal with them. It tells the story of a couple who break up and then come back together over a weekend. I originally envisioned Michael Douglas and Jill Clayburgh starring, and Mark Rydell directing. Goldie Hawn got involved at one point. MGM tried to get Jack Nicholson. The studio execs refused to work with Mark Rydell.

Then enter Coppola.

He says to me, "We've gotta make this movie cheap. I'll get actors to work for nothing.

"But I want three million dollars to direct. I want to get paid to direct what Redford gets paid to act."

Oh, crap. What happened to our *little* picture?

I go to Richard Shepherd, the head of the MGM studio, and this is what I hear: "Ed, you tell that son of a bitch I won't pay more than two million!"

No director had ever gotten more than $1 million before then. MGM was offering double that.

"No, Ed, I want three million."

I got back to Shepherd.

"Look, you'll be a hero with Kirk Kerkorian for bringing in Coppola. A genius, even." (Kerkorian owned MGM.)

"OK, two-and-half and that's it!"

Back to Coppola.

"Ed, here's the deal. They pay me three million dollars. *And I'll pay for the movie.*"

Fateful words.

One from the Heart was a disaster but I was long gone by then. Coppola re-created a fantasy, stylized downtown Las Vegas in a studio. It became a musical. Whatever life musicals had left in them in the early 1980s was snuffed out by *One from the Heart.*

The picture ended up costing around $27 million—that would be pushing $100 million today—and grossed $2.5 million.

This big, bloated mess crashed and burned, and took Coppola's studio with it.

And all I wanted to make was a little romantic film.

"Look, my son is going to Northwestern this year whether you make the movie or not."

Then I added, "I'm a very rich man."

The people in the room look at me incredulously. They know that really rich men don't have to tell everyone they're rich.

Leon Brachman, the head of business affairs for Fox, says, "What the hell are you talking about, Ed—you're a *very rich man*?"

Such is negotiation. My partner, Ted Witzer, and I are being muscled out of our own movie, *Six Pack,* and Fox wants to pay us only an extra $25,000 each to step away. It really didn't matter whether I was rich or not. I had something they needed and it was worth far more than $25,000.

My partner and I had envisioned *Six Pack,* a heartwarming little story about a down-and-out race car driver and his kids-only pit crew, as a small picture with James Brolin starring. CBS was ready to finance it and even guaranteed us a TV series deal.

Fox had other ideas. "I don't do movies with James Brolin," one executive said.

I had a development deal with Fox—only the second one I've ever had in my career—so I had to play along with them.

Before long, *Six Pack* is a Kenny Rogers vehicle with his ex-brother-in-law producing. There was no room for Ed Feldman and Ted Witzer on this bus.

We would receive executive producer credits, the twenty-five grand extra, and that was it. We walk away. Except Fox apparently forgot that we owned the rights and they needed to finalize their deal with Rogers, pronto.

They didn't really believe I was a very rich man, but they knew I wanted more than their meager offer. So even though the Fox business

affairs lawyer was one tough negotiator, Witzer and I ended up with
another $275,000 each for the project.

The movie was made and Kenny Rogers starred. But he wouldn't
sing in the movie except over the credits. America's top singing star of
the time and he wouldn't sing!

James Brolin would have sung.

If you look at a list of my film credits, you see a very curious thing.
Reading the list chronologically—newest to oldest—you come to this:
Witness (1985). Then drop down to the next line below and you see
this: *Hot Dog . . . The Movie* (1984).

What the hell, Ed?

Look, I'm a professional movie producer. I have to make a living.
Not all my pictures can be upscale A-listers with Harrison Ford starring and Peter Weir directing. *Hot Dog . . . The Movie* wasn't great art,
but it found an audience and made a ton of money.

Well, it made a ton of money eventually, but I had a long series of
anxiety attacks before that. It was my project and I financed the $2.5
million budget through a bank, as you normally do with an independent movie, with the loan guaranteed by the investors. I was responsible for 20 percent of the budget (half a million dollars), another guy
had 20 percent, and eleven attorneys at the big law firm O'Melveny &
Myers put up the remaining 60 percent. If all went well, the bank
would be paid out of the proceeds of the movie. But if the picture
went bust, the bank would call on all of us to make good on the loan.

Here's what I had on the line: my house in Beverly Hills. For the first
(and last) time in my career, I actually risked my own money on a picture. If the movie didn't pay off, a big mortgage went on my house to
pay the bank loan.

What was I thinking? The movie was a sophomoric little sex comedy with crude, corny jokes. Big-breasted women. And perpetually
horny young guys.

And you know what else it had? And in abundance.

Snow!

As in, "Snow don't go."

The movie was about ski instructors and their snow bunny girl-friends. "Hot Dog" in the title refers to a skier who does flashy, show-off-y tricks.

I said we found an audience. Guess what audience? You're right. Perpetually horny young guys.

We had former Playmate of the Year Shannon Tweed as our chief snow bunny. She has a nude scene and, between takes, proceeds to walk around the house we were shooting in, stark naked. Guys are bumping into lights, stumbling around.

I said, "Shannon, good grief, put on a bathrobe."

"Ed, all these guys have seen me in *Playboy*. And it's hot in here."

In her nude scene she was in a hot tub with our young male romantic lead, Patrick Houser. Well, before long, Houser gets physically aroused in the hot tub. Naturally, he's plenty embarrassed already. Then I hear Tweed yell out in a loud voice to Houser, "Will you get that fuckin' thing out of there already. Get it down."

I had made arrangements for *Playboy* to shoot still pictures of the hot tub scene for a photo layout in the magazine. We set it up for another night when no one was around. Houser comes over to me. "You know, Ed, I think I should be paid extra for that."

I said, "Patrick, I have thirty guys on this picture who would *pay me* to do that scene with Shannon Tweed. I could call any one of them 'Patrick Houser' and no one in America would know the difference."

So we finish up the shoot and in a few months, my director, Peter Markle, shows me his cut of the movie.

Omigod. My house is on the line for a picture about snow skiing and racing, and Markle's cut has just a few quick minutes of *skiing*. I visited the bathroom five times during the hour-and-forty-five-minute screening—my bladder was out of control.

After the screening, Markle says, "Well, Ed, what do you think?"

I said, "Peter, I don't want to get into an argument but your services are no longer required."

This was a nonunion picture, so getting rid of Markle was easy. On a union picture, the Directors Guild makes you jump through hoops to fire the director.

Apparently, Markle didn't like the ski director, so he hadn't used much of the ski footage. So the editor; the writer, Mike Marvin, a ski director himself; and I reedited the movie. We didn't have much money in the budget for the skiing sequences, so in the big finale race, everyone is wearing helmets and we don't show any close-ups.

With the picture finished, I needed a distributor. I sent the editor with the picture around to the studios for them to take a look. He shows it to three studios the first day. They say, "Thank you very much, Ed, but we're not interested."

Next day, he shows it to two more studios: "Thank you, Ed, but it's not for us."

He shows it to MGM late that day and I'm sitting at home in a fitful state of anxiety. I look around at my beautiful house—it's on the line as I wait for the call.

At 7 P.M., the phone rings and the sales manager at MGM says, "Ed, you hit a home run. We want you to take the picture off the market. Come in tomorrow morning at nine-thirty with your lawyer. MGM wants the picture."

The next day, my lawyer, Charles Meeker, and I are driving over to MGM, and I said, "Now listen, whatever they offer us, take it. Take it. I don't care what it is—just whatever they want."

But we got a fantastic deal. My house was safe.

Lorraine and I attended the first public showing in a theater in Westwood. I'm sitting there and the audience is howling. It played like dynamite. I turn to Lorraine, "What are they laughing at? What's funny?"

I had a scene with a ski gondola with a couple inside and you couldn't see what they were doing. But the gondola was shaking and you knew the couple was doing something. The audience thought it was a comic masterpiece.

Our biggest laugh came near the end, right before the climactic challenge race. Since everyone would be wearing helmets during the race because of our limited funds, we called the race the Chinese Downhill, a name we made up. So the characters are saying, "Chinese Downhill. Forty bucks a man. Winner takes all."

"This is the only way—Chinese Downhill."

"The Chinese Downhill will decide everything."

"It is agreed. Chinese Downhill."

A Japanese character appeared throughout the movie and has said nothing. Well, he listens to this talk about a "Chinese Downhill" and finally speaks up.

"What the fuck is a 'Chinese Downhill'?"

And the audience explodes! Howling with laughter.

I shrug my shoulders at Lorraine. Must be a generational thing.

Hot Dog . . . The Movie was a huge success. My house was safe and I made some money.

Two snow movies were big hits for Ed Feldman.

"Snow don't go?"

Don't you believe it. Snow goes just fine.

In 1990, Disney hired me to executive-produce *The Doctor* for their Touchstone division. Randa Haines, the director, had done *Children of a Lesser God* a few years before. *Children of a Lesser God* was only her second feature film, but it was nominated for five Academy Awards, including Best Picture, winning one: Marlee Matlin as Best Actress.

But Haines didn't get along with the producer of *The Doctor,* Laura Ziskin, so I was basically brought in to referee and get the picture moving. Haines also had a problem with our star, William Hurt, who had starred in *Children of a Lesser God* and was nominated for Best Actor for that work. She had had a terrible time with him on that picture but was willing to give him another go. Because he was a brilliant actor.

Hurt had won the Best Actor Academy Award for *Kiss of the Spider Woman* and had also been nominated for *Broadcast News.*

William Hurt is a great actor but he has his quirks. He is relatively unconcerned with money. As a leading man, he was at his career zenith at the time of *The Doctor.* After that, he has mostly played character parts.

Hurt had a well-known drinking problem and was a recovering alcoholic when I worked with him. He was very serious and diligent about attending AA meetings. But our twelve-hour shooting days were taking their toll on him.

He comes in one day and says, "Ed, I can't work a twelve-hour day. I've just got to get time off. It's too strenuous. I have to go to the AA meetings."

I said, "Bill, don't worry. We'll work it out so you work eleven-hour days."

We start him on eleven-hour days. A week later, he comes back to me. "Ed, it's still no good. I can't work more than ten hours a day."

"Well, Bill, I have no authority to knock it down to ten hours a day. Have your lawyer or agent call Disney and tell them about your problem."

That didn't work, so I say to him, "Bill, I've got a great idea. Why don't we go to French hours? That means, you work from eight to six with no time off for lunch. You use a walking lunch, and people go and have lunch when they can."

"Ed, you're a genius."

But the picture had already started and I had to get a majority of the crew's approval—union rule.

The crew didn't much like that idea because with those hours, there would be no overtime. But I worked it hard and convinced a majority to go with the French hours.

That was the crew's union—IATSE. The Screen Actors Guild was another matter. SAG wouldn't approve French hours for us because they were going into a new contract that summer and planned to use that as one of the bargaining tools.

So I tell Hurt, "Bill, I really tried to get it through but your Guild turned me down."

Hurt flares up at me. "You double-crossed me, Ed. You set me up. You've sold out to *The Suits.*" He meant the studio executives at Touchstone.

I was indignant. "Sold out to The Suits? Bill, you're making forty thousand a day on this picture and you're accusing *me* of *selling out to The Suits?*"

So he wouldn't talk to me after that. The silent treatment. I double-crossed him. I sold out to The Suits. Go figure.

Even on the last day of shooting when it was time to say good-bye, he told everybody he couldn't find me. Like I was some mysterious, missing person.

Later on, when Hurt's post-synchronization session was scheduled, I figured I'd go over to the dubbing studio. Show up just to agitate him a little.

"Agitate," my ass. Hurt comes in the studio, sees me, and literally runs across the stage to throw his arms around me and plant a big kiss on me.

Hurt fired his agent of seventeen years after *The Doctor.* Word was he thought the agent was taking his career into too much of a commercial area. What was the agent guilty of? Getting him the fattest paycheck of his career. What a business!

I believe that William Hurt is one of America's greatest actors. His work on *The Doctor*—as a vain, arrogant physician who learns humility and caring when he comes down with cancer—is brilliant.

But like a lot of people, William Hurt ended up being his career's own worst enemy.

Six of the eight movies I produced or executive-produced in the 1990s were Disney films. I became the "go-to" guy for big, expensive, complicated movies shot in faraway places. The farther movies went away from Hollywood, the more it seemed they needed Ed Feldman.

You can't get much farther from Hollywood than India, so that's where I showed up in 1993 to work on the live-action version of *Rudyard Kipling's Jungle Book.*

Disney hadn't started out to remake *Jungle Book* in live action. The original *Jungle Book* animated film is one of the treasures of the Disney library and was the last animated film to be worked on by Walt Disney himself.

But this *Jungle Book* originated with a producer named Sharad Patel, who was born in India but lived in Kenya. Patel had made a fortune by showing old American movies from screens attached to the tops of trucks, encamped around the wilds of Kenya for sponsors like Coca-Cola.

Patel and his son, Raju, had commissioned a screenplay of Kipling's *Jungle Book.* The original book had been published in 1894 and was in the public domain. So anyone could produce a film based on *Jungle Book* and include the original characters like Mowgli, the boy raised in the jungle by wolves, and Baloo, his bear friend. (Remember that Academy Award–nominated hit song "The Bare Necessities" from the animated film?)

Patel and his son took the script to Disney. Now Disney had no real interest in remaking their classic film in live action, but they were concerned about protecting the "Jungle Book" name, especially in foreign countries. Patel was substantial enough that he could get *Jungle Book* off the ground and into theaters worldwide—with or without Disney. There had been another live-action *Jungle Book* in 1942, but it was pretty stiff and unappealing to kids. Patel's *Jungle Book* could have been a threat, especially if made by Warner Bros., who was showing some interest.

Disney brought me into the project with the assignment of making a carefully budgeted *Jungle Book* in India. The Patels' script was terrible, virtually incoherent. Through Disney, I brought in Stephen Sommers to write a new script and direct. Sommers had just done a Huckleberry Finn picture for Disney and they liked him.

Sommers was a real find. He went on to write and direct the monster hit *The Mummy* with Brendan Fraser, the sequel to *The Mummy*, and the big 2004 picture, *Van Helsing*, with Hugh Jackman.

The Patels told Disney they could make the film for $15 million in India. That got Disney's attention. But as we're developing the budget, I realize that the $15 million figure is unrealistic.

So Disney ups the budget: "Ed, we'll go to $20 million to make the movie."

We get Sommers's script and I go back to Disney: "Fellas, this is more expensive. This is not $20 million."

The original deal had me working for the Patels. Now they were nice men but they had little feature-film experience. I went back to Disney again and laid it on the line: "This picture cannot be made for this kind of money, and I'm certainly not going to go to India not knowing what my parameters are—what I can and can't do."

They made a new deal with the Patels, upped the budget again, and put me in charge of the movie. So off we go to India.

And you have no idea how much trouble that damned rat caused me.

Uh, Ed, I've seen the movie. I don't remember the movie featuring a rat.

No, no, no. Not a rat in the movie. The stray rat that got electrocuted on the set. His little fur was smoking up a storm. I'll get back to that.

You must understand that although India has a thriving film industry, churning out many more movies than Hollywood—it's even nick-named "Bollywood"—it's still very primitive there.

Why film in India? Well, it was cheap and it had The Look. For ex-ample, the story has man-child Mowgli traveling to the Blue City, which is under the shadow of the five-hundred-year-old palace fort in Jodhpur, part of Rajasthan—Mehrangarh Fort. It is a fabulous place. You think it's wooden but it is actually carved out of stone. It gave me a fantastic location—impossible to reproduce somewhere else on our budget. But I had to take out all traces of electricity and lighting be-cause of our nineteenth-century time period.

I was negotiating with the powers that be in the Blue City and they kept changing the deal every day. Because Indians are very smart busi-nessmen. Finally we had a deal, and then one night, that damn rat was electrocuted in a fuse box.

And then they started with me that the gods are angry because of the rat being electrocuted. That really meant, give us more money and all will be settled. The gods will be pacified.

If you think that was a bad sign, try this. Our first day shooting in Rajasthan, and I walk by this huge elephant. He watches me saunter past and then passes a big cloud of gas at me. I didn't know elephants could smile but this one was grinning from big floppy ear to big floppy ear.

The company stayed in the famous Palace Hotel in Jodhpur, Ra-jasthan. Half the place was the maharajah's palace and half was the ho-tel. I used to put tape over my mouth when I took a shower because I heard if you drank the water around there, you'd be dead.

I brought over 250 syringe needles from London and frozen blood for twenty-five people. I brought a doctor up from Bombay who was with us twenty-four hours a day.

Lorraine came over for two weeks and I planned a little Feld-manesque surprise. I dressed up as a maharajah, with the hat and the beard. And she comes to Jodhpur on the plane. Now Jodhpur Airport looked like something out of an old Warner Bros. movie. You expected to see Sydney Greenstreet over here and Peter Lorre over there.

Lorraine comes through the gate and she's only hoping that someone greets her with a "Mrs. Feldman." All right? So I go over to her in my maharajah getup and I say in an accented way, "Welcome to Jodhpur, memsahib."

She walks right by me, like I don't want anything to do with this bum. She continues on, then suddenly whirls around. "Ed, is that you?"

I take her to the Palace Hotel and it's beautiful at night—all lit up. And I say, "I told you, Lorraine, I always promised I'd take you to the palace."

Lorraine stayed with me in Jodhpur and then the company moved to Bombay (renamed Mumbai in 1995) for soundstage work. Our hotel in Bombay was terrific—very elegant. You *could* drink the water. Most civilized.

That's what Lorraine thought until she goes outside for a stroll on our second day in Bombay. She notices a stream of red liquid coming down the street. Oh God, it's blood. A man is being macheted to death in broad daylight. A local labor dispute.

A very shaken Lorraine calls me at the studio. "Ed, I'm a loyal person but I'm leaving tonight."

If you could stand the bloodshed, Bombay was great for making a big movie. The English production coordinator said to me, "You know, Ed, we had 120 guys working today on the set and you know how much it cost—$680."

Disney wanted to know why we weren't paying everybody by check. Like all these Indians had checking accounts to deposit their $5 a day. My driver got $2.50 a day. Well, I didn't know he got $2.50 a day until I gave him $3.00 every night and he almost carried me into the hotel. He thought I was Diamond Jim Brady.

I brought *Jungle Book* in for $32 million, about $2 million over our final budget. Filmed in the United States, the movie with the same look would have cost $90 million.

After India, we completed the movie back home—some jungle waterfall scenes in Tennessee, and the rest of our jungle scenes on Fripp Island, South Carolina, on the Atlantic coast.

In Tennessee, we stayed in a small town where the big thing was a Wal-Mart. Our English comic actor John Cleese, so memorable in *Monty Python,* was fascinated by this Wal-Mart—it was much bigger than anything back home. He's strolling around the store and goes over to the gun counter. There's a guy in a white T-shirt working there, probably named Bubba. Cleese says to him, "My good man, I'd like to purchase a gun. Can I buy a gun tonight?"

Bubba says, "Used-ta ya could, but 'cause-a the goddam Brady Bill, it's gonna take five days now."

Cleese says, "Well, I can't wait five days because there's someone I really don't like, and I may not feel this way in five days."

We had a number of trained animals in our *Jungle Book,* and those scenes were filmed in Tennessee and on Fripp Island. There was this terrible jaguar who used to look at me in a bad way and I was terrified. We had a collar on him. The cameraman says, "We got to get the collar off that thing. We can't shoot him with the collar on."

I said, "You can shoot him with the collar because I'm not standing here without the collar. All right?"

But we eventually took the collar off because there was a scene where Mowgli as a boy is holding the tail of the jaguar and he's leading him through the jungle. You don't see it, but I had six guys, three on each side, with steel chains holding the jaguar. And we took them out optically in post-production. I wouldn't risk a kid's life. No movie is worth that.

I had lunch one day with the tiger trainer, who said to me, "Ed, no matter what you think—I've had some of these cats for fifteen years—you never can forget that they're wild animals. Don't ever let your guard down."

And he added, "Ed, the only thing they're really afraid of is fire."

Fire. Gotcha.

So later, I happen to wander into a shot by mistake—there was no crew member to stop me—and all of a sudden, this huge tiger is barreling right toward me. But we have a big fire going in the shot. I remember the trainer's words, "Ed, the only thing they're really afraid of is fire."

Fire. I'm OK.

Oh, shit. The tiger jumps right through the fire, on toward me, full speed.

Finally the trainer says, "Dorothy, stop."

And the tiger stops on a dime. I can tell you, my undershorts took a beating that night.

We had real bears playing Baloo. We had rehearsed one of the bears for three weeks to dance with Mowgli. The day we came to shoot it, we brought the bear in . . . and he wouldn't dance. Stage fright, I guess. The trainer tried and tried. The bear wouldn't dance. Just looked around. Then sat down.

We all stared at him. He stared back.

Well, the director, Steve Sommers, loses it. In front of the entire company, he starts screaming at me, "Goddammit, Ed, you promised me the bear would dance. You promised . . . YOU PROMISED ME THE BEAR WOULD DANCE."

I'm a producer, not a magician. And bears don't listen to me. Never have.

But I'll tell you this:

Zeljko Ivanek would have danced.

EDDIE AND MEL

"WHERE'S EDDIE?"

"I don't know. Haven't seen him."

"We can't find him. We looked in his trailer."

"None of his people are here either."

"The shot's ready except for Eddie. What do we do?"

"Call the front gate. See if he left the studio."

Finally, the word gets to me.

"Ed, we think Eddie must have gone home. He's not here and his friends are gone too. He didn't say anything to anybody."

It's 5:10 P.M. on a shooting day of *The Golden Child* in 1986. We're scheduled to work until 7 P.M. We're about three weeks away from finishing the picture.

And Eddie Murphy, our star, is gone.

Everyone is panicked, excited, hysterical, even. It's clear that we won't be shooting anymore Eddie Murphy scenes that day, so I wrapped the company at 5:40 P.M.

I have to file a production report with the studio, Paramount, at the end of each day. On this day's production report, I write the following:

"Eddie Murphy left the studio at 5:10 P.M. without permission. Company was dismissed at 5:40 P.M."

Although this sounds innocuous, the production department at Paramount didn't want to accept it.

At this time, Eddie Murphy was Paramount's biggest star. Maybe the biggest star in movies after his rapid-fire successes in *48 HRS., Trading Places,* and *Beverly Hills Cop.* The production department didn't want anything appearing on a formal production report that would reflect badly on Murphy and would require someone at the studio to take some sort of action.

They wanted it to go away like it never happened.

I told you earlier that I'm always very upfront with the studio. And I wasn't going to lie on a production report.

I was told later that Murphy had just gotten bored and left. Gone home.

Well, the next day, I get word that Murphy wants to see me in his trailer. Not really a trailer—it's a big "star bus."

I go in and Murphy's sitting there, holding a copy of yesterday's production report.

He's not looking very happy.

"Ed, I gotta ask you. Why did you do this?"

And he gestures to the report.

"Eddie, you left the studio. You may want to be on this picture all summer, but I would like to finish it."

Murphy's somber expression doesn't change. "You're treating me like a child," he says.

And he didn't mean a *golden* child.

I look at him. I decide not to weigh my words.

"Well, yesterday you behaved like a child."

I reflect on this conversation today and it seems pretty ill-advised on my part. Eddie Murphy might phrase it, "A risky-ass thing to say. *Damn* risky-ass."

But I told him the truth.

Now try to guess what happened next.

Really, try to guess. Don't cheat. Don't look down the page.

What do you think happened next?

Murphy looks away for a moment, reflecting on my words.

Then he responds. "I understand," he says.

For the rest of the picture, Murphy called me *The Man*. "You want to know something? Ask The Man," he would say.

He had more respect for me than you could imagine. We got along just fine.

People sometimes think that working with big stars is difficult. That they're demanding, petulant, pampered, and overall, a big pain.

This hasn't been my experience at all and I've worked with some of the biggest stars around. But I have to tell you that the big stars have achieved a level of power that is held by very few people in Hollywood. You do have to be flexible in your dealings with them but not unreasonably so. For instance, it was well known in the 1980s that Eddie Murphy had an entourage of fellows about his age. They had gone to Roosevelt High School on Long Island with him, and they were his friends and he kept them on payroll. They were always around.

Starting *Golden Child,* I knew this. So the first thing I did was learn all their names. On the set, I considered them part of the company, and chatted and joked with them. They were nice, pleasant fellows and it was no trouble having them around. I earned their respect and Murphy's respect.

You have to be a big, big star for the producer of the movie and the studio to allow this sort of thing. And back then, Eddie Murphy wasn't just a star, he was a constellation.

Golden Child started as a script that I acquired from a writer named Dennis Feldman (no relation). I originally intended it for Mel Gibson, but when I showed it to Paramount, they asked me if I could switch it over to Eddie Murphy. Were they kidding? In a heartbeat.

With *48 HRS., Trading Places,* and *Beverly Hills Cop* in quick succession, Eddie Murphy was striking gold for Paramount, and the studio was looking for projects that would fit Murphy's unique brand of hip, urban humor, yet would appeal to a mass audience. Murphy himself wanted to move on to projects in which he could be more of an action movie star and less of a comedian. *Golden Child* seemed to fit the bill.

In the film, Murphy plays a Los Angeles investigator who locates missing children. He is hired to find a small Tibetan boy who is the Golden Child, a sort of Buddhist messiah with magical powers. Murphy has a love interest, played by Charlotte Lewis, and the villain is the devil personified, portrayed by urbane English actor, Charles Dance.

I had just delivered a huge critical and financial success for Paramount, *Witness,* starring Harrison Ford, so I had their full confidence and backing.

The biggest problem we encountered on *Golden Child* was locating a director. Now you might think that directing a big Eddie Murphy picture would be a plum assignment. But the conventional wisdom seemed to be that if the movie was successful, it was because of Eddie Murphy. If the movie failed, it was because of the director.

For a while, the Australian director George Miller was interested. Miller had directed the three *Mad Max* movies with Mel Gibson, and Miller himself was a hot property in 1985. As an Australian, Miller wasn't fazed by that "conventional wisdom" downside of directing a picture starring the American icon Eddie Murphy. But Miller was a unique personage for a director. He always wore little clip-on pink plastic bow ties. Plus, he had originally been a practicing medical doctor. Murphy and Miller would not necessarily be a good matchup.

I took Miller east to meet Murphy. This episode was so bizarre and Kafkaesque that I will tell it to you in some detail. Here's a little background first . . .

Eddie Murphy was discovered by Robert Wachs and Richard Tienken, who co-owned a New York comedy club called the Comic Strip. Wachs and Tienkin basically launched Murphy's career and became his managers. As Murphy's star rose, he began to take greater control of his projects. On *Golden Child,* Wachs and I would be the producers, and Murphy and Tienkin were two of the executive producers.

I arrange to take Miller to meet Murphy at Tienkin's apartment in New Jersey, just over the George Washington Bridge from Manhattan. Wachs picks us up at the airport—Miller's girlfriend is with us.

We're supposed to be having a dinner meeting with Murphy. Miller and his girlfriend want to stop off at our hotel, Le Parker Meridien, on Fifty-seventh Street in Manhattan, to freshen up after the long cross-country flight from L.A., but Wachs says there's no time. Murphy is waiting for us. And in those days, when Eddie Murphy was waiting for you, you went.

So we arrive at Tienkin's apartment. Murphy is there with Tienkin . . . plus Paramount executive Lindsay Doran, the Roosevelt High School entourage, and others. Some twenty people, all told.

After the introductions, Murphy decides that he and Tienkin will go to the supermarket to buy food for our dinner meeting, since Tienkin didn't have very much to eat in his apartment. So we wait for forty-five minutes while they go on the shopping trip. They return with shopping bags full of cold cuts and paper plates.

We sit down at the table—all twenty of us—it's very cozy, I might add, and everyone is given a paper plate except Murphy. His plate is china. The rest of Tienkin's china is being used as serving plates for the cold cuts.

I survey this situation and I'll be damned if I'm going to eat off of a paper plate at a production meeting for a big Paramount movie. So I skim the food off of one china plate onto another, and now I'm eating off of china, along with Murphy.

This turned out to be one of the strangest meetings I've ever attended. We've got Eddie Murphy, his managers, the producer, an A-List director, the director's girlfriend, a Paramount executive, Tienkin's girlfriend, the mother of the girlfriend, and the Roosevelt High entourage seated around a table eating cold cuts from mostly paper plates, ready to discuss megastar Eddie Murphy's next picture.

Whenever something came up that Murphy needed to discuss with Wachs and Tienkin, they would get up without a word, retire to the bedroom, and close the door. A few minutes later, they would come out, take their seats, and the discussion would continue. This happened several times.

Then as if on cue, a friend of Tienkin arrives at the front door: a very heavyset comic, dressed in a leather jumpsuit—it was summer, for God's sake—with the zipper undone down to his navel. He cruises into the dining room where we're meeting, interrupts our conversation, greets us amiably, and introduces us to the woman with him. She's a flashy, curvy, blonde number. "I want you to meet so-and-so. This is a *bimbo* I picked up in Boston."

Could anything else go wrong?

Well, after this disastrous dinner, Miller, his girlfriend, and I end up at the bar at the Parker Meridien. Miller asks me, "Ed, do you think I should do the picture?"

"George, I do not think this is a picture for you."

Miller agreed. Although Murphy liked him and vice versa, his Australian pictures had been relatively uncomplicated. He didn't want to tackle the convoluted personal relationships involved on this one.

After several more directors pass, we sign the late Michael Ritchie as our director. (He died of prostate cancer in 2001.) Ritchie was an established director of big movies early in his career—*Downhill Racer, The Candidate,* both with Robert Redford; *Semi-Tough;* and *Smile,* a classic satire of beauty pageants. He wasn't really known as a tried-and-true comedy director, but he had done good work on the comedic elements of his films. He had just come off the Chevy Chase comedy *Fletch,* and did well with it. By all expectations, Ritchie should have worked out fine. But he didn't.

The problems with Michael Ritchie on *Golden Child* can be summed up as follows: (1) the picture wasn't as funny as it could have been, and (2) he wasn't very attentive to his job. (Some might describe it as laziness.)

Ritchie was directing America's greatest comic of the day and he wasn't very funny. Murphy is one of the best improvisers of all time, but he still wasn't very funny. Ritchie didn't have a clue how to make him funny, either. In fact, Ritchie thought he *was* funny in the movie. But no one else did.

Early in the shooting, I tried to replace Ritchie, with Bob Wach's blessing. I met with Dawn Steel, the legendary tough-as-nails Paramount production chief. I said, "Michael's got to go. You see the dailies. He's not working out.

"Dawn, I don't want to get you aggravated, but I would like your permission to go to Marty Brest and beg him to take over the movie." Martin Brest had directed Murphy's *Beverly Hills Cop,* was already under contract to Paramount, and had an office on the lot.

Steel ignores my wish about not getting aggravated and blows sky high. She starts screaming at me at the top of her lungs, "GET OUT OF HERE! GET OUT OF HERE! I DON'T CARE WHAT'S FUNNY OR NOT! I'M *NOT* FIRING THE DIRECTOR ON AN EDDIE MURPHY PICTURE! YOU FIX IT, ED!"

Feldman the Fixer. Sounds like *The Sopranos.*

I exit Steel's office—my ears are still ringing—and decide to go for broke. Wachs and I meet with Ritchie in his office. Wachs lets me do the talking: "Look, Michael, the picture's not funny. And it's a fantasy and there's no smoke for the Far Eastern shots. It's a fantasy and everything is flat and there's no movement of the camera. The camera's very static. It doesn't look like a fantasy to me. But the most important thing is, we have an Eddie Murphy picture that isn't funny."

Ritchie reflects for a moment, then says, "Ed, I don't use smoke. I don't move the camera a lot. If you want someone who does that, I suggest you get another director. And I think the picture is funny."

That night, I toss and turn. I was sure Ritchie would go back to Paramount and say, "I can't work with Ed Feldman." Even though I was producer of the movie, they could pay me off and tell me not to show up again.

I arrive at the set the next morning, expecting the worst. Any minute, a Paramount exec will walk up and say, "Ed, you're off the picture." Then I will leave, hat in hand, and Ritchie will continue to direct *Golden Child* the same way he had before, but minus Feldman.

But surprise!

The first thing I notice are the smoke pots positioned around the set. *I have my smoke.*

Then I see the crew laying dolly tracks for the camera. *I have my camera movement.*

Apparently, Ritchie had a sleepless night too. And I guess he didn't know that Dawn Steel was not about to . . . FIRE THE DIRECTOR OF AN EDDIE MURPHY PICTURE!

So he stayed until completion but the movie could have been much better. Michael Ritchie's career was its own "downhill racer."

The late Dawn Steel was about as tough a studio executive as you can imagine. Unfortunately, she passed away at a very young age after a bout with cancer. When we were in pre-production on *Golden Child,* I'm in a meeting with her at her office. The budget was coming in at about $26 million, a little on the high end back then. She says, "Ed, I know how to save three million dollars."

"Tell me, Dawn."

"Go across the street to Raleigh; they're much cheaper than us."

She meant shoot the interiors on soundstages at the Raleigh Studios. Even on a Paramount film, Paramount would charge the production much more than the smaller, no-frills Raleigh Studios. I knew that this would be a political disaster, though.

I say, "Dawn, if you do that, you'll lose your job. Because Paramount wants you to use the facilities of the lot, not across the street."

So I talk her out of that idea. But then later, I'm back in her office and she's on the same cost-saving theme: "I know how to cut three million dollars out of this picture."

"I'm listening."

"You don't go to Katmandu. You shoot all the Katmandu stuff in Lafayette Park in Los Angeles. You do this, you do that, you do this, you do that. You cut half the special effects out."

Now I never expected Eddie Murphy to shoot any of the picture in Katmandu. At this point, he didn't even like to travel to San Francisco. But I didn't want to start skimping on the special effects or other essentials in a big Eddie Murphy picture.

So I reply, "Has anyone discussed this with Eddie Murphy?"

Well, she comes over to where I'm sitting on the couch. She's holding a heavy Lucite paperweight, sort of playing with it as she walks.

Now she's standing over me, glaring. "I want you to understand something once and for all, Ed. *Eddie Murphy does not run Paramount Pictures.*"

"Oh yes, he does." Maybe it came out a little snide.

Steel swings the heavy paperweight like she's going to throw it at me. I put my hands up quickly to protect my face.

She didn't actually throw it but I'll bet she wanted to.

"You've got to be very careful, Ed. I can't have Eddie Murphy playing with a white girl, a Caucasian girl. She's got to be a mixture of something."

This is a Paramount executive talking about casting Murphy's love interest in the movie. Back then, the studios were very nervous about this sort of thing. He's the boss, so we find Charlotte Lewis in London. A very pretty eighteen-year-old with an exotic look, like she could be a "mixture of something."

But I'm not going to ask her. So I just make something up to tell the studio—"She comes from a Portuguese father and an English mother."

I was full of shit but they were satisfied.

The *Golden Child* shoot was pretty unremarkable and routine. For next to nothing, I hired an Indian second-unit crew to film establishing shots and other exteriors in Katmandu, which we combined with our L.A. footage during editing.

I continued to be frustrated by Michael Ritchie's inability to make Eddie Murphy's performance funnier. One day we're filming a scene in which Murphy's character is chasing after the bad guys. He jumps over a wall, right into a Latino family's backyard cookout. They're terrified, so he tries to calm them down, then waves his gun around in the air to keep them quiet.

The scene wasn't funny at all. True, the words in the script weren't inherently funny, but Eddie Murphy could make my wife's shopping list funny.

After the take, I go up to Ritchie. "Michael, it's not funny."

"You could do better, Ed?"

"I think so."

I went over to Murphy and said, "Eddie, forget the dialogue. You go over the wall, you've got a gun in your hand, and you come upon these four Latinos. What would you say?"

He looks over the setting, reflects a bit, and says, "OK, I'm ready. Let's do it."

So he goes back to the starting point. Action. He jumps over the wall, the Latinos are panicked.

He ad libs, "I'm not going to hurt anybody. I don't want no trouble."

He pulls out his gun and waves it. "Ah, ah, no trouble. I just . . . I'm sorry. I just . . . want some chips. I want some chips. That's all." He scoops up some potato chips from the picnic table. "See, chips. That's it."

Then he sees that the barbeque fire is flaming up over the hamburgers. "Turn it over, man, it's burnin'. TURN IT OVER, IT'S BURNIN'." He motions to the grill with his gun.

Finally, he puts a chip in his mouth and exits. It's as if he had held up the family at gunpoint for some potato chips.

It was hilarious. The crew applauds and cheers. Ritchie disappears into his trailer and refuses to come out. We had to wrap for the rest of the day.

Murphy's double got a lot of screen time on this picture. I would say that Murphy himself appeared in only about 40 percent of the shots that included his character. In long shots or back-of-the-head shots, it was always the double.

It wasn't that Ritchie was in awe of Murphy, and wanted to take it easy on him and let him rest in his star bus all the time. I theorized that Ritchie was just being lazy—he didn't want to deal with Murphy unless he absolutely had to. And it wasn't because Murphy was difficult. Except for that incident when he left early one day, Murphy was very easy to get along with. A decent, cooperative colleague in the making of the picture.

———

We have a rough cut of the picture and it's time to test it with a real audience. We arrange a screening on the Paramount lot on a Friday night and bring in a recruited audience. The film plays badly. It's not very funny. The audience doesn't laugh and seems disappointed in an unfunny Eddie Murphy picture.

After the picture ends, a twelve-year-old boy pipes up, "I think the director of this movie sucks. He should be shot." And there's the director sitting three rows behind him. Ouch! It takes a thick skin to attend these screenings.

The next day we meet in the office of David Kirkpatrick at Paramount to discuss recutting the movie. We agree on the changes that Ritchie will make and decide the movie will be rescreened the next Saturday night, a week later.

Monday morning, I get a call at home from Kirkpatrick. "Where's your director?"

"Well, David, he's either on the soundstage or he's in the editing room."

"NO, HE'S NOT, ED! HE'S IN LONDON! He had a free ticket to London and he took his wife TO LONDON!"

It seems that Ritchie left for London with his wife on Sunday after leaving the list of changes with the editor. He never said anything to me, the producer of the movie. Paramount was crazed.

So I call him up in London. "What the hell are you doing, Michael? I know the editor can do the recutting, but who's going to remix the sound on the movie?" We had to have the revised version ready for the Saturday screening and it was Monday. Ritchie was scheduled to be back from London on Thursday. (He eventually did come back a day early.)

Then he says an amazing thing to me: "Well, Ed, God knows you know how to remix a movie."

I was stunned, simply stunned, because most directors would go to the grave before they'd let a *producer* touch their movie.

The picture plays better in the next screening but not by much. I knew we were in serious trouble. We scheduled some reshoots that included Murphy. He was very cooperative, as usual.

But at this point, there's not a whole lot you can do except reshoot the whole movie with a new director like Ray Stark did on *Suzie Wong*. But that wasn't going to happen on an Eddie Murphy picture. Paramount had a firm Christmas release date and Murphy had to move on to his next project.

Golden Child opened to good business, propelled by the public's adoration of Eddie Murphy. Eventually, it did about $80 million at the domestic box office. That was acceptable business, but it pales in comparison to the $235 million domestic gross of *Beverly Hills Cop*.

Here are two postscripts on *Golden Child*—

Somewhere in the bowels of Paramount Pictures there resides a complete movie score by the famed English film composer John Barry. We had hired three-time Oscar-winner Barry for *Golden Child,* and he turned in this lush melodic score, which we recorded in five sessions with a full orchestra of ninety-two musicians. (Our director, Michael Ritchie, bothered to show up for only three of the sessions; he disappeared to New York for the other two.)

Barry is a world-class composer but this wasn't *Raiders of the Lost Ark*. The score just didn't fit a streetwise Eddie Murphy picture. So we engaged a French composer, Michel Columbier, who in two weeks did a terrific job of supplying just the right edgy musical accompaniment for the film.

That full John Barry score, bought and paid for, still resides at Paramount, almost twenty years and several managements later, unused and gathering dust.

I devised a teaser for the film that we shot up in the snow at Mammoth, California, near Yosemite, during principal photography on the film. It was a takeoff on that famous scene in *Lawrence of Arabia,* when a lone figure on a camel (Omar Sharif's character) appears as a speck far off in the desert and then approaches the camera, becoming recognizable as he rides.

Our teaser starts with a lone figure in the snow riding an animal of some sort. There is a voice-over by our villain, Charles Dance, but in reverent, dulcet tones: "Every hundreds of years a special person comes along who can do this, and do that . . ."

And the figure is coming closer to the screen and he's on a yak. He's got all this snow gear on him. We realize it's Eddie Murphy.

"And he is known as the Golden Child."

And Murphy looks at the camera and says, "Sure, all these guys at Paramount are sitting in their warm offices and I'm freezing my ass off."

When that teaser-trailer appeared on the screen, people went bananas. Murphy's line was so unexpected and we were ribbing the studio. I think we were the first ones to poke fun at studio executives, which is now a time-honored tradition.

Eddie Murphy, like a lot of superstars, wants to control his own projects. And a very effective—and potentially profitable—way to do this is by getting into the producing end. This was one of the most significant elements of *Golden Child*. For the first time, Murphy and his managers were actively involved in producing a movie, through his Eddie Murphy Productions.

At this point, Wachs and Tienkin weren't bona fide producers. So I basically managed the film as I had done on other projects. But by working on the picture, they learned what a producer does and, eventually, went forward on their own.

I provided essentially the same function with Mel Gibson's Icon Productions on *Forever Young* in the early 1990s. This film marked the first time that Icon was the producing entity on a movie. Gibson's partner in Icon was Bruce Davey, an Australian who had been Gibson's accountant back in Gibson's "struggling actor" days. Davey had even helped Gibson set up his first personal checking account.

Although Gibson was a big star in 1990, he and Davey had little producing experience. That's where I came in. I would manage *Forever Young* with the assistance of Icon executives in a way that was similar to my relationship with Bob Wachs on *Golden Child*.

Murphy, Wachs, and Tienkin had split up in the late 1980s about the time Gibson and Davey were gearing up for their Icon effort.

Through Icon, Gibson and Davey went on to make *Braveheart,* directed by Gibson, which was an enormous critical and box office success. It won five Academy Awards, including Best Picture and Best Director, out of a total of ten nominations.

Icon, with Gibson and Davey in charge, became a powerhouse in the film business, racking up a string of big hits over the years. Their controversial *The Passion of the Christ* is one of the biggest-grossing, most profitable films in history.

But it all started with a film called *Forever Young.*

Golden Child had been my project, with Eddie Murphy joining the picture as its star. With *Forever Young,* Gibson had acquired the project through Warner Bros., and I was brought in to produce it.

Forever Young was written by J. J. Abrams, who went on to create the hit TV shows *Lost* and *Alias.* It is about an air force test pilot in the 1930s whose fiancée—the love of his life—critically injured in an accident, is in a coma and not expected to survive. With nothing to live for, he volunteers for a risky experiment to be cryogenically frozen and revived later. Circumstances intervene and he is unintentionally left in this state of suspended animation for fifty years, when he is found and accidentally revived by two boys. The film is heartwarming and funny, and it has some great action. A good film for the very, very likable Mel Gibson.

My involvement began when I got a call from my agent, John Ptak, about doing the picture. I then called Nigel Sinclair, Icon's attorney who had been my attorney at some point. It seemed liked a good assignment. Icon really wanted me.

I first met Gibson over a two-hour lunch at a restaurant in Burbank. We talked about the picture at length and I was struck by his enthusiasm and savvy. I'm in.

It really hit me head-on what a big, important star Mel Gibson was when I arrived at his office on the Warner lot and there was Terry Semel, the president of Warners, sitting there with him. Most actors, even important ones, go to the president's office, not the other way around.

One of the first things Gibson says in the meeting is, "I think I can get Sydney Pollack to direct."

Now, who wouldn't want to work with Sydney Pollack? A–list all the way. But *Forever Young* was going to be a modestly budgeted picture. Gibson was even taking next to nothing upfront. So I made an observation:

"Listen, Mel, you hire Sydney Pollack to get you a star. We've got a star. Why do we have to pay a director five million dollars?"

Well, I thought Terry Semel would rush over right then and give me a big, wet smooch.

"Ed's right, Mel. Let's listen to him on this."

We talked to several directors with no luck. John McTiernan, the big action-director (he had done *Die Hard*), turned us down. He couldn't accept the picture's basic premise that a man could sleep for fifty years and come back to life. It was probably just as well. McTiernan was pretty expensive too.

We're stuck when Bruce Davey's girlfriend says, "I know a director you should use. His movie was very good." She had just seen a Disney film, *Wild Hearts Can't Be Broken,* directed by a former TV director named Steve Miner.

I didn't really believe this would work out. Mel Gibson was a huge star and I doubted whether he would agree to be directed by someone who had spent most of his career directing TV pilots.

Gibson and I screen the movie at Warners and he is enraptured by it. We bring Miner over to meet us at Bruce Davey's house. It goes extremely well and much to my surprise, Gibson is sold on him.

This is a huge, huge step in Steve Miner's career—to direct a big Mel Gibson movie. As we're walking out of Davey's house, I say to Miner, "Steve, I think you should fly to Las Vegas right now and put all your money on the table because you must be on a streak—this has got to be the luckiest day of your life."

We cast a very young Elijah Wood as the lead boy and Jamie Lee Curtis as his single mother. Gibson's character moves in with them for much of the movie. Curtis is a potential love interest for him.

Elijah Wood was the ultimate child actor. His family lived in San Francisco and they never treated him any differently from other members of the family.

Elijah was the most respectful kid you ever met on a set. He was always on time; he knew his lines. He was perfect. I wish the average adult actor were as easy to work with as he was. A terrific kid.

I'm delighted with Elijah's success as Frodo in Peter Jackson's *Lord of the Rings* trilogy. He is a most deserving young man.

Forever Young went well. Steve Miner did a very good job. I used him again two years later for *My Father the Hero,* starring Gérard Depardieu.

Mel Gibson was a prince. Very easy to work with. When we were traveling to northern California for some of the shoot, I asked him what kind of accommodations he would like.

"Ed, all I ever do is go back to the room and watch TV. A big room but nothing special."

So I get him a basic room and his partner gets a nice, luxurious suite. This did not go over at all well, however, with Mrs. Gibson.

One day during filming will always remain with me. It speaks volumes about Mel Gibson, and his love and compassion toward people. It was arranged for a terminally ill girl—a big fan of his—to visit the set. Many stars will do this, invite the person to the set, say hello, and sign an autograph book. But he spent the entire day with her except for the time he was in front of the camera. He had lunch with her in his trailer. He gave her the day of her life before she died.

Forever Young is exactly the kind of picture that fits Mel Gibson like a glove. It's exciting, romantic, heartwarming, funny. And it was a good choice to launch Icon as a producing company. Even with much of it being set in another era and with some elaborate action sequences, we brought it in for a very modest budget. Yet it has a great look to it.

I hired the production manager on the film, a young man I had known before named Steve McEveety. He and Gibson and Davey really hit it off on this picture. McEveety joined Icon as an employee and went on to produce many of its projects, including *The Passion.*

Forever Young did OK at the box office but not great. I'm sure Warners and Icon eventually made good money on it after video and TV revenues were included.

Eddie and Mel. I really enjoyed working with both of them and I feel that I helped each understand the producing business a little better.

Even people who have worked a long time in the movie industry aren't always clear on exactly what a producer does on a day-to-day basis. A producer has a lot of responsibility on a picture and manages a boatload of money. An army of people answer to him or her.

Sometimes it's easy to get a swelled head. If we do occasionally, the fall back to reality can be swift and jarring. And it might just be a real *fall*.

Consider this producer parable—

We're on location with *Golden Child* in the Boyle Heights section of Los Angeles. I had to attend an important breakfast meeting that day, so I was wearing my dress shoes when I arrived at location later. Usually I wear running shoes on the set because of all the walking and standing.

We're changing locations by a few blocks, so I'm walking along the sidewalk with a crew member when suddenly I slip in my leather-soled dress shoes and hit the pavement.

My God, it hurt. I'm writhing in excruciating pain on the sidewalk. It turned out that I had torn a quadriceps muscle in my right leg. Eventually, I had surgery and was on crutches for weeks.

So I'm on the ground and they call for the rescue squad. I continue to endure this horrible pain but help is on the way.

I look up and I see Eddie Murphy and Bob Wachs looking down at me. Murphy shakes his head and turns to Wachs: "This is our opportunity to take over the movie. You can now run things, Bob."

Finally I hear the siren approaching, the rescue unit stops, and the attendants rush out. I expect them to hover over me any second and begin preparing me for transfer to the ambulance.

No one appears. I wait. Still no one. What the hell?

I lift my head a bit and see the attendants . . . they're crowded around Murphy, completely oblivious to me and my suffering. Turns out, they were trying to score tickets to his next concert.

Mr. Producer, no matter how much in charge you are, always re-member your place in the pecking order. You may not be as fortunate as I was. They *did* eventually lift me onto the stretcher. But get ready for the alternative—you might just have to hobble over to that ambu-lance and climb in yourself.

9

OTHER THAN THAT, MR. BELUSHI, HOW WAS THE FILM?

FOR A SOLID TWO MINUTES, JIM BELUSHI TRASHED MY OFFICE. He turned over furniture, scattered files, tore phones from their plugs, pulled things off the wall. It was mayhem. Luckily, I was home recuperating from a leg operation for my *Golden Child* injury and didn't receive the brunt of his wrath directly.

Belushi was furious that I was turning the book *Wired,* the tragic story of his brother John's career and untimely death by overdose, into a feature film. So he arrived unannounced one day at my office suite at Paramount, demanding to see me, not even giving his name. That day, I had a temp in, manning the phones and greeting visitors.

The temp told Belushi that I wasn't in but he barged by her and commenced trashing my private office.

When he was done, he reemerged into the reception area and strode up to the scared, bewildered woman. In his toughest tough-guy, Cagneyesque voice, he told her, "You just be sure and tell Feldman who did this."

The temp blinked at him.

"You got that?"

She still looked at him, blinking.

"Well?"

Finally, the temp answered in a small, weak voice, "I would give that message to Mr. Feldman but . . ."

"But what?"

"I don't know *who you are, sir.*"

Belushi must have deflated before her very eyes.

Jim Belushi was the least of my problems on *Wired*. Over the four years that it took to make the film and get it into theaters, I had been subjected to forms of harassment and interference rarely seen in the film business. Things were rocky from the start, but on the day I received an ominous call from the most powerful man in Hollywood, I knew this project was in serious trouble and my career was hanging in the balance. Jim Belushi was a man of big moxie, tiny clout, but the man on the other end of the phone . . . well, he was the Don Corleone of Hollywood moxie *and* clout. He was used to having his way and his way for *Wired* was oblivion—and me with it, if necessary.

But let me start at the beginning: Vito can wait for now.

The book of *Wired* was published in 1984. It was written by Bob Woodward of Woodward and Bernstein, *All the President's Men,* Deep Throat fame. The book chronicled the life and demise of John Belushi, the well-loved, extremely talented television and film comedic actor. *Wired* became an immediate best-seller.

John Belushi grew up in Chicago and got his professional start with the legendary Second City improvisational group. He eventually moved to New York and appeared in the Off Broadway show *Lemmings* in 1973, then became part of the original cast of *Saturday Night Live* in 1975. Belushi helped create some of that show's most memorable sketch characters including the "chizzburger" short order cook and the Blues Brothers.

But it was the film *Animal House* in 1978 that really launched Belushi's star. Between 1978 and 1982, the year of his death, Belushi's professional life had mixed but solid success while his personal life disintegrated with his increasingly heavy use of cocaine and finally heroin. On March 5, 1982, Belushi died in a bungalow at the Chateau Marmont hotel in Hollywood, from a heroin overdose. He was thirty-three years old.

Woodward's book was a well-researched, insightful account of Belushi's rise and fall. It pulled no punches—it named names, including some of Hollywood's biggest stars as Belushi's cohorts in cocaine. The book was highly controversial, hated even, especially with fans and Hollywood types who preferred the memory of the uproarious funny-man of *Animal House* over the coked-out wreck lying in an L.A. morgue.

No one wanted to touch *Wired* as a film. No one, that is, except two fellows trying to take their production company public. One Ed Feldman and his partner, Charles Meeker. Feldman-Meeker was up to the challenge of making *Wired, the Movie*. And we weren't about to be deterred by some rumblings, some talk in the business. Mere chitchat. Batten the hatches, boys. Full steam ahead. Don't fire until you see the whites of their eyes. But don't take the call from Don Corleone. Well, we missed that last one.

"This is Michael Ovitz."

Michael Ovitz, I thought. Why is *he* calling me?

Selznick was clearly exaggerating when he told me he was "the most important man in the history of this business." But it was no exaggeration to say that in the mid-1980s, Michael Ovitz was the most powerful man in the industry. Bar none. In fact, there has been no one since his fall to be anywhere near as powerful. Not even remotely. On a scale of one to ten, Ovitz was a twenty.

I had never met Ovitz but I knew a call from him, in show business, was a call from the President, or the Pope, or the Emperor of the World, even.

Just a couple of days before, the *New York Times* had published a major story about the optioning of *Wired* for a motion picture by Feldman-Meeker. We had fed the story to the *Times* ourselves but never imagined it would be this big.

It dawned on me that Ovitz could be calling about that news, but somehow I didn't think he was calling to offer the services of his agency in arranging actors, a writer, and a director for us. It turned out I was right on both counts. But I *never* expected what came next.

"Ed, I hear you're a very nice man. But if you proceed with this Belushi project, I wouldn't give you five cents for your future career in this business."

Don't you just hate it when someone minces words. I know I do. Why doesn't he just come right out and tell me I'm finished in Hollywood if I produce *Wired*? He's softening it by telling me I might be worth *five cents* instead of *zilch*.

Considering how shocked, aghast, and stunned I was, I thought I was pretty cool in my response:

"Well, Michael, I will certainly listen to your advice. But I don't think anyone has the right to tell me what movies to make. And I am very interested in making this project. I think it's a good idea for a movie."

Ovitz says nothing and hangs up the phone.

And I sit there in my chair thinking, "Oh, God. Now what?"

Michael Ovitz was the Center of the Show Business Universe in the 1980s because he and the talent agency he headed, Creative Artists Agency (CAA), began packaging motion picture projects. In other words, he put a script, director, and actors together in a package deal and studios could then just sign on the dotted line. But these weren't just any old garden variety writers, directors, and actors in the package. They were the top people. The Robert Redfords, the Steven Spielbergs. If you were a producer for a big-budget action picture, for example, Ovitz and crew would put the package together for you—kind of a one-stop-shopping arrangement.

Don't like Stallone for your picture? That's OK, we represent Bruce Willis and he's available. Want Streep outside of a package? Well, too bad because she's committed to this package deal next door.

Get the idea?

Ovitz was able to do this because of a void that existed in the industry then. Packaging had always been a common practice in television, while the major studios had traditionally packaged their own movie projects through producers. But the old studio system was crumbling in the 1970s. Conglomerates were buying up studios and MBA types were taking over. The MBAs tended to be generalists—they could sell Muenster cheese or *The Munsters,* whatever. They were plenty smart and competent as business people, but their mind-sets were different from the tradition-bound movie moguls, the Cohns and Zanucks of old.

And this created a power vacuum that Ovitz and CAA were poised to exploit. And did they exploit it to the hilt.

The power to control high-quality, extremely marketable projects from the get-go script stage and then grant or deny big stars and directors was a tremendous drawing card for CAA's client list. Clients were flocking in and they were getting richer thanks to Ovitz. So his power was getting stronger and stronger. And it was pretty damn strong when Ed Feldman crashed into that wall circa 1985.

Things were quiet at first, then the Ovitz Machine reared its head. We needed a writer for *Wired,* someone to take Woodward's book and turn it into a movie script. This shouldn't have been too difficult—it was a pretty big-time project: A movie of a very high-profile, best-selling book by a Pulitzer Prize–winning author. And I was no slouch, either. I was producing *The Golden Child* at the time, a big-budget studio picture with Eddie Murphy. Even though *Wired* was controversial, normally you would expect several established writers to emerge as candidates.

We got nothing.

No writers came forward on their own. And when we contacted writers through their agents, they weren't available, or they weren't interested, or they were out of town, or they had to walk the dog. Nothing. The well was dry.

No one ever said to me, "Look, Ed. Joe would love to work on *Wired,* but if he does, it's the last Hollywood script he'll ever write. He'd be finished. Maybe they'd give him a dog food commercial, but I doubt it."

No one ever said, "Ed, you schmuck, don't you know Ovitz has put the word out on *Wired*? Don't get near it. Stay away. We all love you dearly. And I'd put Susie on your script in a heartbeat. Probably win an Oscar for it. But Susie'd like to work again after *Wired*. And so would I, as a matter of fact."

No one ever said these things. All we got was nothing. Not interested. Out of town. Gotta go. See ya, Ed.

Later, Ovitz told *Time* magazine that he was just giving me some "friendly advice" with his phone call.

Finally, we did sign up a very good New York writer, Earl Mac Rauch, for *Wired*. Rauch had written *New York, New York* for Martin Scorsese, and the cult science fiction classic, *The Adventures of Buckaroo Banzai*. He did a nice job on *Wired*, putting some interesting twists to what could have been just a linear telling of Belushi's rise and fall.

I signed my good friend Larry Peerce to direct. He was an established director who had done the classic *Goodbye, Columbus* and *Ash Wednesday* with Elizabeth Taylor and Henry Fonda. I had worked with him before, most notably on *The Other Side of the Mountain,* and knew he would do well with *Wired*. Besides, he solved a major problem—he was too loyal to me, and too much of an iconoclast, to worry about Ovitz.

With a good script in hand and a solid director, now was the time to cast the film. Certainly, actors would see the merit of the project and sign on. If nothing else, there are plenty of hungry actors out there, right?

Wrong. Not hungry enough, apparently. Gotta walk the dog, feed the cat, clean out the birdcage. You name it, they had to do it. Except act in *Wired*.

Now, I'm a pretty savvy guy. I've been around. I know we don't stand the slightest chance of signing any CAA clients. And that by itself is a formidable problem. CAA represented some awfully good people, and that whole list was unavailable. I knew that from the day of Ovitz's call.

But I never expected to be frozen out by the other major agencies. For one thing, Hollywood is a competitive town. Agents who didn't work for CAA had to come into the office every day and face the CAA-Ovitz juggernaut in trying to get work for their clients. Now here's a chance to sign people to a big project and not have to worry about squaring off against the Don and his men.

I had forgotten the power of one thing, though. Hollywood is competitive but it's also very fluid. Work for William Morris one day, work for CAA the next. My enemy, my friend.

Or if you got too cozy with Feldman and *Wired,* work for William Morris one day, *not* work for CAA the next. My enemy, my enemy, my enemy . . .

Life was just too short to go up against The Most Powerful Man in Hollywood. Whatever short-term benefits accrued from *Wired* would be quickly wiped out by the long-term, you'll-never-work-in-this-town-again banishment that would surely follow. It would be the Hollywood version of being dumped in the East River with your feet encased in cement. Most of the Hollywood players just weren't in a frame of mind to take a nighttime swim with the fishes.

> **Fact:** Actor J. T. Walsh, who played Bob Woodward in *Wired,* showed up for work on a later film, *Loose Cannons.* He was fired after one day, reportedly because his presence on the set would "upset" star Dan Aykroyd.

We finally cast *Wired* with a good but relatively unknown slate of actors. Seems there were enough hungry actors out there, after all. Walsh, Lucinda Jenney as Belushi's wife, Patti D'Arbanville as the woman who administered Belushi's final heroin injection, Gary Groomes as Dan Aykroyd, and Ray Sharkey as the mythical "Angel." Groomes, a comedian from Minneapolis, was once asked, "Don't you think this is going to adversely affect your film career?"

Groomes responded, "Until now I didn't have a film career."

J. T. Walsh's career picked up quickly and he worked on fifty-two theatrical and television films from *Wired* until his untimely death in 1998. Here's an interesting tidbit—Walsh played Bob Woodward for us; he was John Ehrlichman in Oliver Stone's *Nixon.*

In dead center, though, was Michael Chiklis, who played Belushi. Significantly, he was a twenty-three-year-old unknown New York actor who had little to lose from an Ovitz cocktail. But he *was* worried about one thing: Chiklis swore me to secrecy about his age. He was afraid everyone would think he was too young to play Belushi.

Chiklis had a thankless task on this picture. Everyone remembered the real John Belushi whether they liked him or not. So there would be the inevitable comparisons—does he look like Belushi, sound like Belushi, ad nauseam. There was no way he was going to be funnier than Belushi. And there was a large contingent of Belushi worshippers out there who would never admit that Chiklis was funny at all, no matter how well he did.

Compare this to Jim Carrey as Andy Kaufman in Milos Forman's *Man on the Moon*. Carrey was wonderful but he didn't have many of the built-in obstacles Chiklis did. Kaufman was not as well known as Belushi, not as well liked as Belushi, didn't live the tragedy of Belushi. And let's face it, many people didn't think Kaufman was all that funny.

For my money, Chiklis did a terrific job under the circumstances. He gave a powerful, assured performance. This is all the more amazing given his youth and relative inexperience at the time.

One reviewer in 1989 said that Belushi was played by "unknown—and soon-to-be-unknown—Michael Chiklis." Here's hoping that reviewer was tuned into the 2002 Emmys thirteen years later, to see Chiklis pick up the award for Best Dramatic Performance in a TV Series for *The Shield,* besting Martin Sheen and Kiefer Sutherland. And this was following Chiklis's five-year star turn on ABC's *The Commish.*

So even with the Ovitz posse on our tail, we had a script, a director, and a cast. Surprisingly, though, we even had trouble lining up our technical people, director of photography, editor, and others. But it finally came together.

But then the Ovitz juggernaut hit us where it really hurt—in the wallet.

I've been asked why Ovitz was so dogged in his determination to scuttle *Wired*. Was it a genuine devotion to Belushi (John not Jim)? Was it the product of an oversized ego? Why go to the trouble?

My best guess is that Ovitz had made a promise to Dan Aykroyd and Jim Belushi—both CAA clients—that *Wired* would never see the light of day. Ovitz understood the extent of his power and also the level of opposition to the Belushi story in Hollywood. Plus he had an enormous ego. I think he just concluded that *Wired* was stoppable, if not dead in its tracks, at least through a process of wearing us down. Every step of the way was a major hurdle. I had made a lot of movies by then and was amazed at how difficult every single thing was on this project.

But finally Ovitz went too far in my mind.

Here's what happened.

We needed at least $9 million to make *Wired*. The studios and all the other traditional financing sources had been scared off. With considerable difficulty, we finally found an unconventional source: Lion Screen Entertainment, a unit of Lion Nathan Ltd., New Zealand's version of Anheuser-Busch, in some sort of a tax shelter arrangement.

Now, with independent, non–studio-financed movies like ours, it's important to sell off as many of the financial pieces as possible to raise production capital. We had a deal with HBO in which they would front us money in return for the video rights to *Wired*. One day I got a call from HBO and their executive said, "You've got to let us out of the contract. We're getting killed." Which we did. Although *Wired* appeared on videocassette, to this day, it's never been on HBO or Showtime or any other premium cable channel.

Even with the setbacks, somehow we muddled through, and now we had a finished picture that we believed was pretty good. Finally, I thought, with the product in hand, we can sell the distribution rights and get *Wired* in theaters. I knew how to do this and thought we had a good shot at a major distributor.

Wrong again, amigo.

Some of the studios didn't even want to look at it. Not at all. Not a frame. Sorry, Ed, not interested.

Now, the truth of the matter is that it's unheard of for a studio not to look at a finished picture. What does it cost them—two hours of screening time?

You would have thought this was a porn film or a snuff film, the way we had to sneak around. We had to go to one studio early in the morning before everybody came to work. God forbid people should know they were seeing the movie.

No interest. Not even a little. We were totally shut out of the majors.

Then we went to secondary distributors like Samuel Goldwyn, who was going to distribute the picture, and then turned on us in a minute and a half.

Finally, though, we had a pretty firm deal with a small company called New Visions. It had been set up by the director Taylor Hackford after he had success in producing *La Bamba,* the Ritchie Valens biography, in 1987. New Visions had as its mission the production and distribution of "quality, yet modestly budgeted films."

We would have preferred Paramount or Fox, but Hackford had a pretty good little company—classy. New Visions's later successes would include *The Long Walk Home* starring Sissy Spacek and Whoopi Goldberg; *Queens Logic* with John Malkovich and Jamie Lee Curtis; and Demi Moore and Bruce Willis in *Mortal Thoughts.*

Now we had a respected distributor who believed in the film and would get it into theaters. No more sneaking around at dawn.

Take that, Michael Ovitz! We're bloodied but we're still standing.

Well, is that right, Mr. Ed Feldman? Not so fast, pardner.

We're set with Hackford, we think. Then all of a sudden, one day he calls up and says, "Ed, I can't do this." Taylor Hackford and New Visions are out, and we don't have a distributor.

So far, I couldn't quite connect the dots back to Ovitz. The manipulation and intimidation I was so sure of could have been explained away. Until now. Ovitz's fingerprints were everywhere.

You see, Hackford was a CAA client. Dots connected.

It seems that Hackford's New Visions and our company were customers of the same bank based in Rotterdam. We had taken out the *Wired* production loan, guaranteed by Lion Nathan, through this bank. So the bank had a very real interest in the distribution of *Wired,* because it would generate the money to repay the loan. Word got back to us that even the bank knew that it was no coincidence that the New Visions deal had come undone. As *Time* magazine would later put it, the deal dissolved "suspiciously."

There is a legal concept called tortious or wrongful interference in a business relationship. I'm not a lawyer, but as I understand it, it prevents people from meddling in the business affairs of other people when the purpose is to intentionally harm those people.

My God, that's just what Ovitz was doing, I was sure.

Woodward even put us in touch with a big and powerful Washington-based law firm and they were talking $25 million in potential damages.

But I couldn't do it. That's just not my business style. Never has been, never will be.

I want to make movies, good ones, I hope. I don't want to spend time in a courtroom playing *he said, she said.* That's not the life of Ed Feldman.

Case closed.

We finally got another distributor, one Taurus Entertainment Co., a new joint venture half owned by United Artist Theater Circuit. Our release was sandwiched in between two of their other big movies: *Beverly Hills Brats* and *Martians Go Home.*

We didn't have a ghost of a chance.

We opened on some twelve hundred screens and promptly died an excruciating death from inattention.

On opening weekend, only five of the twelve hundred theaters reported a box office take in four figures. If you're a little weak in math, that means 1,195 theaters each sold less than $1,000 in tickets.

After two weeks in theaters, *Wired* vanished into thin air. Kaput. Sayonara.

I had given it my best shot. I went on the free publicity circuit. I appeared on *Larry King* and *Good Morning, America.* There were articles in *Time* and *People.* We tried everything we could. Tried to capitalize on the controversy. But we sank like a rock.

After the fateful call from Ovitz, Lorraine and I had a frank conversation that night. My loving—and very smart—wife told me to drop *Wired.* "Ed, you're going to kill yourself," she said.

And you know, she was right.

The last two years on *Wired* were the worst, most stress-filled, anguished years of my life. It had been a living hell.

One of my best friends ran Paramount then and wouldn't even let me rent an office there on a pay-as-you-go basis. He later apologized.

One of Ovitz's CAA partners stopped by my table in a restaurant and said, "Ed, I am embarrassed by what we're doing." I appreciated the gesture but he was still screwing me.

Ultimately, there was only one guy who stood by me—Jeffrey Katzenberg, now head of DreamWorks, who feared no one. During this time, he was the only studio head who would give me development deals.

I'd like to look heroic in all of this. Hollywood Medal of Honor and all that.

But you know, if I had it to do all over again, I wouldn't. There would have been no *Wired*. I would have produced some other movie and would have been happier and no doubt richer.

But I just wasn't going to let some guy, no matter how much of a big shot he was, call me and tell me not to make a movie.

Remember how Jim Belushi trashed my office? Then he thought my temp would just naturally know who he was? And she didn't? Well, the head of Paramount security told Belushi's manager that more behavior like that and he was barred from the studio lot.

But now here's the most amazing thing of all. *People* magazine asked Belushi about the episode of his hands and my office, and here's what he said, quote: "Warriors have cleared villages for lesser reasons."

Fast Forward:

The screening for Disney of the live-action *101 Dalmatians* has arrived. The word of mouth on the picture is strong. Expectations are sky-high. I'm feeling very confident as I take my place in the screening room next to the Disney brass. I had executive-produced the picture and it looks like a big hit.

I glance over two seats and there is Michael Eisner, head of Disney. Then I look at the seat next to me. Of all the people on Planet Earth I should be seated next to, it is none other than . . . Michael Ovitz!

Maybe for a very, very brief instant, I thought, "Don't sit in that seat. He's probably got it *wired* and you'll go up like a Roman candle." The Don's last hit: Feldman's Finale.

And right before I blasted off, Ovitz would snarl, "I told you not to make *Wired,* didn't I? But no-o-o-o. You just wouldn't listen."

But Ovitz was cordial, as befitting the new number-two man at Disney. The screening went well, and afterward he shook my hand and warmly congratulated me on a great picture. We chatted like old friends. Well I'll be damned.

Ovitz didn't last long at Disney—about a year. He wasn't a good fit to follow in the footsteps of the esteemed Frank Wells, but he did make a ton of money in this brief stint, reportedly $140 million. Ovitz was in the spotlight in 2004 with the mega-lawsuit over his Disney severance package. A few years before, he had surfaced in a big way when he was ranting on and on about being the victim of a Hollywood Gay Mafia. Now, if that malarkey were true, wouldn't that be something?

The Gay Mafia sticks it to Don Vito himself.

That, my friend, would be poetic justice . . . in spades!

You know, it's funny—I was supposed to be worth a nickel or less if I made *Wired.* Yet here I am. Nine years later, I produce *101 Dalmatians*—for Ovitz's company, yet. And it grosses $320 million worldwide. Then I produce *102 Dalmatians* and it grosses $180 million worldwide.

Now, that's half a billion dollars for Disney on a guy who was supposedly worth five cents.

That's as good a return on an investment as Peter Minuit's deal when he bought all the real estate in Manhattan for $24 in 1626. That stuff is worth several hundred billion now, easy.

Everybody's right. Disney really does love a bargain.

"WE DON'T DO RURAL MOVIES": THE STORY OF *WITNESS*

I TOOK KELLY MCGILLIS'S HAND IN MINE. SHE WAS TREMBLING, almost shaking. There were audible sighs. "Oh, Ed."

I grasped her hand even tighter, trying to give her confidence, to allay her fears.

I had known Kelly only a short time but that was long enough to know we had a very special relationship. And now that relationship was being put to the test.

What could I say? What could I do?

I looked at her—the unconventionally pretty face virtually exclaimed, "Oh my God, I am so afraid."

She had never done anything like this before. But it seemed so right, so natural.

We sat there in the dark sharing an intimacy unbounded by time, by space . . .

Now wait a minute . . . don't jump to conclusions.

The fact is, Kelly's nude scene in *Witness* was about to be projected for the first time and she was a basket case.

You must understand that this was only Kelly's second feature film. Five months before, she had been serving lattes in a Greenwich Village coffee bar. And now here she is, the female lead opposite Harrison Ford in a big-budget, high-profile studio picture.

The script called for Kelly to be naked from the waist up, washing herself, when Harrison passes by her open door. They exchange meaningful, seductive looks.

Almost twenty years later, this is a classic scene in a picture with more than its fair share of classic scenes. But in that screening room, Kelly wasn't thinking "classic scene," she was thinking "nude scene." Her body was being magnified on the screen by about forty times.

Now, as is the normal practice on feature films, we held a screening of the dailies at the end of each shooting day. They usually covered the previous day's filming. The dailies were very well attended—probably seventy to eighty people came by. That's kind of an amazing attendance figure in general but it makes sense because this was a Peter Weir film. Attendance at dailies is always high on a Peter Weir film.

And what they saw was fantastic.

Harrison was in his breakout dramatic role of police detective John Book. Before *Witness,* Harrison had achieved movie star status with the *Star Wars* films and the first Indiana Jones picture. But John Book was the role that would establish Harrison as a true leading man superstar.

In addition to Kelly, *Witness* launched the film careers of Danny Glover, Patti LuPone, and Viggo Mortensen, among others. It established Peter Weir as a major international, A-list director and John Seale as one of the cinema's great cameramen.

But back to Kelly's situation.

Now, I'm sensitive to what actors go through, so on the day her nude scene was to be shown, I asked Kelly, "Would you like me to close the dailies down tonight? I don't want you to be embarrassed."

Kelly looked at me with an almost indignant expression.

"What are you talking about, Ed? I'm a professional actress. That's a scene in the movie and I have no objection to anyone seeing it."

OK, that's in the morning. At 4 P.M., she comes into my office, crying and singing a different tune.

"Oh, Ed, I can't bear the thought of everybody looking at me."

And I understand that.

I said, "Look, Kelly, I'll close the dailies down. We'll do the first part of the dailies, and then I'll ask everybody but a few of us to leave. Don't worry about it."

That's what I did. Almost everyone cleared out. Even Harrison and my wife left. There were about ten of us in the room as the nude scene dailies went on. Besides Kelly and me, it was only Peter, the cameraman John Seale and his crew, and a couple of others.

But Kelly was still very nervous; her hand felt clammy and sweaty in mine.

The picture comes up. The scene is gorgeous. Beautifully filmed. But Kelly is still tense, shaking like a leaf.

I decided we needed an icebreaker.

With Kelly on the screen in all her natural glory, I yell out, "What a set of tits!"

A couple of beats and then uproarious laughter. Kelly laughed right along with the rest of us, and that was that.

Hindsight is great. Someone suggested to me recently that it must have been a cinch to set up *Witness* with a studio—that they were waiting to sign on the dotted line.

"Pick me, Ed, Sweetie."

"No, me, Ed, Darling."

"Ed, I've always admired your work. Give it to me, you great big hunk of genius, you."

But there was no Sweetie or Darling or genius or anything else re-motely like that.

Here's what I really got when I was out peddling *Witness* (and these are exact quotes):

"Ed, we don't do rural movies."

"Ed, Harrison Ford can't act."

Who said these things that seem so outrageous now?

Only the head of production at 20th Century Fox, Joe Wizan; and a very senior executive at MGM.

Every major studio that was pitched *Witness* passed on it, except

Paramount, then headed by Barry Diller, Michael Eisner, and Jeffrey Katzenberg.

And who are three of the biggest names now, twenty years later, in entertainment and media?

That's right, Barry Diller, Michael Eisner, and Jeffrey Katzenberg.

I've been talking all along about the risks of moviemaking, and here's another one for a short list—the risk of Clouded Vision.

To make unconventional, unprecedented, great movies takes Vision with a capital V.

It takes very little vision to make repetitive action movies with big stars. It takes very little vision to make sequels of hits with the same team. Just make your best deal and go.

In 2003, _Chicago_ almost swept the Academy Awards. Producer Marty Richards held the rights to that project for twenty-seven years with several false starts. Director Rob Marshall had never directed a feature film before. And who knew Gere, Zellweger, and Zeta-Jones could even sing?

Even Westerns had more life in them as a genre than musicals.

But _Chicago_ cleaned up at the box office—$300 million worldwide—and garnered big awards including the Best Picture Oscar. Who could have predicted this level of success? There were people out there who had considered _Chicago the Movie_ unmakeable.

Great Vision made _Chicago_.

Look, Hollywood loves precedent. If space movies are selling, let's make umpteen space movies until they start flopping. If the public wants gangster movies, let's give them a zillion gangster movies. Comic book heroes? We'll just dust some off and follow the green lights.

So how about _Witness_?

Well, here are the negatives for a major studio in 1983:

★ It's set in Pennsylvania Amish Country. Never been a hit movie about the Amish. (_Friendly Persuasion_ was Quaker, not Amish.)
★ Harrison Ford may be a popular star, but in effects-heavy action movies.
★ Peter Weir . . . great director, but of art house movies.

★ Do people really care about that "turn-the-other-cheek stuff"? (Yes, *that* was said.)

See the dilemma the studios are in? You can't do research to see whether *Witness* will be a critical hit and box office smash. In 1983, pre-*Witness,* you can't ask people if they want to see a movie about the Amish. You can't ask them whether they want to see Harrison Ford as a tough but sensitive cop when they know and love him as Han Solo. Or whether they want to see a movie directed by an Australian they've never heard of. Potential audiences have no frame of reference for that sort of angle. How should they know until you show them the outcome?

It would be circular—you have to show them the movie for them to know but you won't make the movie unless they answer yes.

So what's the secret? How do the *Witness*-es of the world get made by the studios?

Great Vision.

Great Vision is when the decision makers combine confidence in the creative and financial elements with good judgment and astuteness about what makes for exceptional, captivating cinema.

Unfortunately, Great Vision is in short supply in Hollywood, and that's why the risk of Clouded Vision looms so large.

I received the script of *Witness* in 1983. It was written by two television writers, William Kelley and Earl W. Wallace, and the title was *Called Home,* which is the Amish term for dying. *Witness* ended up being their first feature film credit and, interestingly, pretty much their last.

The script was far too long—182 pages—and spent an inordinate amount of time describing the customs of the Amish. While this may have been interesting in another context, we weren't making a documentary.

The script for *Witness* had been kicking around Hollywood for many years in different versions. Pamela Wallace, Earl Wallace's wife, had come up with the idea for the story, apparently as a result of some

Amish themes Kelley and Wallace had worked on when they were writing for *Gunsmoke* in the 1970s.

Several big-name directors had worked on the *Called Home* script over the years. But it was still available in 1983, when I was in a first-look development deal at Fox with my Edward S. Feldman Co.

The late David Bombyk worked with me then as a development executive. When the script came to him, his immediate reaction was, "This is a very good cop movie, but it's diluted by all the Amish stuff. But I think you could rewrite it down and make it into a real vehicle for an actor."

Overall, I thought it was a terrific piece to make a movie out of because no one had ever done a real picture about the Amish. And to mix the Amish with a detective thriller was a good combination.

So I made a deal with Kelley and Wallace's agent for a one-year option and one rewrite for $25,000, against $250,000 if the movie were actually made.

Now, I didn't check with Fox on this. I just naturally assumed they would back me on the deal. So I sent the script to Joe Wizan, and later Bombyk and I met with him.

This is when I heard those immortal words, "Ed, we don't do rural movies." Wizan didn't believe that movies about rural communities make money. Of course they can—plenty have. Look at *The Last Picture Show* or *Paper Moon*. But at that time and place, Wizan had no faith in "rural movies."

I was very disappointed walking out of Wizan's office, but Bombyk took it especially hard. With tears in his eyes, he said to me, "I can't believe it that they wouldn't back this movie."

Considering I'm on a first-look deal and they have money invested in the deal, you'd think they would do it for that reason alone.

At this point, I turn to Bombyk and say, "David, we're going to grow up, right now. I'm going to buy the option. And I'm going to buy the script. I'll pay the $25,000."

And I took the money out of the bank and paid the $25,000, and proceeded to rewrite the script with the two writers—whether Fox liked it or not.

Witness was on its way.

Kelley and Wallace were seasoned pros and they knew the big problems with the script already—problems caused by so many hands tinkering with it over the years. If you figure one page of script equals about one minute of screen time, then in this incarnation, *Witness* would run over three hours. Most features run between ninety minutes and about two hours and fifteen minutes. *Witness* was good but it didn't merit the *Gone with the Wind* treatment.

Here were the instructions I gave them for the rewrite: "Set up the picture. Get us to Philadelphia as quickly as possible. And get back to Amish country as quickly as possible."

If you remember the plot, at the beginning Kelly McGillis's—Rachel's—husband has died, and after the funeral, she and her son, Samuel, played by Lukas Haas, set out by train to spend time with her sister in Baltimore. But at a layover in Philadelphia, Samuel witnesses a brutal murder in the men's room of the Philadelphia train station. John Book—Harrison—investigates and then realizes that Samuel is in grave danger because the murder is tied to some very high-level police corruption.

So now with the rewrite, only about 40 minutes of 120 is spent in the early Amish scenes and the Philadelphia scenes. That leaves 80 minutes for the heart of the movie, which is the time Book spends with Rachel and the Amish, and for the story to be resolved.

It took Kelley and Wallace only about five to six weeks to do the rewrite. Now we had something that we could really sell.

Robert Cort was a development executive and vice president at Fox, and a friend of mine. He was assigned to my projects by the studio. Although Fox had passed on the picture initially, I showed the rewrite to Cort and he thought it was terrific.

Cort went on to produce or executive-produce forty-eight feature films to the date of this writing, including *Mr. Holland's Opus* and *Runaway Bride*. Cort has a very interesting background—he had been a CIA analyst in the 1970s before he joined the film business. Draw your own inferences.

Now with a first-look development deal, I'm required to take the script back to Fox and let them consider it again, even though they had turned it down before. This is called "changed elements." They have forty-eight hours to make a decision about producing the film.

Joe Wizan came back very quickly with this: "The script is much, much better, but we still don't make rural movies here at Fox."

I have lunch with Bob Cort and he's singing the praises of the rewrite. But he says to me, "Look, Ed, let's analyze what we've got to do. I think you need a star."

I really thought about this. Who would look good in a big black hat (when Book is incognito among the Amish)? And I think back to Gary Cooper in *Friendly Persuasion*. Well, then, who is a Gary Cooper for today? Strong but likable. Tough but vulnerable. A man of few well-chosen words. Possessing an enormous amount of inner strength.

Harrison Ford.

I had seen Harrison in a number of pictures, some successful, some not so successful. But Harrison was hot as fire then. Cort thought Harrison was a fabulous idea.

I didn't know Harrison at the time, but I sent the script over to Phil Gersh, Harrison's agent, on a Thursday. And on the next Monday, Harrison committed to the project without a formal deal.

But now it's "changed elements" again. I have to go back to Fox and they have another forty-eight hours to decide whether they want to produce it.

My deal at Fox wasn't really that good, and as the project was coming together so nicely, I'm thinking, now I'd be better off if they passed.

I got my wish.

Here's Wizan again: "Ed, we love Harrison Ford around here. *(They'd better: the* Star Wars *saga was a major cash cow for them.)* We think he's a great actor. But we just don't do rural movies at Fox."

My God, that rural movie thing was turning into a Fox mantra.

I was quite surprised they passed again. I had thought that with Harrison Ford on board, and with a cop thriller, and with a not-outrageous budget, even with Harrison's salary, they would finally see the light. But they didn't. I was now free to place *Witness* at another studio.

I hired Phil Gersh to represent me in shopping the project around town.

Warner passed. They didn't want to pay Harrison's fee, which was $2 million. (The total budget was $12 million, which would be about $50 million nowadays.)

MGM passed. "Harrison Ford can't act," said the executive.

Harrison passed on Universal. Something about they had replaced him with Mel Gibson on a picture and he wasn't happy about it.

Finally, Paramount, God love them. Yes, Paramount adores the script. Yes, Harrison Ford will star. Yes, Ed, you will produce. But we need a director.

I came up with the name of Peter Weir myself. My wife, Lorraine, and I had attended a screening of Peter's *The Year of Living Dangerously.* As we were coming out of the theater, I told Lorraine, "Now *that's* a *director!*"

So I give the script to his agent, John Ptak, who is also my agent. But Ptak tells me that Peter is preparing his first American movie, *The Mosquito Coast,* for Warner and is unavailable.

We go through an assortment of directors over a period of four to five months with Harrison sticking with me all the way. Peter Yates *(Bullitt)* wants to do the movie but he leaves me in a couple of months because a little picture that he wanted to make his whole life has come together. Arthur Penn *(Bonnie and Clyde)* is interested but Paramount declines. John Badham *(Saturday Night Fever)* dismisses it as just another cop movie and passes. (I didn't tell Harrison what Badham said—I was afraid it would spook him.) I knew Ed Zwick's television work and thought he had great potential, but Paramount wouldn't approve him back then. (He later did *Glory* and *Legends of the Fall.*)

Now we're going months upon months, and people are starting to recommend less than A-list directors, but I won't give in. It's hard to find a piece of merchandise like this. And I knew Harrison wouldn't perform for a director he didn't have confidence in.

Finally, they're so desperate that they want me to use an English director who had done a famous historical piece for British television. But I say Harrison would never approve him—too inexperienced. They say, "Ed, keep him happy for now anyway. Take him on location, show him what you're going to do."

I knew this was a waste of time and I hated doing this to him. He was a decent man but he would never direct *Witness*.

All of a sudden in my moment of desperation, I get a call from somebody at Warner telling me that Peter Weir's picture is in turn-around. And I call up John Ptak. John says, "Peter will never do this kind of movie, Ed. He's not going to do a cop movie."

"John, if you don't send the script to him, I'll send it."

So off goes the script by FedEx to Peter in Australia. Four days later I get a call from him in Sydney: "Ed, I like your script very much and I want to get to work. I'm coming up soon and I want to do the picture."

And I was absolutely in fantasyland. I told Jeffrey Katzenberg and you would have thought he had just been injected with adrenaline. He was so thrilled I thought he would fall down. Peter was hot and he was relatively inexpensive.

We have the script, the star, the studio, and the director. *Witness* is a go. The light is green and the road is clear . . . but we'd better step on it. Because a possible Directors Guild strike is looming very large, almost five months away.

Michael Eisner opened the lunch meeting this way: "You know, the word is out that you're going to direct this movie, Peter. I got a call this morning from Robert Redford's agent. He would like to do the movie."

How things can change almost overnight. All of a sudden, *Witness* and Peter Weir are very hot properties in Hollywood. In February 1984, Robert Redford was a star of enormous stature. And he wanted to do *Witness*. A proven dramatic actor and a proven box office draw in his own right. Tempting, very tempting.

But pay close attention, all you aspiring producers out there, because Redford, as talented and desirable as he was, would have been a risky idea. Here's what I told Peter then and I will always believe it: "Peter, listen to me. You'll spend the next year rewriting the script a dozen times and at the end of the year, who knows? Redford could find another project that he would be happy with."

We were ready to go right then—top director, A-list actor, possible strike looming large. Most superstar actors want rewrites when they enter projects. It just happens. If we had gone the Redford route, tempting as it was, it could have been disastrous and I knew it.

After I said my piece to Peter, there was silence. I looked around the lunch table. Diller, Eisner, Katzenberg, Peter. No one said anything for a moment, and then Eisner spoke up, "Peter, listen to Ed."

Paramount wanted to go ahead and make the movie, and get it done before the potential strike. They were set. Besides, at this point, they were more excited about Peter Weir's directing his first American movie with *them* than anything else. They loved the script and were excited about Harrison, but they were *ecstatic* over Peter. So ecstatic that they were willing to sacrifice Harrison to keep Peter happy. Listen to this—

Later in the lunch, Diller says to Peter, "Look, I'm sending you to Wyoming to meet Harrison Ford. But I'm telling you right now, Peter, if he doesn't want to do the movie with you, *you're* doing the movie and we'll get another actor."

Then he added for emphasis, "*You* are the director of this movie."

Now, I had never worked with Peter and Harrison before, so Diller's statement, though a wonderful affirmation for Peter, was guaranteed to give me heartburn. If Harrison didn't like Peter, we would be out looking for another top star, and the movie would almost inevitably be delayed.

But I shouldn't have worried. Peter is a winsome, intelligent, engaging man. Peter and Harrison fell in love. They got along famously and, by the end of the shoot, had bonded like brothers.

Before you knew it, they were working together again—on Peter's project that had gone into turnaround earlier, *The Mosquito Coast*.

We had only ten weeks to prepare the picture, but with Peter directing we were in great shape.

Casting the female lead, though, was somewhat problematical. Peter originally was very interested in Glenn Close for Rachel. Glenn had just opened in Tom Stoppard's *The Real Thing* on Broadway, produced and directed by Mike Nichols and costarring Jeremy Irons. And it looked like they were settled in for a long run.

But Glenn, in turn, was very interested in doing *Witness*. Her show had been on for about three months, and her agent said to me, "You get her the part and I'll get her out of the show." And I said, "That's impossible. Mike Nichols would never allow it. Brand new show on Broadway." She and Irons were hot items in New York right then.

Peter then wanted Isabella Rossellini. But she and her agent wouldn't wait for two weeks so we could get her approved. She went over to the Mikhail Baryshnikov picture, *White Knights*. Peter eventually did work with her on *Fearless*.

Then Peter decided we should use a German actress to play Rachel because Amish women typically learn German before they learn English, and he has someone in mind. He tells me that she speaks perfect English. One day she calls the hotel in New York to speak to Peter, and I pick up the phone.

"Hallo, Mr. Veer, this is so and so. Not Mr. Veer? Vell, I vant talk to hum ubot *Veetniss*."

I called to Peter, "Your English-speaking actress is on the phone."

Then there was Kelly McGillis. When she came to read for us, she had done one other feature, *Reuben, Reuben*. She arrives and the first thing out of her mouth is, "Well, I hadn't had a chance to read the script."

I figured Peter's going to pass on this girl fast, but he said, "I want you to read the script and come back two days from now." And she was great. So we do a screen test. There wasn't much money in the budget for tests, so we film it in sixteen millimeter and I'm reading the part of Rachel's Amish grandfather. (Needless to say, *I* didn't get the role.)

Kelly does well in the test and it looks like she'll be Rachel. But Harrison is unimpressed. He doesn't feel she's right for the part.

And then Peter says something that sends chills down my spine and a burn to my heart: "Harrison, if you're going to work with me, you've got to trust me. And if you don't want to trust me, *you shouldn't make the movie*."

Did I just hear, "You shouldn't make the movie"?

I'm stunned. No one says anything. I'm guessing Harrison might next say something on the order of, "I'm sorry, Ed, Peter, but I'm out of here."

But that doesn't happen. Harrison slowly turns to me and says, "Well then, I guess she's in the picture."

Paramount originally wanted me to film in Washington State because there's an Amish community there. They figured the very strict Pennsylvania Amish would never cooperate with us. Well, one thing about the Amish is that they do like money. Now they won't appear on film but they're great carpenters and electricians. And so I promised them if they worked on the movie, they would never be shown on camera, even as extras. So the barn-raising scene is basically populated with Mennonites with beards.

We shot everything in Lancaster, Pennsylvania, and Philadelphia. We did some interiors—the police station and the train station men's room—on stages we constructed in an old factory in Lancaster. All the rest of the interiors were in real buildings or houses.

The shoot was very smooth. Everyone worked hard, things came together, and we wrapped up on June 28, 1984, three days before the threatened Directors Guild strike, which never materialized, by the way.

I came in within the 10 percent budget contingency. We had been very efficient in our spending—so much so that I cautioned Jeffrey Katzenberg about not coming out to the set in a helicopter. It would've looked bad because I had been crying poor to the production the whole time. He drove a rental car instead.

Incidentally, the title changed from *Called Home* to *Witness* about halfway through the shoot, when a frustrated marketing department at Paramount decided that it would be an uphill battle to try to sell a *Called Home*.

The picture had gone extremely well . . . until we got to the editing. We had a famous world-class editor on the picture from New York, but he had no concept of the movie. When he showed us the first half of the movie cut together, it was very disappointing. He had cut all the classy, atmospheric footage out—the wheat moving and the Amish in their day-to-day activities. His cut played like a routine episode of a cop show on TV.

The day we had seen the cut, Peter came to me after dailies. There was a ferocious storm outside and I suspected it might be an omen of what was ahead. Peter said, "This guy doesn't understand the movie. What are we going to do?"

I said, "Well, we're going to let him go, and I will put all the dailies back into individual takes." In other words, undo everything the editor had done.

We did that but it was surprisingly hard to get a new editor because Peter wanted to work on post-production in Australia. We said to prospective editors, take your wife, take your girlfriend, whomever you want, but still it was tough getting someone to commit. Finally, we sign Thom Noble, who had done *Fahrenheit 451* with François Truffaut, and he and Peter went to Australia for ten weeks and I never heard from them.

Then one day, I get a call from Peter: you and Harrison come down and see the picture. Now, it's a long way to Australia, but Harrison and I wanted to see the cut before Paramount did. So we fly to Sydney with our wives to see Peter's cut of the movie.

Now, Harrison is pretty nervous before the screening—this is the film that could take his career to new heights as a dramatic actor. And I was pretty tense too. We get a few Scotches under our belts and then go off to see the picture.

It was terrific. Peter and Thom Noble had done a brilliant job. We exit the theater, Harrison looks at me, and he gives me the biggest wink I've ever seen. He says, "Ed, I think we've got something very big here."

Boy, was he right.

I couldn't have been any prouder of *Witness.*

In 1986, we were nominated for eight Academy Awards including Best Picture. Harrison was nominated for Best Actor; Peter for Best Director; John Seale for Best Cinematography; Maurice Jarre for Best Original Score; and Stan Jolley and John H. Anderson for Best Art Direction–Set Decoration.

William Kelley and Earl Wallace, along with Pamela Wallace, won the Academy Award for Best Original Screenplay. And Thom Noble won for Best Editing.

We were nominated for six Golden Globes and seven BAFTAs (British Academy of Film and Television Arts). Kelly McGillis was included in these nominations.

We did very well at the box office, with a total worldwide gross topping $100 million, which would be around $200 million today. The movie opened to moderate business and then stayed in the top ten for months as people discovered the film.

Remember how John Badham had dismissed *Witness* as "just another cop movie"? Many years later, one night he and I had a drink. And he's laughing. "Consider the irony, Ed. I, who have made some of the least successful cop stories in recent memory, dismissed *your picture* as a just a cop story."

After *Witness,* Peter's career exploded, as he worked steadily on high-profile, unique films that garnered him accolades everywhere.

With *Witness,* Harrison had made the jump to dramatic leading man and proved he could play almost any lead role in the film universe with skill and conviction—drama, comedy, action, villain. Harrison Ford—Everyman and Movie Star.

For me, *Witness* was one of two major career turning points. The first was *Save the Tiger,* where I established myself as a true movie producer, and *Witness,* where I showed I could delivery a high-quality, artistically strong but popular major studio feature.

Witness was the opening-night film at the Cannes Film Festival. Harrison, Kelly, Maurice Jarre, the writers, Peter, and I were all there.

Let me tell you that Cannes is one of the toughest audiences you'll ever encounter. But after the end credits rolled, the audience gave us a standing ovation. They cheered and applauded for several minutes.

Now, I know that Cannes is for the creative people—the directors, actors, writers—and it should be. The lights came on and the searchlights come down and the searchlights are on Kelly and Harrison, on Maurice Jarre and Peter Weir. My wife is sitting between Peter and me.

And amid this thunderous ovation, Peter reaches across Lorraine and grabs my hand for me to stand in the spotlight and share it with him.

I don't know how many directors in the world would ever do that.

There we were. Peter and I, standing together, hands clasped, bathed in the glow of our little "rural" movie.

It was the most exciting moment of my life.

RISKS AND REWARDS:
THE TRUMAN SHOW

LAUREN HOLLY IS PLENTY UPSET WITH ME: "ED, YOU TOLD US we would have a GIII. That Westwind is *not* a GIII."

"But Lauren, the Westwind is almost the same size as the GIII and they both go five hundred miles an hour."

I had gone to a lot of trouble to set this up. So I might have said, It's the Westwind. Take it or leave it.

But Lauren was married to the proverbial eight-hundred-pound gorilla, Jim Carrey, one of the biggest stars in the business. And you did not dismiss such a personage lightly.

Especially when he's starring in a $70 million picture you're producing, *The Truman Show.*

How did I get into the world of GIIIs and Westwinds? Such is the life of a movie producer.

We were shooting *Truman* in the panhandle of Florida, near Panama City. Lauren's new movie with MGM, *Turbulence,* was premiering in Los Angeles, and Lauren was to make her big entrance. And by the way, MGM wanted to make sure Lauren's husband, Mr. Carrey, was there too.

We had arranged the shooting schedule to work around Carrey's absence and I assumed MGM would send over a jet. Wrong. It turned out *we* were supposed to provide the plane in addition to covering for our star. No one ever explained to me why *The Truman Show,* a Paramount film, was absorbing the cost of Jim Carrey's attending an MGM premiere.

Now, in the overall scheme of things, it wasn't a huge amount of money. But I was the one person primarily responsible for the *Truman* budget. Paramount and Scott Rudin looked to me to manage the money and to spend it wisely. That's what they pay me for.

I had arranged for Carrey and wife to fly to L.A. on the Paramount jet, a Gulfstream GIII. And I'll have to say, this is a very fine way to travel. The GIII can easily accommodate ten people, but it would be only the two of them on the round trip.

Unlike Warners, which had several jets, Paramount had only one and I was not able to book it for the return trip. Sumner Redstone, the CEO of Paramount's parent company, Viacom, was using it and he outranked even Jim Carrey.

To rent a GIII to bring the Carreys back from L.A. would cost around $33,000, and it would be charged to my budget, as was the flight out to L.A. So I did some shopping around and found I could rent another jet for $18,000 less. This plane was that Westwind Lauren was railing about. It would get Carrey and wife back to Florida in about the same time but it wouldn't be quite as roomy. That didn't seem a problem to me; after all, there were only two people, right? Plus the plane suited its owner, an important man and connoisseur of air travel.

But it was a big problem for Mrs. Jim Carrey.

She's sitting in my office near the *Truman* set and has rejected the Westwind outright. "It's not adequate, Ed. It's just not adequate."

Then she says something guaranteed to chill the spine of a producer down to his soul: "And if we don't get a GIII, then Jim may not be back on Tuesday to resume production."

Whoa there. That crosses the line. Remember how Steve McQueen had told me something like that in connection with not riding his motorcycles during the shooting of *Bullitt* before we had insurance coverage? That the main things in life he cared about were his *balls* and his *bikes*? Then he showed up anyway, right on the dot—albeit with slightly shrunken gonads.

For an actor not to show up on the set is a very serious breach of contract. So at this point I say, "Lauren, this is beyond me. I think you should have your lawyer call up the head of Business Affairs at Paramount, Bill Bernstein, and tell him that."

Understand, I wasn't talking to Jim Carrey himself in my office. After having worked with him closely on this picture, I suspect he didn't care a whit whether he flew on a GIII or a Westwind. He was much more concerned with his personal safety and privacy. Plus he was about as nonconfrontational as you could imagine for a megastar. Very collegial and cooperative. A wonderful man.

No, this was the wife's idea and she had her mind made up.

So how did all this work out?

The studio told me, "Ed, don't hassle Jim Carrey for eighteen thousand dollars. Get him whatever he wants. Keep him happy."

So the Carreys flew back in a GIII and that was that.

I don't want you to get the impression that *The Truman Show* was one headache after another. Far from it. The GIII situation was an aberration. Aside from having to replace Dennis Hopper with Ed Harris, as I recounted earlier, the shoot went very smoothly. I was working with Peter Weir, one of a handful of outstanding directors in the business; Jim Carrey, a talented and cooperative star, giving the performance of his career; and a dynamite script, one of the most original in years. We had a dream cast: Laura Linney, Natascha McElhone, Holland Taylor, Noah Emmerich; then later, Harris.

But producing a film, any film, especially a very expensive, high-profile film, consists of hundreds of individual decisions in which one miscue can be very troublesome and costly. In addition to managing the money, it is my job to keep things humming along smoothly, so that the creative talent can do their jobs to the fullest.

People will flourish on a happy, pleasant set and that's the atmosphere I always strive for, usually successfully. For me personally, *Truman* was a wonderful experience, and I think it was for everyone else.

———

I became attached to *The Truman Show* in 1996, while I was finishing *101 Dalmatians* in London for Disney. I got a call from Peter Weir, telling me about the project and asking me if I'd like to executive-produce. *Truman* had been developed by Scott Rudin, probably the most astute judge of high-quality material in the business. I had never worked with Rudin before, but my son, Richard, had when Rudin was head of production at Fox.

This film was truly a Scott Rudin Production, but Rudin has his hands in many different projects at one time. So it was important to have a strong, empowered executive producer on site to manage the production. I had worked very successfully with Peter Weir before on *Witness* and *Green Card,* and I was the one he wanted on *Truman.*

You must understand that *Truman* was considered something of a risky project. Although Jim Carrey was aboard and he had a string of hits behind him, plus a regiment of devoted fans, he was known as a very broad, physical comic. On *Truman,* he was playing essentially a dramatic role. Now there were humorous moments in the picture and Carrey was laugh-out-loud funny. But it was definitely a drama, not a comedy.

This picture would eventually be shooting 2,200 miles away from studio headquarters, with an untested dramatic actor and a very big budget. A lot could go wrong, and that's when the studio is happy to have me sign on the dotted line.

For *The Truman Show* to work—for the audience to believe that a man could be the unwitting star of his own life as a twenty-four-hour-a-day TV show—the details of the script had to be as plausible as possible. The original script I saw when I returned to L.A. from my stint in London had Truman living in a large, fictional U.S. city and taking the subway to work every day.

This setup was problematic. We were asking the audience to believe that a man lives a cocoonlike existence, his friends and family are all paid actors, and his life is scripted and choreographed in every detail. *And* that this could be carried out in the middle of a large city. It required far too much suspension of disbelief.

We solved the problem by moving Truman to a fictional beachfront town, large enough to give him a good quality of life but small enough so that the audience would believe the town could fit into a domed soundstage in Los Angeles, between Hollywood and Burbank. Even as a small town, this studio was, according to the picture, the largest man-made structure in the world.

Our problems dealing with this setting were not unlike the problems facing the producers of the fictional TV series—we had to film this picture in what would pass for a controlled setting but was plausible as a real town. We couldn't just use any old real town because Truman's town was the ultimate planned community. It was another person's view of an idyllic life, created just for Truman. It was as if a designer were given a blank slate and told to fashion the "perfect" town. It wouldn't look like what we have now. It would be "perfected."

Just the setting itself was clearly going to be very expensive.

I meet with Paramount chief Sherry Lansing about the budget and she says, "Look, Ed, I can't make this movie for more than fifty million."

I had reviewed the financial commitments we already had—talent, script, producers—and they added up to some $31 million. And it wasn't mainly that Jim Carrey is high-priced. He was earning good money on the picture but nowhere near his usual $20 million. Now $50 million less $31 million is $19 million, and that wasn't going to be enough. So I said to Lansing, "But I've gotta have some money to make the movie." I didn't want to start the movie fearing we would go into overage and have a lot of pressure on us.

So Lansing says, "All right, I'll get you sixty million."

By Hollywood standards, this is a fairly modest budget for a major picture with a big, big star and significant special effects. We just didn't have the money to build our fictional town from scratch and have it be believable as a place where a man could live captive for thirty years in modern times and still have a good quality of life.

We had to find a real place and that place turned out to be Seaside, Florida.

We had decided Florida was the place where we would shoot *The Tru-man Show*. We needed a coastal community with warm weather be-cause we would be filming in winter. And Florida had the advantage of being a "right to work" state. Although this was a union picture, the unions were fairly easy to work with there.

We sent location scouts around the east coast of Florida, but it was too developed for us. Then Wendy Stites, Peter's wife and collaborator, told us of a place she had read about in an architectural magazine that might fill the bill. Peter and the production designer, Dennis Gassner, went there and it was as if God had spoken to us. It was perfect.

Seaside is a planned community developed by Robert Davis. Davis's grandfather had purchased the property—eighty acres with a half mile of beachfront—in 1946 with the intention of building a recreational camp for the employees of his company. But the property was still un-developed when Davis inherited it in the 1970s.

Davis's idea was to create a community of homes that would reflect the old idyllic building designs and construction methods of a bygone era. These would be basically wooden beach cottages, but upscale.

The houses were built in three-quarter scale. They all had to have a widow's walk. They all had to have only foliage in front, no gardens. And each house on each street had to have a wooden picket fence, but no two fences on the same street could be the same. When Davis sold the first houses, they went for $20,000, $22,000. Now they're worth millions. And the fact that their size is three quarters of the size of a normal house made it look interesting. No rambling houses. It was like an organized, structured community where you could believe such a fantasy was going on.

Now all we had to do was get the approval of the people who ran Seaside. This turned out to be not an insignificant task, even though Peter Weir had really turned on the charm in the initial meeting.

Now wait. Let me back up, ". . . not an insignificant task." No, actu-ally this was the toughest deal of my career. For one thing, the Seaside residents were pretty well off. We would be paying substantial location fees but they didn't need the money. Plus we would be a major incon-venience for about three months. Closing streets, telling people they couldn't go to their own houses. It's fun to watch moviemaking for a few days, get a glimpse of Jim Carrey, maybe even serve as an extra for a few scenes. But eventually it becomes tiresome and disruptive. The residents weren't exactly welcoming our film company with open arms.

They were saying things like, "We don't *need* you here and we don't *want* you here."

But what they *did* need at Seaside was a new schoolhouse and we could provide it. Now *that* was interesting to them.

There was a strong vocal group of opponents to our coming to Seaside and they made things difficult from the beginning. Luckily for us, Robert Davis was in favor of it and he carried a lot of weight.

Davis is a businessman and he could see that being featured in a major movie could only enhance the reputation and visibility of Seaside. He was right. Much later, after Seaside had signed on, Davis and crew sent promotional material to people throughout the Southeast, inviting them to come to Seaside, stay in one of these quaint old-world cottages, and watch a big Jim Carrey movie being made. And while they were there, think about buying into the Seaside dream.

But going back to the beginning, after five weeks of negotiation, we still didn't have a deal with Seaside. Suddenly I said, "Look, the problem you have is that you don't understand the motion picture business. Paramount will pay for any lawyer you want who knows something about the business. Paramount will pay his fee." They had lawyers but not someone versed in movie production. So they picked a lawyer in Atlanta and he was someone of reason we could talk to. We closed the deal and we paid them several millions of dollars to shoot the film. Plus the schoolhouse.

By the way, I figured if we were paying their lawyer, closing the deal was the only way that lawyer was going to get paid. A strong incentive for the deal to get done.

Now, I appointed myself Goodwill Ambassador to the people of Seaside. I would give talks to the residents, going over our plans in detail and trying to extol the virtues of having a movie company in their midst. I would occasionally trot out my secret weapon, Peter Weir, before these groups, and, as usual, he was charming and winsome.

One day, we're shooting on a street and an assistant director begins to push back the people who are watching the shooting fifty yards. He was brusque and it was getting a little tense. Finally I said, "Listen, this is their street. Be careful what you say. These people could easily tell us to drop dead and go find some other street."

I first met Jim Carrey at a meeting attended by Carrey, his manager, Peter, and me. He had been attached to the picture for a long time, well before I became involved. In fact, Peter had to wait a year for Carrey to finish another film before he could start *Truman*.

Let me tell you that Jim Carrey is not at all like his public persona. He is soft-spoken, polite, self-deprecating. As my late mother, Gertrude Feldman, would say, "a very nice boy."

Unlike many comics, he doesn't feel the need to be "on" all the time. And he is a very good actor. I believe that to be a good comic, you have to be a good actor. And he took direction well.

But Jim Carrey has built up a huge career on doing certain tried-and-true bits. For the first three days of shooting, he was over the top, doing that Jim Carrey shtick that is his trademark. And Peter just let him go. Do whatever he wanted. Then on the third day, Peter says to him, "OK, Jim, are you finished now? I mean, you've done your number. Now we're going to make a movie, right?" And Carrey was fine after that. He had gotten it out of his system. (Peter had done the same thing with Robin Williams on *Dead Poets Society*.)

Jim Carrey was a pretty undemanding superstar, but he did want a nice place to live during the shoot. We located a wonderful beach house right on the Gulf, about five miles from the set. We had looked at another house earlier, and he was OK with it. Carrey, a location manager, and I met at this new house, and he was now ecstatic. "Where did you find this, Ed?"

It was new, very lavishly but tastefully furnished, and relatively secluded. This was good because Carrey was very particular about security and privacy. Many times, big stars just stay in a hotel during a shoot. Harrison Ford stayed in a downtown Toronto hotel on *K-19*. (Don't need much security in Canada.) I personally was staying at the Hilton in Destin, Florida, during *Truman*.

But it was much easier to guard Carrey if he was in an out-of-the-way house. You see, he was almost obsessed with the fear that someone would shoot him during the filming. He has his own personal security people and then we augmented those during the production. But he was afraid of crowds and preferred to stay in the back. I kidded him once, "Jim, when was the last time you ever heard of an actor getting shot on location?"

I could protect him from gun-wielding crazies but I couldn't protect him from acts of God Almighty. One night we were filming on the beach with Carrey and Natascha McElhone, and suddenly lightning is upon us. I didn't know this before, but Carrey is deathly afraid of electrical storms. He runs over to his car, jumps in the back, gets down on the floor, and tells the driver, "Take me home." And we are done for the night.

Peter Weir has always been a past master of casting. Think about *The Year of Living Dangerously,* starring Mel Gibson, one of Peter's early successes. Who would have thought to cast a Caucasian woman as a small Oriental *man*? Peter did, and Linda Hunt won an Academy Award for her portrayal. Many actors and actresses, well known now but relatively unknown before, got big breaks in Peter Weir films: Kelly McGillis, Danny Glover, Viggo Mortensen, Andie MacDowell, Natascha McElhone, Paul Giamatti, Peter Krause.

The part of Truman's wife was absolutely critical to our film, almost equal in importance to Christof, the show's creator and director, and was a casting challenge. This actress would portray a woman who had been hired to be the wife in a TV series. An actress playing an actress playing a devoted wife. But her character would be on call to provide love and affection to Truman twenty-four hours a day, even though, in all likelihood, she really didn't care much for him personally.

Peter originally cast Mary-Louise Parker, a fine stage and film actress, to play Meryl. (Meryl was the character's name on the show itself. Her "real" name was Hannah Gill.) Parker has made a specialty of playing rather offbeat, slightly off-center characters. Not long ago, she won a Tony Award for her portrayal on Broadway of a mathematical genius's mentally unbalanced daughter in *Proof*. (That part is played in the film version by Gwyneth Paltrow.) And she won Emmy and Golden Globe awards in 2004 as the unstable Mormon wife in *Angels in America*.

When Peter saw her, he fell in love with her for the role of Meryl. He thought she was incredible. So Parker is set for Meryl and we're ready to go. Then I get a call one day from the William Morris Agency telling me, "Listen, she's got another picture, but she can do both pictures simultaneously."

I said, "Well, maybe you think so, but Peter Weir doesn't do that with actors. If she wants to be in *The Truman Show,* she's not doing the other picture."

Acting in a Peter Weir film is a full-time job, not something you do in your spare time. Sometimes you'll see actors doing two projects at once, especially when a television star is doing a film. But it's very difficult to coordinate this and it's especially hard on the actor, who has to shuttle between two sets and go in and out of two different characters.

So for reasons unknown to me, she did the other picture. For posterity, Mary-Louise Parker turned down the third lead in *The Truman Show* directed by Peter Weir, the picture *Esquire* called "the movie of the decade," to do a small, forgettable independent movie that pretty much went straight to video.

Peter is now very disheartened because he had his mind set on Parker. I said, "Look, Peter, she's not the only woman in the world. What if she didn't exist? There's got to be someone else."

So our casting director, Howard Feuer, found Laura Linney, and Peter met with her in Atlanta and naturally fell in love with her for Meryl. And she was cast in the part. *Truman* was Laura Linney's big breakthrough role. Laura was a graduate of the Juilliard School in New York, one of the premiere acting programs in the country. She had performed in many stage productions and appeared in a number of pictures, with her stature constantly on the rise. She received strong notices on *Primal Fear* as the chain-smoking, salty-tongued D.A. with the All-American, blond good looks. She was the female lead in the action film *Congo,* and had just wrapped as Clint Eastwood's daughter in *Absolute Power* when she came with us.

Laura meshed with this role so well it's hard now to imagine any other actress as Meryl. Over the course of the picture, Meryl slowly comes apart at the seams. The pressure to be Truman's wife, especially when Truman is coming to the realization that things in his life are staged, is becoming too much for her. She has to maintain her perky wholesomeness and hawk sponsors' products to boot, while dealing with the increasingly suspicious and erratic Truman.

Laura really shone in the climactic scene between Truman and Meryl, when she has to keep up the wifely facade and counter Truman's accusations: "Why do you want to have a baby with me? You can't stand me."

Meryl then finally unravels completely: she steps out of character and addresses Christof in his heavenly control booth: "How can anyone expect me to carry on under these conditions? It's not *professional!*" It is a terrific scene, a highlight of the movie, and often cited by critics in giving strong reviews to Laura's performance.

Laura always comes well prepared to a role. She even devised a backstory that had Meryl being paid an extra $7,000 every time she had sex with Truman. We were PG, so that would have been off-camera.

Laura was nominated for a Blockbuster Entertainment Award for *Truman*. She went on to garner an Academy Award nomination for *You Can Count on Me* (losing out to Julia Roberts), and a Golden Globe nomination for that same role. Within a two-year span, Laura was nominated for an Academy Award, nominated for a Tony Award for Broadway, and won an Emmy Award for television. The big three— film, stage, and television.

In 2004–2005, Laura repeated the cycle again: Academy Award and Tony nominations, and an Emmy win.

For Ed Feldman, movie producer, Laura Linney will always occupy a very special place in my heart, beyond even for her exquisite performance in *Truman*. Over my long career, only three actors I have dined with have picked up the check—*Harrison Ford, Jack Gilford,* and *Laura Linney.*

The Truman Show is but one more lesson that the film business is incredibly risky. Let's review why. For starters, movies with big stars and top directors are usually very expensive, routinely approaching $100 million. Plus it can cost upward of $20 million to market the film. And there are few guarantees that a movie will be successful. Granted, the huge DVD market, a fairly recent phenomenon, can cushion part of the risk. But the opening weekend of a movie sets the trajectory for the film's entire income cycle from theatrical release to home video to cable TV to broadcast TV. Tens of millions of dollars hinge on the first three days of theatrical release. (Or if there is a Wednesday opening or if a holiday is involved, up to five days.)

The box office gross from those three days is maddeningly difficult to predict even just a *week* before opening day. Imagine trying to predict these numbers *two or three years* in advance before okaying a $100 million outlay.

Studios try to manage this risk in any number of ways. Much of the time they do this by investing in big stars with a proven box office track record. But this is far from foolproof. Think of all the big movies with bankable stars that have tanked at the box office. Jim Carrey's third dramatic film, after *Truman* and *Man on the Moon, The Majestic,* did that.

Another approach is to diversify their offerings. Any serious investor knows the importance of a diversified portfolio. So the studios will offer a variety of genres—big action movies, lighthearted comedies, slasher pics, serious dramas. This also allows a diversification across budgets. Big action movies will always cost the most, but slasher pics usually come in for a fraction of the top budget offerings.

The upfront sale of foreign distribution rights is a huge source of money to finance the film and to reduce the risk exposure of making it. It is much easier to market these rights if a big star is attached; hence, another incentive to sign on the Tom Hanks and Julia Roberts of the world, even at massive salaries.

Yet even with all these precautions, the average studio picture loses money.

My contribution to this unbalanced equation is at the production end. It is my responsibility to manage the making of the movie so that it is a high-quality product but brought in at its budgeted amount. I try to ensure we get the most bang for the buck. That's why I get so upset with "dead overhead," such as the money we spent to fly the Carreys back on a GIII instead of a Westwind. The movie is no better or worse because of that expenditure. The $800,000 for Ed Harris to replace Dennis Hopper was money well spent and, in my opinion, made *The Truman Show* a considerably better film. True, it would have been better (and cheaper) if we had cast Harris to begin with. But such is the nature of moviemaking that we are just not able to make the optimum decisions up-front all the time—we have to try things and sometimes they don't work out. We hope they will most of the time.

Another way for studios to manage risk is to partner on individual films. I mentioned earlier that Fox had partnered with Paramount on *Titanic*. That turned out to be a bonanza for Paramount, whose investment was capped at a fixed amount. So when the picture went wildly over budget, Paramount was protected from the overage, yet shared in the enormous income.

Paramount partners on almost every big-budget picture it makes. And it did so in 1997 except on one picture—*The Truman Show.* Paramount was shouldering the entire cost and this created pressure.

Sherry Lansing agreed to increase the *Truman* budget to $60 million pretty soon after I got involved. But even that was unrealistic. We ended up at $70 million, and let me tell you, there was very little fat in that budget. People sometimes marvel that I can command the details of these enormous budgets or that I would be concerned over a $33,000 airplane expenditure, an almost infinitesimal portion of the total budget. But remember, this is what I do for a living and I believe it is one of the keys to my success as a producer. These relatively small amounts can add up quickly.

I had a tense exchange with Dennis Gassner, our production designer and a perfectionist, over money matters.

"Ed," he sniffed, "I don't design to budgets."

Wrong thing to say to Ed Feldman.

"Well, Dennis, do you design to *unemployment*?"

"But Ed," you may protest, "it's not your money. Lighten up. Come on, these big studios are rich. Live a little."

I firmly believe that you cannot have that attitude and be a successful film producer. You have to *manage the money as if it's your own.* For one thing, the studio can sense your attitude toward their money. Paramount might have told me to back off on the GIII issue, but they certainly weren't mad at me for it, for watching their interests.

I think I did a pretty good job of managing Paramount's $70 million on *The Truman Show.* The movie came in on time, almost at budget, and was in very good shape. All that, even with having to replace the second lead after we had begun his scenes.

The first test screenings of *Truman* didn't go very well. Not many people know this, but the initial cut of the movie started with the introduction to the *Truman* TV show: "Coming to you now from Seahaven Island . . . It's *The Truman Show!*" The audience knew immediately that they were watching a movie about a man whose life is a TV show. And it just didn't work. The audience was in on too much, too early. I was one of a chorus of people who saw an easy fix to this problem.

Peter simply moved the revelation of the TV show to about the sixty-minute mark, with miraculous results. The audience was now merely watching this man's rather humdrum life, knowing something is out of kilter but not being able to pinpoint the reason. As the film reaches a dramatic crescendo, all is revealed. The test scores went up.

But *Truman* never tested all that well for reasons unknown to me. This was somewhat surprising, given that it became a smash hit.

Now it's time to show it to Sherry Lansing, chief of Paramount. I had no dealings with Lansing during the actual production. Michelle Manning, president of production, was my contact on the film.

So Peter, Scott Rudin, and I trek to Paramount one afternoon to screen the movie for Lansing. Now in the movie business, timing is essential. And our timing on this screening, to put it bluntly, stank.

Lansing had just screened *Titanic* that morning. "Ah ha," you're thinking, "Ed, *The Truman Show* is a great picture . . . but it's no *Titanic!*"

Wrong you are. That wasn't the problem.

Paramount was very nervous about *Titanic.* The company had put tens of millions of dollars at risk in a picture that a lot of people thought would, well, sink . . . a picture a lot of people thought would *tank.* OK, try *croak.*

Hollywood didn't know *Titanic* would be a megahit until it opened in theaters. Until then, a potential disaster . . . er, *debacle.*

So Lansing saw *Titanic* in the morning and *Truman* in the afternoon. As I cited in Chapter 1, she thought *Truman* was an art film, which really means: good picture but no big crowds.

Then she proceeded to express her problems with the film in very forceful language to Peter Weir, and he quickly exited her office. Scott Rudin and I walk her to her car, and Rudin asks, "Sherry, what's wrong? I've never seen you like that."

Big risk exposure will do that to people. Tons of money on the line and no guaranteed payout. We've bet the store, and do we win or do we crap out?

Well, we and Paramount won, and won big. The only big movie Paramount didn't partner on that year was a critical and financial smash. Paramount didn't make nearly as much as it did on *Titanic,* but *Truman* went on to gross a quarter of a billion dollars worldwide. And it was the most prestigious mainstream picture Paramount made and distributed that year. It garnered enormous critical acclaim. It elevated Jim Carrey from ha-ha funnyman to dramatic leading man—he even won a Golden Globe as best dramatic actor.

Peter, Ed Harris, and the writer, Andrew Niccol, were nominated for Academy Awards. The film and its producers were nominated for Best Dramatic Picture in the Golden Globes.

But for some reason, we weren't nominated for Best Picture in the Academy Awards. I would be a prevaricator if I said I wasn't disappointed. Hell, I was devastated. But you never know about the Academy Awards. You could be just one vote away.

A film depicting media manipulation and exploitation of people, no matter how well done, is not a guaranteed crowd-pleaser with Hollywood insiders. A lot of them make a good living doing just those things.

So we've screened *Truman* for Paramount and Sherry Lansing is in an art-film funk as we put her in her car and say our good-byes. Scott Rudin and I take Michelle Manning, the executive on the picture, to La Luna, a nice Italian restaurant near the studio.

We all agree *Truman* is a great picture but its commercial outlook is iffy. The Paramount marketing people will have to do one heck of a selling job to get the crowds to come for our offbeat film about a man whose life is a TV show. Even if the marketers can get people into theaters the opening weekend, word of mouth on films spreads quickly. If folks are turned off, if Jim Carrey fans are disappointed that he's not talking out of his rear end, then we could be toast by Weekend No. 2.

From out of the blue at dinner, Scott Rudin turns to me and says the most extraordinary thing: "Ed, it's just not fair that you're an executive producer on this film. You should get a producer credit. If we should happen to win Best Picture, you should be up on that stage."

I will tell you that it's almost unheard of to have a contractual credit changed from executive producer to producer after a picture is finished. Just doesn't happen.

We didn't end up on stage at the Academy Awards, but Rudin's generosity is one of those moments when all the Hollywood cynicism fades, the pressures dissolve into the past, and a nice pat on the back feels really good.

DREAMING IN
BLACK AND WHITE

ABBY GRESHLER LOOKED LIKE A MAN WHO HAD BEEN EMBALMED and then had come back to life. When he spoke, it sounded like someone revealing a deep, dark secret while straining to go to the bathroom. He made a lot of money as an agent but was as cheap as they came.

But, by God, I loved Abby Greshler.

I had known Greshler during my Seven Arts days in the 1960s. I was based in New York but traveled frequently to L.A., where I often crossed paths with Greshler. When I moved to California to join Warner Bros., my welcoming present from that big spender was a five-dollar box of Whitman's Sampler chocolates from the corner drugstore.

Abner "Abby" Greshler started out booking local comics into small theaters in his Lower East Side neighborhood in Manhattan. Over time, he expanded to booking acts into venues in the Catskills (the so-called Borscht Belt) and beyond. His roster included Danny Thomas, Milton Berle, and Red Skelton. And a very young comic named Jerry Lewis.

Greshler booked Lewis into the Havana-Madrid nightclub at Fifty-first and Broadway, Manhattan, where up-and-coming singer Dean Martin was already headlining. Martin and Lewis began clowning around in each other's acts. They had a great rapport. Later they both appeared at the 500 Club in Atlantic City, where they began to gel as a team. And one of the most successful and famous comedy duos of all time was born.

Greshler moved to California because of Martin and Lewis's burgeoning movie career and to capitalize on television. At one time or another, he represented Tony Randall, Jack Klugman, Zsa Zsa Gabor, Jayne Mansfield, and many other stars.

One reason I liked Abby Greshler is that you could always do a deal with him. No matter how difficult things became, he would never let a deal die—he would find some way to make it work out.

And he was untiring in promoting his clients. I was looking for an actor to play Robert Preston's son in an ABC TV movie called *My Father's House.*

Greshler says, "Ed, I've got the perfect actor for you. Perfect. He looks just like Robert Preston. His name's . . . Jack Klugman."

I ended up using Cliff Robertson for the role—Robert Preston and Jack Klugman as father and son? Nope. (I did hire Klugman, a great actor, later for *Two Minute Warning.*)

One time, I asked Greshler about an actress he represented. "Oh, she's thirty-two years old." She was forty-eight. Those sorts of details never mattered much to him. He always had a client who would somehow fit into any part you asked for.

Abby Greshler was one of television's top agents but, God, he was cheap. When he came to visit me in my office, he would catch up on his long-distance calling on my nickel—New York, London. And he would never pick up a lunch tab. *Never!*

But one day, I decided to change that.

I was meeting Greshler for a one o'clock lunch at the Hamburger Hamlet in L.A.'s Century City. He was the only person I ever knew who could reserve a table at Hamburger Hamlet. I told my assistant, "Don't expect me back." I wasn't leaving Hamburger Hamlet until Greshler picked up the check.

So Greshler and I have lunch at Hamburger Hamlet. And the check arrives at 2 P.M. I don't pick it up, and, of course, neither does Greshler.

I just keep on with the small talk. Two-thirty, three. More small talk. The check sits there. Greshler watches it out of the corner of his eye.

Finally at 3:30 P.M.—an hour and a half after the check arrived—Greshler gives up and says, "All right, already." And he picks up the check. To this day, I wish I had had a camera crew there to record that historic moment.

"Man Walks on the Moon."

"Abby Greshler Picks Up Check."

But I bring all this up to set the stage for one very memorable event.

I'm having lunch with Greshler and his number-one client, David Janssen, at the Warner Bros. commissary during post-production on *The Green Berets,* in which Janssen had one of the starring roles.

Janssen was a big TV star then. He had done *Richard Diamond* and *The Fugitive,* both negotiated by Abby Greshler.

Greshler had built Janssen's career and made him very wealthy. But Greshler had a habit that really grated on Janssen. During business meals, Greshler would take off his wristwatch—a very fine $3,000 model, $10,000 now—and set it on the table facing him, so he could monitor the time constantly.

Janssen hated this. It made it seem like Greshler was putting a time limit on everything.

So we're sitting there, finishing our lunch at Warners. Greshler's watch is in its usual position on the table.

Without any warning and in one quick movement, Janssen reaches under the table, brings out a hammer, and proceeds to smash Greshler's watch into pieces.

Greshler watches in horror.

A gear and a spring land in my potato salad.

Janssen says nothing, puts the hammer away, and resumes munching on his pastrami on rye.

Greshler looks down wistfully at his obliterated timepiece. Then as if "snapping out of it," goes back to his own sandwich, chatting away as though nothing had happened.

———

Abby Greshler was an agent, not a producer. But his broken watch was a testament to a maxim that I would call the First Rule of Producing:

Treat everyone on your picture with personal respect.

The movie business is about people and relationships. That's why it's so hard for some folks—especially overly analytical types—to be successful in it. Abby Greshler was successful and he fought hard for his clients. But sometimes he came across as insensitive and not caring about people, even ones close to him. His watch bore the punishment for that.

When you produce a movie, you're the general manager of a massive undertaking in which the lion's share of the success or failure is the direct result of the contribution of diverse human beings. Actors, directors, writers, cameramen, editors, costumers, grips, gaffers, and the list goes on. Every person on that film is important and every person deserves your respect if you're the producer.

On my films, my office door is always open to anyone on the picture who wants to talk with me. On one film, an assistant director came to me with the news that the director was talking terrible to the minor actors. Well, you can't do that because it affects everyone's morale. The major actors don't want that—they're not looking to knock their fellow actors.

After we had a talk about it, the director was very apologetic. "Ed, I'm under great pressure. I didn't mean it and it won't happen again."

When something gets to my office, it's usually pretty serious because most of the time, people will work through the production manager.

Most often, though, it's actually the director who comes in to see me. The pressure of filmmaking is intense, and he or she is feeling overworked and put upon. You try to calm him or her down. That's about all you can do. We have a saying and I've said it to many directors: "If it was easy, everybody would be doing it."

Over the course of the book, I've talked about rules of producing from time to time. Since this is the last chapter, I thought I would summarize my highly personal list of rules of producing for you. There are only seven. But it could have been a hundred. These are seven I consider particularly important, in rough order of significance.

Now, I know that most of you reading this aren't producers or even aspiring producers. Many of you aren't directly connected to the movie business except as fans and customers. But these rules can easily be generalized to managing any creative project where art and commerce unite in a salable product or service.

Take a look at number seven. You may be surprised to see it here. And it could just as easily have been number one—

Don't skimp on the catering.

In a movie, food costs are a relatively small expenditure. But you'd be surprised how many producers try to economize there. Bad idea, as far as I'm concerned.

I have plenty of good food on set for lunch and breaks. And everyone on the crew eats the same food—cameramen, grips, extras. If you had visited the set of *K-19* in Toronto, you would have seen Harrison Ford go through the food line with everyone else.

A happy and contented crew goes back to work happy and stays happy the rest of the day. And makes a better movie.

You don't see any "Thou shalt not"s on the list because these rules are not etched in stone. You probably won't fall off a mountain or get swallowed by a whale or end up in the gutter if you ignore one or more of them. But I do believe that following them will make you a better producer—they made me a better one.

Rule number four, managing the studio's money as your own, may give the wrong impression. Lorraine and I used to travel to Las Vegas at times and we always enjoyed seeing Don Rickles perform. I had offered Rickles a part in a movie not long before one of these trips. But I didn't have the money to pay him what he thought he should get.

Well, Lorraine and I are sitting there, enjoying his show, when all of sudden he stops and makes an announcement to the crowd of about a thousand. "Ladies and gentlemen, we have a very special guest in the

A Few Rules of Producing

1. **Treat everyone on your picture with personal respect.** *A film's success or failure is the direct result of the contribution of many diverse human beings. Every person on the film is important and every person deserves your respect if you're the producer.*

2. **Respect the creative process.** *Movies should be magic. To get that magic, you have to let the creative process evolve without a lot of interference and micromanagement. It needs nourishment, not oppression. Hire good people and let them do their jobs.*

3. **When producing a big-budget picture, you are always better off telling the studio the truth, no matter what.** *Studio executives hate surprises. I'm not an alarmist, but if there's a problem, I want them to know about it.*

4. **Manage the money as if it were your own.** *Studios can sense your attitude toward their money. They won't get mad at you for watching their interests. You might even be a hero.*

5. **You can manage the people risk about 99 percent of the time. It's the other 1 percent that will get you.** *You can have people risk from directors, crew, and actors who are not at the very top. Not just the A-Listers. But there is a much heavier concentration of risk in the A-List.*

6. **The risk of the lure is strong: Manage it as if it could cost you millions.** *The entertainment industry has more than its share of temptations, sexual and otherwise. In filmmaking, the risk of the lure is always there, and it can be very expensive and disruptive. But the risk is manageable.*

7. **Don't skimp on the catering.** *A happy and contented crew goes back to work happy and stays happy the rest of the day. And makes a better movie.*

audience tonight. I want you to meet Ed Feldman, the movie producer. Ed, would you stand up?"

The spotlight hit me. I stood up and gave a little wave to the crowd.

Rickles continues, "I wanted you to meet Ed because he's a very important man. He once offered me a part in one of his movies. But the offer was so low that I learned something. I learned that . . . Ed Feldman is the *cheapest man in show business!*"

One producer and his director blithely ignored rule number three about telling the truth to the studio . . . and it almost cost me my life.

At least that's the way I remember it.

You may recall that I was head of advertising and publicity for Seven Arts during the making of *The Night of the Iguana,* produced by my old boss and friend Ray Stark and directed by that venerable icon of filmdom John Huston.

The Night of the Iguana was a high-class production. Richard Burton, Ava Gardner, and Deborah Kerr starring. From a play by Tennessee Williams. Stellar supporting cast.

And they decided to make it in black and white.

Now, *The Night of the Iguana* was being filmed in a seaside location in Mexico near Puerto Vallarta. The location was gorgeous and looked great in color.

Still Stark and Huston decided on black and white for artistic reasons.

I produced the "Making of . . ." featurette for *Iguana* and I thought color would be just fine for my opus. I was trying to sell the picture, not establish myself as an artist of the cinema.

Now, here's something amazing—MGM, the film's distributor, didn't know the picture wasn't in color.

Even in the 1960s, studios generally had an aversion to black-and-white movies. Some thought they looked overly "artsy." And the marketing types considered them a harder sell for television as the networks were moving everything to color.

The MGM executives watched the dailies and yes, they were in black and white. But they thought the lab in Mexico City couldn't make color prints for dailies in quick turnaround. Plus my featurette was in color and they just assumed the real picture was in color.

Stark and Huston didn't want to break the illusion. Actually, "afraid to break the illusion" was more like it.

But MGM had to find out sometime. Stark and Huston decided I'd be the one to break the news, so to speak, when I took the finished picture to MGM headquarters in New York to be screened for the first time for MGM executives. Stark was conveniently in Los Angeles that day and Huston had scurried off to his manor house in County Galway, Ireland.

I just knew the dung was going to strike the blades, so I called up Huston in Ireland for some instructions.

"John, what do I tell these people when they ask, 'Where's the color?'"

There was a pause at the other end of the line.

Finally, Huston speaks up in those wonderfully melodic bass tones of his, "Ed, just tell them that 'We dream in black and white.'"

Huston was brilliant. I never would have thought of that in twenty-six eons.

We dream in black and white.

So now I'm screening the picture at MGM for Morris Lefko, the cigar-chewing head of sales. The picture starts and in a couple of seconds, Lefko shoots up like he's been given a fifty-amp shock to the rear.

"Wait a minute! Wait a goddam minute!"

He's waving the stogie at the screen. I hold my breath and close my eyes. Here it comes.

"WHERE'S THE FUCKIN' COLOR?"

Now he's in my face. The stogie jabs ominously.

"WHERE'S THE FUCKIN' COLOR?"

I get my composure together and in a calm voice, I deliver my message: "Well, Mr. Huston told me to tell you that we dream in black and white."

"WHAT ARE YOU TALKING ABOUT, YOU LUNATIC? WE DREAM IN BLACK AND WHITE! THAT'S HORSESHIT!"

I thought Lefko was going to throw me out of the eighth-story window. I would be this body hurtling out of the MGM building onto Broadway below. My life passing before my eyes.

But in black and white.

Stark and Huston were among the legendary, almost mythical people I've had the good fortune to work with over my many years in the movie business. Filmmakers, studio heads, big stars. Some were so mythical they carried their own set of myths around with them.

When I was a publicist at Fox in the late 1950s, I was handling a press luncheon for *An Affair to Remember,* starring Cary Grant and Deborah Kerr. We were all mesmerized by Grant then. He was perfection— classically handsome, urbane, impeccably groomed. I never saw him with a wrinkle in his pants or jacket, even offstage.

I thought it would be fun to surround Grant at his table with a gaggle of women but with an added little twist of my own. After they're comfortably seated, Grant introduces himself to them.

"I'm Cary Grant."

"Nice to meet you, Mr. Grant. I'm Judy Green."

"My pleasure, Judy."

"I love your work, Mr. Grant. I'm Judy Smith."

"Hello, Judy."

Grant greets all six of the ladies and each one is named Judy. Grant corners me.

"Ed, I know what you're doing. You want me to keep saying Judy, Judy, Judy. But I never said that. That's from guys in Las Vegas—comics who imitate me with Judy, Judy, Judy."

Charles Einfeld, another legendary personage I worked with, was one of the most significant influences on me, personally. He was head of advertising and publicity at Fox when I was just starting out. I talked about him much earlier.

Einfeld was the toughest SOB around. I told you how he would berate his publicists if their front-page *Variety* stories were below the fold

instead of above it. But I learned from Einfeld the importance of diligence and attention to work. To always strive for my very best—lessons
I brought with me from then on. This is perfectly enshrined in an image I carry in my mind—of myself, in a tuxedo following a premiere,
waiting patiently at 3 A.M., on South Street, the Bowery, lower Manhattan, to plant a photograph in the next day's *New York Journal-American*.

A lone figure, dressed to the nines, waiting on a seedy New York
sidewalk. How's that for showbiz glitz and glamour?

I still stand up whenever an actress enters the room to read for a part
because I think that's one of the most horrifying things any human being has to do. To go into a room with four people who don't know
much more than she does. To perform for these people cold. And her
life depends on their decision.

I've always worked well with actors. One reason for this is I constantly look out for anything that can go wrong in their performance.
Gena Rowlands was one of the stars of *Two Minute Warning*. On one
particular day, we shot an important scene late in the afternoon. In the
dailies, I just didn't think she looked her best. She was obviously very
tired and was having trouble with her facial expressions. Without con-
sulting the studio (which is a no-no), I took it upon myself to reshoot
the scene two days later in the morning. Gena knew I was looking out
for her and she was grateful.

Did I break my own rule number three? Maybe a little technical vi-
olation. So throw me out a window.

I don't think producers should ever refer to a film as "my picture." For
one thing, moviemaking is a highly communal experience. The work
of hundreds of people has contributed to the project. Each doing his or
her job and making a distinctive mark. Many times, you don't know
where the creativity comes from. It could be an assistant wardrobe person saying "Why don't we try this?" or "Have you ever thought about
that?" You have to be open to other people's ideas and not be dismis-
sive out of hand.

Also, most of the time the director has the real power on the picture, not the producer. The day of the producer running the movie, in most instances, is over. Now the director runs the movie whether the producer likes it or not.

The producer has to be very careful how he or she contributes to the movie. Some directors like and appreciate input. Other directors think you're the evil baron if you make even one suggestion. But a good director will find a medium ground because most producers have some very good ideas. And again, it's a collaborative effort.

One of the hardest things in the world is to fire the director on a picture, and that's because of the union rules. When I was producing *My Father's House* for Filmways and ABC TV, I ran into a problem with the director, Alex Segal, four days before the end of shooting.

Now, Segal was a very well-respected director—he had done *All the Way Home* and the TV version of *Death of a Salesman*—and he was head of the cinema program at the University of Southern California. But he was having emotional problems and behaving irrationally on set, and it had finally reached a breaking point.

We had children in the cast. The state of California welfare worker assigned to us, a woman I knew very well, came to my office. Segal had been berating the children's mothers in front of the children in rude and abusive language. The welfare worker was direct: "Ed, one more time and we're putting Filmways on notice, and the penalty is, for two years, you can't make a picture with a child."

So I fired Segal and then had to defend the action before the Directors Guild. We did that successfully but it was very difficult to find a replacement director. Finally, I secured William Graham, a top-notch TV director, to finish the picture, but he wanted to work anonymously and would take scale only, Guild minimum, in payment.

Sadly, Alex Segal passed away two years later.

Working with an actress as accomplished and intelligent as Glenn Close is more of a mutual collaboration than anything else. We were extremely fortunate to have Glenn as Cruella DeVil in the two *Dalmatian* films. I am convinced that Glenn deserves a big chunk of the credit for the films' combined worldwide gross of half a billion dollars.

Glenn had already signed on when I joined the first picture, *101 Dalmatians*. John Hughes had written the script and was a producer of the film. The very competent and cooperative Stephen Herek was directing.

Joe Roth, the head of the Disney studio at the time, had championed the project and Disney considered it integral to the studio's transformation toward more live-action family films. The success of our *Jungle Book*—with that damned dancing bear—was a motivator for this.

Hughes has an incredible number of big hits on his résumé, including *The Breakfast Club, Ferris Bueller's Day Off,* and *Home Alone*. A large share of the classic youth films and comedies over the last twenty years are his. He almost single-handedly invented the "brat pack," the group of hot young actors in the 1980s that included Emilio Estevez, Andrew McCarthy, and Molly Ringwald.

Hughes had personally recruited Glenn to *101 Dalmatians*. She was not overly enthusiastic about playing Cruella when he visited her in New York during her run as Norma Desmond in *Sunset Boulevard* on Broadway. Before that show, she had appeared in nine Broadway productions and sixteen feature films, and had received five Academy Award nominations. She was a film and stage diva in the best sense of the word. Cruella DeVil was not a role she would have been likely to jump at. Sure enough, she balked.

When Anthony Powell, the costume designer for *Sunset Boulevard,* heard Hughes's pitch and Glenn's reaction, he said, "Glenn, are you kidding? This is the kind of movie that will make you an international star. Every child and grown-up in the world will be talking about the movie and you." He was persuasive and Glenn signed on. Powell, who became our costume designer on the picture, did a spectacular job, by the way.

Once Glenn joined the project, she was totally professional and very enthusiastic, despite her earlier misgivings. She put all her efforts and energies into making her character come alive and ensuring that *101 Dalmatians* was a success.

As an aside here, let me say that I always believe that in a fantasy movie, you're better off hiring the best actors you can because they will energize their characters—which tend to be inherently artificial—the way Glenn did.

For example, we tested about twenty well-established English actors, some pretty substantial, for the parts of Cruella's henchmen, Horace and Jasper, who provide much of the picture's comic relief. During the auditions, we paired them off differently to see which combination would work the best. We ended up with Hugh Laurie as Jasper, and Mark Williams as Horace. These two were accomplished actors even then. Laurie had attended Eton and Cambridge, where he headed up the famous Footlights comedy troupe. He went on to star in the *Stuart Little* movies and now has his own dramatic TV series, *House*. Williams attended Oxford. He has appeared in eleven feature films since our movie, including *Shakespeare in Love*, and is Ron Weasley's dad in the *Harry Potter* series of films.

In one scene in the movie, Cruella drives up to her office building and is greeted by the doorman. The part of the doorman is very small, with one line of dialogue. On the set, I recognized the actor—he was the main supporting player in the Jane Tennison *Prime Suspect* series on TV, playing Helen Mirren's superior. His name is John Benfield and he is a classically trained Shakespearean actor. I went over to him and said, "Geez, I'm really embarrassed that I don't have more for you to do."

And he replied, "Listen, I am a professional actor. This is as important to me as anything." That remark captures the spirit of English actors—the most important thing to them is the work.

I've often said if you can't cast a picture well in England, you should leave the business.

I enjoyed getting together with Glenn for dinner in London. Unlike some actors, Glenn has a broad range of interests and is a knowledgeable, charming dinner companion. It's funny, though—the first time we were going to meet for dinner, I asked her what she'd like. "You know, Ed, I am just *dying* for a pizza."

So we ended up in a pizza joint in Soho.

John Hughes's script was in very good shape except for the last few minutes. This is when the puppies are escaping the clutches of Cruella and her henchmen, and the villains all get their painful, humiliating comeuppances. There was physical humor and there were sight gags in the script, but Glenn didn't think that stretch was funny enough. The dialogue especially didn't measure up to the rest of the picture.

Glenn is smart about filmmaking and she knew this was a serious problem with the movie. Hughes promised to make revisions.

Except for these revisions, Hughes's work on the project was pretty much finished by the time we began shooting in England. He'd leave his home in Chicago and show up in London on a few occasions, and Glenn would question him about the revisions. "I'll get to it," he kept telling her.

You must understand that Glenn would never have taken the part unless the finale of the movie was going to be strong for her character.

Finally, as the shooting date for these scenes approached, she started asking *me* to ask Hughes to do what he had promised. I called him in Chicago.

"John, I've got an actress here that you've promised to do certain script changes for. And she's expecting you to follow through."

"Look, Ed, you just tell her the following: She's the actress and I'm the writer. She speaks what I write."

"That's easy for you to say, John. You're living in Chicago and I'm down the hall from the actress."

Well, even with all the hounding, we never got what we needed from Hughes. So the dialogue got enhanced by the director and Glenn, and we winged it. The finale ended up being hilarious.

When a collaborator like Glenn Close is working with you, quality will prevail. I guarantee it.

Mel Gibson produced and directed one of the top-ten-grossing movies of all time, *The Passion of the Christ*. Not many months before its eventual release, he couldn't even get a distributor.

Mel's business sense is terrific. He always knows what direction to take. On *Forever Young*, although he was a megastar, he knew we shouldn't spend $50 or $60 million on that picture, and he was willing to work with a director who was amenable to bringing it in for a much lower budget.

Without a doubt, Mel possesses some of the sharpest acumen in the business.

Harrison Ford is my all-time favorite actor I've worked with. Harrison stood by me, uncomplaining, for six months while I found a director for *Witness.*

Not only is Harrison a very fine and versatile actor, but he is highly intelligent about the business. He knows filmmaking so well, he could easily have been a director if he had wanted to (and been willing to muster the patience).

I was fortunate to receive the Producer of the Year award at the Holly-wood Film Festival in 2001. On his own, Harrison flew in from his ranch in Wyoming just to attend the ceremony and present me with the award. He even declined to accept a hotel suite from the event organizers.

I will always cherish Harrison's friendship and the kind words he said about me at the award presentation.

Larry Peerce and I became longtime friends over drinks in the TWA departure lounge at London's Heathrow Airport in the early 1970s. I was in England on business for Filmways, and Larry had just finished shooting *Ash Wednesday,* with Elizabeth Taylor and Henry Fonda. I had met Larry a couple of years earlier through the producer Stanley Jaffe. But sitting with him at the airport, swapping funny stories, laughing uproariously, we really clicked.

Not long afterward I was putting together *The Stranger Who Looks Like Me,* a TV movie for ABC, and I thought of Larry to direct.

Larry had done very well since starting out as a struggling director in the early 1960s. His first two features, *One Potato, Two Potato* and *The Incident,* were low-budget, grittily realistic, and very well received. By the way, *The Incident* was the feature film debut for a young actor named Martin Sheen—playing a violent and abusive young punk.

Larry's career skyrocketed. He went on to direct *Goodbye, Columbus* and *A Separate Peace,* both major successes, before we worked together on *The Stranger Who Looks Like Me*. We ended up collaborating on five projects, including *Wired* and the two *Other Side of the Mountain* pictures I talked about before. *Two Minute Warning* was the other one.

With a lot of laughter, my friendship with Larry has endured for over thirty years and his four marriages. I'm delighted that number four is a very happy one. He finally got it right.

They say you can't have long friendships in Hollywood. But you can—if you're willing to put your priorities in order. I was setting up a movie called *Garbo Talks* under my development deal at Fox. Larry was attached to direct but Fox had other ideas. The head of Fox told me, "Ed, if you get rid of Larry, we'll make the movie."

Without even thinking about it, I said to myself, "You know, in this town, it's harder to find a friend than a go picture." I walked away from *Garbo Talks* and it ended up at MGM, directed by Sidney Lumet.

Any time you need emotion and compassion in a picture, you go to Larry Peerce. I would work with him again in a minute.

I believe that my good fortune in getting Peter Weir to direct *Witness* and then working with him again on *Green Card* and *The Truman Show* helped me establish my career more than the impact of any other single person. Peter is a filmmaking genius. He is very strong-willed and he knows exactly what he wants to do. And it's not that he's doing anything frivolously. He believes in what he's doing and you can see it from his pictures. When he makes a movie, it has to be perfect.

Peter and I worked very well together, and a good part of the success of our collaboration is this: I think I know when to push and I think I know when to back off. For example, Peter doesn't just casually hire actors; he looks into everyone very, very carefully.

At one point, Paramount was pushing hard for Shelley Long to star with Harrison Ford in *Witness*. She was in *Cheers* right then, one of Paramount's hot television properties. But Peter would not allow himself to meet her. He knew he wasn't going to cast her in the movie and he thought it unprofessional to bring her in.

I began to pester him: "Peter, why don't you just do it. See her for ten minutes. Take a look. You don't have to use her. It will make Paramount happy."

It was always "No, I'm not going to do it" from Peter, and eventually I dropped it. I learned something from this—don't compromise your standards just to achieve some fleeting advantage or to curry favor with the studio.

One of the pleasures I've had in the business was when my daughter, Shari, worked with me on eight of my pictures as a costume designer or as a costume supervisor. I especially enjoyed her company on *Witness*.

She worked with our director Peter Weir's wife, Wendy, on that picture. Wendy was having quite a bit of difficulty locating the right shirt for our old Amish grandfather. She is a very meticulous person and after much looking, she found the ideal shirt in a thrift store. It was the perfect color and made of just the right material. The problem was that we couldn't reproduce it readily, so we ended up with just that one shirt for the character. Since he was Amish, his shirt had to be the same throughout the film. Shari told Wendy, "You can't have a picture with just one shirt. What if something goes wrong?"

But Wendy was very insistent about it. So Shari became the keeper of the shirt. She had it with her 24/7—it was even next to her while she slept. She hand washed it. No one else could touch it. With Shari's diligence, the prized shirt came through the shoot with flying colors, so to speak.

At the start of the picture, Harrison Ford asked her, "Who's my dresser, Shari?"

"Well, I am, Harrison. You must understand, Paramount is an equal-opportunity employer. So I'm your dresser."

Harrison thought that was pretty funny because he had never had a woman dresser before on a picture.

My daughter dresses Harrison Ford every day for a couple of months. Wait a minute. Come to think of it, she shoulda been paying me!

Being married to Lorraine for over fifty years has helped my career immeasurably. I don't think you can really live with the ups and downs of the motion picture industry without having someone to come home to at night and talk with rationally.

Most every producer goes up and down—some days you're a hero, some days you're a bum. Even superstar producer Jerry Bruckheimer, as invincible as he seems today, has had his share of down times.

As a producer, you must learn how to handle rejection. You must keep your equilibrium. I've had some very tough times in this business. I came to California in the 1960s in the most exalted kind of job, then lost the job. There were those months when they were moving me from office to office at Warner Bros. until I got close enough to the front gate to see it out of my window. My telephone calls went from sixty or seventy a day to two a day. That takes a lot of emotional sting out of you.

And Lorraine was there for me.

When I had my darkest days as a producer—with Michael Ovitz sabotaging my every move on our John Belushi picture, *Wired,* Lorraine was always there to give support and good counsel.

I've been a very lucky man to have had her at my side.

Warren Beatty and I go back a long, long time. It's such a long time that Warren and I are both Old Hollywood *and* New Hollywood, simultaneously.

In fact, it's so long that we're Old Hollywood, New Hollywood, and Baby Boomer Hollywood, all rolled into one.

I first met Warren in the mid-1960s when he did a picture for us at Seven Arts, *Promise Her Anything,* and I was heading up advertising and publicity. I got to know Warren well a couple of years later when I was the assistant head of production for Warner Bros. and we were releasing *Bonnie and Clyde,* Warren's big breakthrough picture, not only as leading man but also as producer.

Warren was a swinging single back then. Nowadays, they would use the term "chick magnet" to describe him. And it was well known that not all of his love interests were unmarried.

Warren was very funny and I enjoyed his company. He would say,

"Ed, let's grab some dinner."

And I would say, "Sure, Warren, but it would be my luck that some irate husband would shoot at you and hit me!"

I talked at the beginning about working as a young man for Spyros Skouras at Fox. Over all those years, Skouras never knew I worked for him. I told you about the time in the elevator, when I encountered Skouras after a screening of *All About Eve*. He smiled at me and said gently, "Tell me. Tell me how you loved the picture."

That was Old Hollywood.

Here's the New Hollywood version.

I attended a preview of Warren's film *Shampoo,* in which he played a studly hairdresser who scooted all over Beverly Hills, bedding his clients. The screening was at the old Directors Guild headquarters.

Now, Warren could be very intimidating. He sees me across the room after the screening and trots over to greet me.

But instead of shaking hands, he grabs my privates and squeezes.

Still holding on, he looks me square in the eye and says in that trademark Warren Beatty style, "Well, Ed . . .

Tell me how you loved the picture."